THE HAZARD OF THE DIE

TOLBERT FANNING AND THE
RESTORATION MOVEMENT

THE HAZARD
OF THE DIE

TOLBERT FANNING AND
THE RESTORATION MOVEMENT

JAMES R. WILBURN

SWEET PUBLISHING CO., AUSTIN, TEXAS, 78751

Library of Congress Card Number
74-77235
Standard Book Number
8344-003-8

Manufactured in the United States of America

CONTENTS

PREFACE

THIS IS MORE than the story of a man. It is the story of a movement. Its own people commonly call it the Restoration Movement for it was born amid early nineteenth-century plans to "restore New Testament Christianity" on American soil. Its heirs number among the larger religious groups in the United States. Those closest to one of its leaders, Alexander Campbell, preferred to be known as Disciples of Christ. Others preferred Christian Church, while still others more often used Church of Christ. Throughout most of the nineteenth century these designations were used interchangeably. Today, Churches of Christ generally is the designation used to refer to independent congregations not related to the Disciples' United Christian Missionary Society. It also usually refers to churches which do not use instruments of music in their worship, although this is not without exception.

Although Tolbert Fanning really belonged to the movement as a whole, throughout this volume I have used the phrase Church of Christ in an effort to achieve some consistency in narration. I have also used it because Fanning himself preferred it (though he did not limit himself to its use), and because his life helps largely to explain how the contemporary heirs of the movement became formally divided, with Fanning's life more closely associated with Churches of Christ. At his death, Fanning still used Church of Christ to include the Disciples, and even today one can find Christian Churches with Church of Christ on the cornerstone of their buildings, or a Church of Christ whose property deed still reads Christian Church, or some similar reminder of the past interchangeability of these phrases.

This is also the story of American life because together, these groups constitute by far the largest indigenous religious phenomenon in our nation's history. But it is more than anything else the story of a man, since so much of history is made up of a series of biographies.

It occurs to me as I contemplate the life of Tolbert Fanning, a man with whose life and times I have lived closely for almost ten years, that we can no longer afford the un-ethical frontier sport of violent charge and counter-charge in either secular or religious circles, although its real presence makes the story of Tolbert Fanning a part of the fabric of our own times. Some recent religious journals, with fearful lashing out against neighbors, almost appear to claim some type of mandate to continue the rough and tumble warfare of "church politics," of which Tolbert Fanning was a victim in the days of our forefathers.

That this is a heritage for which we should be ashamed, not proud, is part of the message of the biography of Tolbert Fanning. He lived in a time when violence, both physical and verbal (it is doubtful that they can be separated), was common. Indeed he suffered greatly from both. He realized that genuine Christianity is incompatible with such attitudes, and in Christ he found his polar star, as "one who never did an injury, and never resented one done to him; never uttered an untruth, never practiced a deception, and never lost an opportunity of doing good . . . his illimitable meekness and patience never once forsook him in a vexatious, ungrateful, and cruel world—*Christ in History.*"

Because one finds the Christ in history in the life of Fanning, though imperfectly, his life should be saved from obscurity. His life has helped to establish priorities in my own personal life, and because he is so much a part of the lives of thousands who today do not even remember his name, his story has to be written. Because the forces which he faced were so similar to many faced today, we may come to know ourselves much better when we have come to know him.

I have often asked myself during these months what Tolbert Fanning himself might feel toward me and toward my work. It is so difficult to know the mind and the life of the living that one comes occasionally to feel ridiculously presumptuous in trying to capture the life of one whom none now living can remember. I have several times contemplated even reneging on the task for fear that the kind of "immortality" which a published biography bestows on a man might be unjust or in error. But I have always returned to Tolbert Fanning, convinced more than ever of the validity of the task.

There are points in the life of Tolbert Fanning which, with the educated eye of posterity, I have been tempted to judge. There are some things which he did and wrote with which I do not personally agree, as must always be the case with a biographer who tries to be objective. On the other hand, it has been just as tempting to engage in praise and excess adulation. Particularly with a man like Fanning, I have found this latter temptation to be the greater of the two, as the reader will no doubt come to recognize. In an effort to solve the dilemma and in a search for that ideal but ever elusive objectivity, I have often retained Fanning's own words, even though with our rapidly changing language they may sound a bit stilted today. My aim has been to see his life and his surroundings through his own eyes and then to let the reader indulge in any judgment which he may feel righteous enough to make. For, in a real sense, Tolbert Fanning belongs to all of us.

I perhaps can best express my personal assessment of Tolbert Fanning, formed, as all important assessments are formed, in the loneliness of my own heart, by borrowing Gibbon's judgment of the great Byzantine general, Belisarius: "His imperfections flowed from the contagion of the times: his virtues were his own."

So many have helped me in this task that I cannot fail to acknowledge my debt to them. When I was sixteen years old and a freshman at Abilene Christian College, I was introduced to many of the great men of the Restoration Movement through a series of lectures by Dr. Frank Pack. In those Wednesday night lectures, Dr. Pack did more than whet my appetite for more knowledge of their lives. He gave me a tremendous respect for them and for their directions in life. Almost a decade later, when I returned to do graduate work, it was from the teaching of Dr. J.W. Roberts that I came to appreciate how much needed to be done in recapturing and reevaluating the lives of these men. More than anything else it was Dr. Roberts' guidance and encouragement which led me to see the need for studying the life and the environment of Tolbert Fanning, both for its own worth and as a valuable avenue into a greater understanding of the Restoration Movement. I am especially indebted to Dr. Roberts for serving as the chairman of my thesis committee, since the first draft of the book was in fulfillment of the requirements for the Master's degree at Abilene Christian College in 1961. I am also grateful to Dr. Frank Pack and Dr. J.D. Thomas who served on the committee and made helpful suggestions. I owe a special debt to Claude Spencer of the Disciples of Christ Historical Society, to Mrs. Mary Harlow of the Abilene Christian College Library, to Mr. C.E.W. Dorris who so graciously opened his personal library to me in Nashville, to Miss Irma Lee Batey of Nashville, and to Mrs. Carol Russell who read the manuscript and made helpful suggestions. I am also obligated to David Stewart, Executive Editor for The Sweet Publishing Company, for invaluable help with the mechanical make-up of the manuscript.

In many respects this volume is but an initial effort. For Vivian I have hopefully reserved the best, which is yet to be.

Unfortunately, as with all who put their work into permanent form, always something short of what they had hoped it might be, I must be responsible for the completed work— hopefully for its virtues, and inevitably for its errors.

James R. Wilburn
Los Angeles, California
September, 1968

CHAPTER 1

HIS BANNER
TO THE BREEZE
BIRTH AND BOYHOOD

*"So soon as we were able to bear the
King's weapons, we threw His banner
to the breeze for a life voyage."*

Tolbert Fanning

WITH BOYISH awkwardness, a nineteen year old son of an
Alabama planter pushed six feet and six inches of rawboned
figure too far through his trouser legs and crossed the Tennessee River. It was October of 1829. The affectionate fare-
wells of his mother and father may not have been immediately
dramatic to the ungainly youth. But the Tennessee River
was the Rubicon for Tolbert Fanning.

Thirty years later, from a posture of maturity and with
his typical editorial "we," he contemplated the scene himself:
"In our 19th year we enlisted as a corporal in the cause of
One who 'has gone to prepare a place' for his friends: So
soon as we were able to bear the King's weapons, we
threw His banner to the breeze for a life voyage."[1]

None of the children at play around Florence, Alabama
could have known that they would most certainly hear again
about this young man passing along their road in the fall
air. The ferryman at the river had no way to divine the
future and could not have understood that his young passen-
ger would face a crisis in a great movement, put his shoulder
to heavy-hinged history and, groaning, make it move. And
not until a century later would men be able to see how
decisively the hinges had yielded.

Exactly two years earlier, to the day, Tolbert Fanning had
been baptized into Christ. His commitment followed a sermon by B. F. Hall.[2]

B.F. Hall was striking in many ways. In contrast to the religious leaders of the neighboring denominations, he claimed no name but "Christian." Young Fanning's ears were more accustomed to the party names of "Baptist" and "Methodist" —so accustomed that he was almost certain that all who did not belong to one party must assuredly belong to the other. Yet for almost five years now he had been familiar with a growing group of people in his neighborhood who preached that there was "but one body of Christ, one faith and one creed for Christians."

Fanning was later to learn that it had been a quarter of a century since Barton W. Stone, along with several other Presbyterian preachers, had withdrawn from the Synod of Kentucky. Their decision to withdraw was an imperative. Their growing conviction that the gospel was for all the world and not limited to a predetermined, select few, left them no option but to withdraw. During the first year of their efforts, Stone and his companions established fifteen congregations and formed the Springfield Presbytery. On June 28, 1804, however, they wrote the "Last Will and Testament of the Springfield Presbytery." The now famous document demonstrated their determination to give up everything of human origin in religion and to follow the Bible as their only guide. They were convinced that their only name should be "Christian."[3]

Young Tolbert also learned of similar efforts, emanating from Virginia and led by Alexander Campbell. Like his father, Thomas Campbell, Alexander was anxious to restore the "ancient order" of Christianity as revealed in the New Testament. With similar ideals, though working separately from the Campbells, Stone became more and more convinced that such a restoration of the essentials of New Testament Christianity could provide a workable basis for unity among all Christians. When Fanning was baptized, never dreaming of becoming anything but a Christian, Barton W. Stone was already publishing his paper, the *Christian Messenger,* with the unity of Christians as his polar star. Alexander Campbell had only recently published a far-reaching and significant series of articles in his *Christian Baptist* magazine entitled, "The Ancient Order of Things."

In the early 1830s, led by John T. Johnson, a former U.S. Congressman, who had determined to use the remainder of his life in preaching a return to New Testament Christianity, those under the influence of Campbell committed themselves in formal action toward unity with those under the influence of Stone. After that the message spread with such rapid impact that in less than a decade the groups were among the largest religious bodies in America.

Among the leaders of the movement in Alabama were those who initially influenced Fanning, including Ephraim D. Moore, James E. Matthews, and Ross Houston. Born in North Carolina in 1782, Moore had moved to Tennessee where he became a Christian. He began to preach in 1807, was in the battle of New Orleans with General Andrew Jackson, and in his prime was one of the most eloquent and moving speakers of his day. During the time that he preached in Alabama in 1826, he taught young Tolbert Fanning to search the Bible for the way of salvation rather than wait for the Holy Spirit to enter his heart through some direct ecstatic stirring. Moore especially impressed Fanning with his care in teaching teenagers.

But James E. Matthews was the man to whom Fanning felt "mainly indebted" for his early religious instruction. Matthews was born in Kentucky in 1799 and also became a Christian under the influence of Barton Stone. He began preaching in Mississippi and Alabama several years later, was a member of the legislature of Mississippi, and also held the office of Auditor of Public Accounts as well as other public positions in the state. He often traveled on horseback or on foot, carrying a change of clothing in his saddlebags, for he made preaching trips away from home for several days or weeks at a time. When Matthews died in 1867, Fanning wrote, "Perhaps, for no man, since the departure of our own father, did we feel a more tender regard than for our deceased brother."[4]

Unlike Moore and Matthews, Ross Houston, another of

Fanning's teachers, never did preach. Still, for many years after the time that Fanning was his student, he quite often sent reports to the religious periodicals to trace his progress in Alabama. Upon occasion his reports betray a deep admiration for Tolbert Fanning, the pupil of his youth who was destined to attain such prominence among his brethren.

It was while Moore, Matthews, and Houston were teaching in the area that B.F. Hall, not yet 25 years of age, visited Fanning's neighborhood. In 1825, at the age of 21, he had been ordained by Stone and during the following summer preached in several series of meetings. He discovered the "mourner's bench" still in use by many of Stone's associates. Hall was disturbed because so many meetings closed without the "mourners," kneeling at the front of the audience, receiving deliverance from their obvious distress. The next year, still troubled by his own preaching, he was visiting on Line Creek which separates Tennessee from Kentucky. In the cabin of a friend he found a copy of the *Campbell-McCalla Debate* and read carefully Alexander Campbell's discussion of the New Testament design of baptism. Suddenly he cried, "Eureka! Eureka! I have found it, I have found it!" The book dropped to the floor as the whole "plan of salvation" became clear to him for the first time. Puzzled mourners did not need to wait in vain for God to enter their hearts miraculously. Confronting Christ, they could respond to God through their own free will and as an expression of their own intellect, being immersed for the remission of their sins. Such was the obvious picture in the first century, and God was the same in 1826!"[5]

When Hall excitedly approached Stone about this, Stone replied that he also had preached baptism for the remission of sins. But its effect on his listeners, he reported, was similar to throwing cold water on them, and so he discontinued the practice.

Meanwhile, down in Alabama, young Tolbert Fanning was about to catch a glimpse of the Bible which would start him on a collision course with its demands on his life. The first lasting impact came on a dark night when he was in the company of Moore, typically spending the evening with young people. They were waiting for the "witches" to come to a "haunted house." The preacher, huddling in the darkness with the lad, told him the story of Joseph in a manner so vivid that he afterwards could never erase the impression. When Moore died many years later, Fanning wrote, "Before we had thought there was anything very interesting in the Bible, he delighted us with the history of Joseph and his brethren; and we doubt if we have ever thought of Joseph since, that we did not call to mind Elder E. D. Moore."[6] The early impression of Joseph's unwavering faith made a permanent imprint. Tolbert, like Joseph, retained a tenacious grip upon God through disparities designed to try even the most determined.

Encouraged by Moore and Matthews, Fanning turned from his efforts to "get religion" to a persistent personal search of the Scriptures. Still using the editorial "we," so characteristic of his style, he later wrote,

> Our first purpose in reading the Bible, was to ascertain which, the Baptist, or Methodist were right in religion, and upon examination, we were quite surprised to find no light on the subject. We found, however, what we could much more clearly understand that Jesus of Nazareth was miraculously born, and after preaching and suffering he was taken to heaven.
>
> We also learned that through his Apostles, a new church—a new order of things, was established on earth.[7]

Unaware of Tolbert Fanning, B.F. Hall made his way to Alabama. On the last day of September, 1827, he preached at Cypress Creek, just north of Florence. He had determined to imitate the preaching of the apostles, and so for the first time he urged his hearers to be baptized for the remission of their sins. To encourage his listeners to respond, he decided to ask the group to sing an "invitation" hymn. His message came through to Fanning "in a manner which was so simple and plain that anyone could understand it." He was convinced of its truth. When the invitation hymn was sung (for the first time among these people), he came forward and confessed his faith in Christ.[8]

Fanning was immersed the next morning by James E. Matthews. It was Monday. As he came from the water, a Baptist friend exclaimed, "Oh bless me, when did you *get religion?*" "Getting religion," Fanning confessed, had never held much appeal for him. But he could never again escape the confidence that God was true and that "in his promises there was safety."

Another confidence was implanted that day. Years later, when he stood near life's terminus, Fanning remembered, "Our determination from the day of our admission to the Savior was to recommend his religion to the lost. We thought it was the duty of all Christians to work in the vineyard."[9]

He read the Scriptures a year before he stood before an audience. As he spoke publicly, he gradually gained confidence and began to take an active role in the Cypress Creek church. Meanwhile he continued his studies with Ross Houston for two years, persevered with his work on his father's land, and pursued his study of the Scriptures.

We had but one book, the Bible—and we really did not suppose that a preacher needed any other. The idea of a concordance, or commentary, had scarcely entered our mind, but we continued our study of the naked scriptures. At that time, we were ignorant of religious papers, but during our first year's work, we read a printed sermon by W. Kinkaid, on Predestination, that we have not to this day, seen excelled. From the fact that, we had no aids in our studies, we were necessarily compelled to become familiar with the different parts of the Bible; and with the scriptures bearing upon special subjects.

In twelve months, we had but little difficulty in examining most subjects before an auditory by turning to, and reading the passages, bearing upon the matters before us. We are now more than satisfied that, we are more indebted to our poverty, in shutting out all books from us, save the Precious Oracles, than any other cause in our Success in comprehending and teaching the scriptures to others.[10]

With the encouragement of the congregation where he had made his confession, Fanning began to preach in schoolhouses and beneath brush arbors. Luke Shirley, the first person he baptized, was twenty-seven years old at the time and later was prominent for his work in the church. Then, on October 1, 1829, Fanning bade farewell to his mother and father and crossed the Tennessee River to preach. Having buckled on the King's weapons, he "threw His banner to the breeze for a life voyage."

CHAPTER 2

THE HAZARD OF THE DIE

CONVERSION AND EARLY INFLUENCES

"We have set our lives upon a cast and we will stand the hazard of the die."
Tolbert Fanning

THE MOLD in which Fanning was cast became a variegated matrix as event contrived with event to fix his destiny. As he innocently waited, and watched, and listened, a fascinating young country matured rapidly. Men anticipated swifter travel on the recently completed Erie Canal. The whole nation talked about Robert Fulton's steamboat. James Madison was president. Napoleon Bonaparte dominated Europe, and international tensions gave birth to the Monroe Doctrine. Henry Clay, John C. Calhoun, and the booming Daniel Webster, with his heavy oratorical artillery, used the Senate floor like an anvil to hammer out the guidelines which would shape their nation for decades.

Over in Pennsylvania a young man named Alexander Campbell preached his first sermon. In the same year, down in Cannon County, Tennessee, Tolbert Fanning was born. The date was May 10, 1810.

Tolbert's parents, William and Nancy Bromley Fanning, both of English descent, had been married in Virginia in 1807. Soon after their marriage they waved brave good-byes to loved ones and crossed the Allegheny Mountains. They settled first in Warren County, then in Cannon County, Tennessee, and before Tolbert reached the age of ten, moved farther south to Alabama where they settled in what later became Lauderdale County. At the time it was still an Indian territory.[1]

Not much is known of Fanning's parents. His mother was a kind and gentle woman with rare natural abilities. His father, though poor, was very industrious and became the owner of a considerable landed estate in Alabama with holdings in both Lauderdale and Jackson counties. Tolbert had two brothers and four sisters, another brother dying in infancy. With the exception of Tolbert, each of these reared a large family.

Shortly after Tolbert left home, his parents and several of the children moved on to Mississippi, settling in the wilderness later known as Tallahatchie County, near the city of Charleston. There his mother died in 1834, and in 1844, his father decided to move still farther west, this time to the Republic of Texas. One or two daughters were still with him in Texas where he died in 1865.

When the Fannings moved to Lauderdale County, they settled in a wild land where bears, wolves, and wildcats occasionally ravaged unattended flocks. Indians still lingered in the wilderness, and neighbors were sparse. The precarious pilgrimage through such surroundings was made bearable by a large company of other Tennessee neighbors and kinsmen who moved with them. Each was lured farther west by a restive thirst for adventure and an impatient hunger for new experiences.

Their dwelling places were crude and well ventilated. Stock and dirt chimneys and puncheon floors seemed luxurious when compared to a wilderness whose threats were answered by the warm security of a wide, spacious fireplace. One post provided an adequate bedstead and half of a neatly peeled gum stick, with rockers, guaranteed sure safety for the baby's innocent slumber. Among household utensils were piggins—small wooden pails, each with an upright stave for a handle—and noggins—small drinking mugs.

Surrounded by such comforts, each family was its own doctor, and home remedies were shared both with neighbors and with future generations. It was fifty years before Tennessee had its first medical school.

Since William Fanning was a planter, young Tolbert spent

most of his time in the field. Necessity dictated that even times of mirth be merged with events of work. At a barn raising Tolbert preferred and was expected to take a corner. His adolescent stature, acting self-assured in its reach for six foot six inches, argued convincingly that for anyone but Tolbert to be the captain of the team at a log rolling or rail splitting contest was inconceivable.

In the absence of professional men, the neighborhood teacher played a multi-sided role and was afforded ample credit for all that he knew. He was regarded somewhat as an intellectual giant who was expected to work hard sums, formulate legal documents, arbitrate neighborhood troubles, judge at shooting matches, pass the hat around for contributions at big meetings, publicly advertise stolen or strayed livestock, and read the Declaration of Independence at the annual Fourth-of-July barbecue.

Though life was never too secure for men in such surroundings and though ignorance in some areas separates them from us, they were often supremely blessed with an enviable sense of spiritual values. They felt their need for leaning heavily on a divine being. Their faith and trust, though simple and innocent, were frequently profound.

One of Tolbert Fanning's contemporaries remembered that many of the preachers of the day were ignorant men who preached "simply and singly for the want of sense."[2] Some, as today, were searching for places of honor and fame. It is also obvious, however, that many sincere and honest men underwent great hardship and sacrifice to infuse into coarse frontier life the wholesome leaven of spiritual concern.

Arminians and Calvinists made up the two major religious parties. According to reputable historians, the cut of the preacher's Sunday coat revealed his partisan creed—whether he got religion, or religion got him!

Nancy Bromley Fanning, Tolbert's mother, was a strict and pious Baptist of the old Virginia school. Her children generally heard preachers who were of the Methodists, the Baptists, and occasionally the Presbyterians.

Another force in Fanning's life was given birth many miles from his home. It was during the early 1800s that the "Second Great Awakening" blossomed fully. It started in a series of revivals among students at Yale and other colleges. But when it reached the frontier, the wilderness captured its captor and placed its indelible mark on the religious resurgence. At river crossings and in private barns there was heard the cry for "revival," as some were "caused to shout, some to laugh, some to dance, some to jerk, and others, when happiest, to sink into a deathlike swoon, and all to act ridiculously silly." As this interest moved south, it grew in intensity. But Fanning remained unaware.

Tolbert's education was decidedly limited in the beginning. From three to six months were devoted to studies each year, and he often regretted that his family had not taken greater care in selecting teachers. He was persuaded that they had wasted a great deal of money by hiring the cheapest teacher, without proper regard for his qualifications.

By the time he was seventeen, his education had included "a little" geography, arithmetic, grammar, and history. He had examined a few newspapers and read the life of General Marion, Goldsmith's *Vicar of Wakefield,* and his grandmother's copy of *Pilgrim's Progress* which she had brought from London. He remembered, "The *Vicar of Wakefield* directed our sympathies aright. John Bunyan gave us an exalted opinion of one Mr. Faithful." He also had devoted three weeks to the study of Matthew, Mark, Luke, and John. His study of American History, at the feet of James E. Matthews, was select though impressive, but he knew little or nothing of the history of the world.

As the stirrings of the Second Great Awakening, which were to lead to his conversion, moved closer, and as he cultivated a taste for literature and puzzled about his inability to "get religion," the eyes of the nation were invited elsewhere. In Washington, D.C., political thunder was already announcing the approach of the dark and ominous clouds which were to disrupt some of Fanning's most fruitful years. On March 4, 1829, a few weeks before Fanning crossed the

Tennessee River to devote all of his time to preaching, Andrew Jackson had been inaugurated. Few knew what he would do now that he was president, but everyone liked him. In Congress, Hayne and Calhoun were upholding the doctrine of nullification. Toward the end of January, 1830, Daniel Webster arose to engage these in tense combat. Like a "great cannon loaded to the lips" (as Emerson liked to say), he thundered his message for a strong federal union. He said the government was made "for the people, made by the people, and answerable to the people." Over in Illinois a young man exactly Fanning's age read Webster's words and they made a profound impression on his mind. His name was Abraham Lincoln.

Webster closed his famous speech by ridiculing the idea of "Liberty and Union afterwards," and called for "Liberty *and* Union, now and forever, one and inseparable."

While schoolboys declaimed Webster's words in class-rooms across the country, the nation waited to see which side Jackson would take. His position was made clear at a Jefferson Day gathering that same year. After twenty-four toasts had been offered by others, he solemnly arose and proposed his own toast. The nation waited. He proposed: "Our Union: It must be preserved."

As the nation's attention was drawn to these events, the stirrings in Fanning's heart were moving toward an important crescendo. Most of his initial preaching, primarily in 1830, was done in Northern Alabama and Middle Tennessee and included the scenes near his birthplace in Cannon County, Tennessee. In later years, Fanning often told of the elderly sister in one of the churches who took him aside during these efforts to tell him, "You have made a failure. You are neither called nor qualified to preach. You ought not to try. You will disgrace the cause." Fanning's clothes were all made at home—grown, carded, spun, dyed, woven, and cut by the women in the family. One well-meaning member took careful inventory of the tall and gangling appearance which he presented in the pulpit. He advised, "Brother Fanning, you never can preach, and will always run your legs too far

through your breeches. Do go home and go to plowing."[3]
Rees Jones, one of the earliest preachers in the American
movement to restore New Testament Christianity, took him
aside one day and confided that he would never amount to
much as a preacher. He advised him to try something else.

But others were more encouraging. His wife later wrote,

> His plain and simple manner of presenting the Scrip-
> tures led hundreds to obey them, understandingly. He
> had the happiness to see many pass from the state of
> gloom in which he had suffered into the glorious liberty
> of the children of God.[4]

And his critics lived to hear him hold an audience spellbound for two, three, and five hours at a time. But this
was only after innocent inexperience had ripened into dis-
ciplined maturity.

Tolbert Fanning was no exception to the tendency of youth
to believe one can revolutionize the institutions of his society
with sledgehammer tactics. In his early years as a preacher
there were examples of his readiness to attack not only doctrinal positions which he believed to be in error among his
own people, but to attack institutions and social practices
of his society which many older and more experienced men
considered to be sacred. One occasion coincided with the
hysteria which swept through the South after Nat Turner, a
pious slave in Virginia, led an uprising in 1831 in which
fifty-seven white people were killed and both the army and
the navy had to be called in to help round up Turner and
others suspected of helping him. About one hundred Negroes
were killed, and Turner was hanged.

Since the South was already learning that slavery was
beginning to pay again, the myth of the "contented slave"
was fairly mature so that the underlying, subconscious feelings of guilt were exposed when the Nat Turner rebellion
came to shock the psychological structure of the whole class
structure. To illustrate that white people had not really convinced themselves of the myth, the Charleston newspaper
even refused to carry news of some slave uprisings for fear
that it might set off a whole series of similar rebellions.

Beneath their protestations of the happy black man, many in the South projected their own feelings onto the blacks and realized that if they were in their position, they would hardly be content.

Mass fear was institutionalized in stronger "black codes," especially in the "deep" South, including Alabama, Mississippi, and Louisiana. These laws often made it illegal for slaves to congregate, to walk on the sidewalk with whites (in some areas), or even to teach a slave to read and write (a practice common with Fanning and his wife in later years).

Into this explosive situation Fanning inserted a dangerous sermon in Murfreesboro, Tennessee. During the week, he stood watching a member of the Church of Christ selling one of his slaves. Even discounting the fact that the slave was also a member of the church, Fanning could not convince himself that the social institution which permitted such injustice could be compatible with the spirit of Christ. Especially piercing Fanning's heart was the fact that the member of the church dragged the black man away from his own wife and children to sell him for profit.

The next Sunday Fanning, though a young preacher, reminded his listeners that the gospel of Christ had demanding social content, and he proceeded to rebuke the Christian slaveowner publicly. Not only because of his youth, but because of the timing of the sermon, many in the community were enraged against Fanning. The church member was so bitter that he had Fanning arrested and filed suit against him for using inflammatory language to the slaves (some of whom were in his audience as members of the congregation). There was probably no more serious charge which could have been thrown at Fanning at that time, especially since he was considered, much like Amos in the Old Testament, to be an "outside agitator" who had come into town to disrupt the quiet and calm which the citizens of the South had worked so hard to maintain. Fanning had touched a raw nerve. It is doubtful that he realized how friendless he would be even among members of the church.

One man who was not a member of the congregation, Mr. Charles Reedy, an outstanding lawyer, became concerned with the dilemma in which Fanning found himself. He especially despised the religious prejudice involved. Reedy took the case voluntarily and without charge, and not only won the case for Fanning, but won a lifelong and grateful friend as well.

Fanning's youthful courage was also evident, even at the age of twenty-one, when he discovered a practice which he believed to be unsound doctrinally. In these first efforts to preach, he displayed an early decisiveness for which he was later remembered even into the years of his maturity. Once, he had gone to preach in the neighborhood known as Owl Hollow, and when he arrived he found a warm camp meeting in progress where he was scheduled to participate. There was straw on the ground around the "mourner's bench" since many in the Church of Christ still retained the paraphernalia for "getting religion." During a recess and before the time for Fanning to speak, he secured some help and gathered up the straw and accessories to the mourner's bench and carried them off to throw them down a nearby hill. One might question his wisdom, but none could deny his youthful determination!

Fanning sat silently while the zealous members condemned the dastardly deed. When his turn to preach arrived, he delivered a sermon on the evils of the mourner's bench system, and the church there never used the method again.

Fanning's maturity during this period emerged, but not without struggle. On one occasion, in Alexandria, he was nearly attacked by a drunken man who did not agree with his preaching. (For a drunken man to be in a worship service was more common then since drunkenness was a greater social problem in America than it is now in public places.)[5] Fanning had returned to the tavern to get his clothes in order to baptize several persons, and the man was waiting in the hallway. A Mr. Griffin, who evidently had not made any claim to be a Christian until recently, was with Fanning. Fanning was afraid that he had not learned the lesson of turning the other cheek. But when the drunken man said, "I suppose you take up for all that Fanning says," the new member simply replied, "I speak to gentlemen, Sir, when I speak." The man left and Fanning was proud of this new friend and fellow Christian. As Fanning's maturity emerged, it showed itself obviously to be of the contagious variety.

But while Fanning was maturing, he also retained much of the fire and righteous impudence of youth. However, the opposition which he encountered among the more educated tended to temper his zeal with wisdom. What at first was little more than a suspicion soon deepened into an obsession. He needed more education if he was to be as effective in serving his Maker as he was determined to be.

In quest of his goal he ginned cotton between meetings, did his own cooking, and saved his money. With his savings and with some help from his father, Fanning entered the University of Nashville in January, 1832, where his first intentions were to secure a degree in law. Several years before Fanning arrived there, Dr. Philip Lindsley, who had been serving as acting president of Princeton University, came to Nashville to become president of the school. Finding himself in a desert of cultural famine, Lindsley had dreams of making Nashville an educational oasis from which to radiate intellectual influence throughout the whole South.

Fanning used the time from 1832 through 1835 not only for his studies, but also for preaching in and around Nashville with another young preacher, Absalom Adams. For the most part, he felt that his time at the university was wisely invested, and he developed a deep sense of admiration for its president. All of his efforts, to be sure, were not so gratifying. He once wrote:

> While a college student, with a professor who claimed to understand no more of the language than ourself, we undertook the study of Hebrew; and at the close of two years neither of us had the least confidence that we could read a verse correctly. Afterwards we read to no profit with persons who claimed no knowledge of the

Nasoretic [*sic*] points. Next we studied with Prof. Palfrey, at Harvard, and then with a Jewish high priest, who looked at everything through German glasses; and at the end of seven years' anxious toil we were taught the Hebrew alphabet, and to spell and read the language by a haggard-looking, poor and threadbare, Free-will Baptist preacher, who had spent many years in Asia, and who was the only man we have seen to this day, that seemed at all familiar with the languages of the East.[6]

Fanning nowhere else mentions any work at Harvard, although he spent some time in Boston upon several occasions. Whether he went to Harvard for the study or simply studied under Prof. Palfrey, who was himself on the Harvard faculty, is not clear. Years later, the Harvard Law School was to use the cover of Fanning's paper, the *Christian Review,* to advertise its curriculum.

One of the most significant facets of the mold which shaped Fanning was the church in Nashville. The group there, which became known as the Church of Christ, actually began in July, 1820, when two Baptist preachers, Jeremiah Vardeman and James Whitsett, visited the city. During their meeting the Baptist Church of Nashville began with five men and fourteen women as charter members. Governed by a creed, the group united with the Concord Baptist Association. At this time they met for worship only once each month, and in 1821, by subscription, they built a building for $6,000 (which served the group until just before the Civil War). The first pastor was Richard Dabbs, and the deacons were Robert C. Foster, Sr., and Nathan Ewing, with Henry Ewing as clerk.

In 1825, the group withdrew from the Concord Association and adopted the biblical practice of meeting on the first day of every week for commemorating the Lord's supper. In the same year, Dabbs died, and in 1826 the group asked P.S. Fall, who had moved to Nashville to teach in the Female Academy, to serve as its "pastor."

On August 12, 1827, the group formally repudiated all human creeds. According to the minutes of the meeting, they decided:

> To adopt the Bible as the only infallible rule of faith and practice and to be governed thereby, that they would, in future, in imitation of the apostolic churches, meet for worship every Lord's day, to break the loaf, unite in reading the scriptures, prayers, praise, and contributing for the support of the poor saints, and that all persons making truly the confession required by the apostles be received by immersion for the remission of sins into the church.[7]

When the vote was taken, twenty-five affirmed their support of the resolution, while three voted against it. Actually, five remained with their former practice to constitute the First Baptist Church in Nashville, meeting in school houses, public halls, and the courthouse. Seven years later they still numbered only about thirty members,[8] but the original group gained fresh impetus from their newly expressed direction.

In 1831, Fall returned to Kentucky because of ill health. When Fanning arrived in Nashville the following year to go to school, he urged the members to continue without hiring a full-time supported preacher to work with them. That all of the elders, as well as most of the other male members of the congregation, participated publicly in the worship services, deeply impressed Fanning. The elders were Moses Norvell, Henry Ewing, Albert G. Ewing, Thomas Claiborne, and Robert C. Foster, and by this time the church had grown to about three hundred and fifty members. About the same time that Fanning moved to Nashville, W.A. Eichbaum was placed in charge of a newly organized Bible school. Soon a weekly visitation program was initiated to discern the needs of unfortunate citizens of the city and to provide for them from a "poor fund"—well before the days of hospitalization insurance, social security, and unemployment benefits.

Since the elders were doing most of the preaching in Nashville, they sent Fanning and Absalom Adams to preach in other Tennessee communities. During his first year at the university, Fanning preached in Rock Spring for a four day meeting where thirty-two were baptized. From there he went to the edge of the Chickasaw Nation in Georgia and baptized three. (This was before the Indians were driven from their land in Georgia and forced to settle in Oklahoma which was thought to be not fitted for the white man to occupy.) The next spring found him in Murfreesboro where, through four months' labor, he baptized fifteen to bring the total number worshiping there to forty.

In August of that year, when Fanning was in Franklin, the Methodists and Baptists both purposely commenced meetings on the same day as his and feelings of opposition grew bitter. In spite of this, Fanning baptized seventeen people. Toward the close of the week he met with them in the Masonic Hall to determine their willingness to begin a congregation; thus the church in Franklin had a promising beginning.

These vacation activities during his second year at the university illustrate how decidedly Fanning's education was a means to an end. His grand design was to "snatch men as branding irons from an eternal destruction."[9]

Young leaders had influenced Fanning tremendously during his teenage years in Alabama, but in his twenties his maturing mind attached its attention to older men. Four were especially significant, but the earliest to touch his life was Barton W. Stone. Out of lifelong esteem Fanning wrote of him,

> To be sure his talent was not, perhaps, quite so brilliant as some others. But his acquaintance with the Scriptures was extensive and critical, and a more humble, conscientious and pious man cannot be found. If justice is ever done to his memory, he will be regarded as the first great American reformer—the first man who, to much purpose pleaded the ground that the Bible, without note, commentary, or creed, must destroy antichristian powers, and eventually conquer the world.

> Although I have heard Father Stone slandered, and his views grossly perverted, yet never did I hear mortal man utter a syllable derogatory to his moral worth. A man more devoted to Christianity has not lived nor died, and many stars will adorn his crown in a coming day.[10]

From Virginia another path moved toward Fanning to intersect his life in a most conspicuous way. Shortly after he obeyed the gospel, Fanning had been told that the "great Baptist preacher," Alexander Campbell, was trying to accomplish the same thing which Fanning's companions were seeking to perform—to go back to the Bible and become simply Christians. Fanning probably met Campbell, however, during one of Campbell's visits to Nashville where his daughter lived while Fanning was a student there.

While young Tolbert was preaching in Middle Tennessee, Campbell made several trips to Nashville. His first trip had been in 1827, the year in which P.S. Fall led the church there to accept the Bible as its only authority in religion. In 1831 he visited the city again and this time had a public debate with Obediah Jennings, Nashville's Presbyterian preacher.

Young Fanning, barely twenty-five years old and nearing the completion of his college course, was permitted to accompany Campbell on a preaching tour in the spring of 1835 through Kentucky and other points East, and again on a more extensive tour the following year. Campbell wrote that Fanning was a "devout, and ardent, and gifted brother, about finishing his academic studies in the University of Nashville." He observed that Fanning was "desirous of fitting himself for permanent and extensive usefulness."[11]

On the first tour they spent some time in the home of the colorful and gifted John T. Johnson, who had played such an important role in bringing union between those under the influence of Stone and Campbell. Later, in the fall of that year, Fanning returned to Kentucky to preach again at Georgetown, Johnson's home.

Fanning's next trip with Campbell lasted longer. In all, it took Campbell ninety-four days, although Fanning evidently did not travel with him the total distance.

Beginning in May, they traveled across the Western Reserve of Ohio, through the New England states, and up into Canada. On the Western Reserve they stopped in Ravenna, where Campbell spoke. Then they traveled on to Randolph with Fanning remaining there to help with a meeting while Campbell proceeded to Cleveland. Because of a four-mile trek in the mud, Campbell came down with a severe cold. When Fanning joined him in Cleveland, they worked together for about three days before embarking on a Lake Erie steamer for New York. They shared a cabin on the journey, and most of the sixty or seventy passengers (including Fanning) were seasick because of rough waters. They spent some time in Canada, but were not able to locate any members of the church there.

In Boston, they decided to try to arrange a public discussion with the Universalists, since this was their headquarters, and they had recently been the center of national agitation. For this purpose, young Fanning was dispatched to visit Mr. H. Balfour, the "father of the system," to determine his inclination to debate the merits of his beliefs. Balfour replied that he would indeed be interested in doing so, especially since the "sects" of the city were afraid of such an engagement.

Later, when the Universalist clergy had gathered to hear Campbell speak, he approached the subject of a debate, but no one would commit himself. In private Balfour said that if Campbell would write a pamphlet, he would answer it, and this ended the matter. Campbell remarked to Fanning, "If I cannot overpower my enemy in all his strength, I will not meet him at all."[12] This so impressed young Fanning that many years later, when he was in the heat of controversy with Robert Richardson, a close associate of Campbell himself, he recalled the words and expressed his desire to emulate them.

While still in Boston, Fanning delivered an address in which he showed the weaknesses of sectarianism and called for unity among all Christians. With well-formed language and symmetrical thrusts of reason he pictured the New Testament plan for unity and painted the beauties of society under such an arrangement. Civic and religious leaders in the city were so impressed with the young man's address that they requested that it be printed in a booklet for distribution.[13]

Alexander Campbell was now about fifty-five years old, and Tolbert Fanning was twenty-six. When they returned from their work together, Fanning spent some time in the Campbell home at Bethany, Virginia. There were many things which deeply impressed him during these days in Campbell's home. For one thing, he was impressed with the maturity in the Wellsburg congregation where the Campbells worshiped. In fact, he was convinced that no church had advanced beyond it. He was also deeply awed by the Christian culture which characterized Campbell's home life in Bethany.

It would be interesting to know more specifically what these two talked about as they rode horseback together through the long and tedious hours of their journey. How much did they confide in each other when they retired for the night at the close of a busy day? One regrets that he does not know more. Fanning had regrets too:

> We have seriously regretted for thirty years that we neglected, in 1835-6, when we spent much of our time with this remarkable man, taking full notes of his frequent recitals of his academic and college life. We think he told us all, but we let much slip from us, which might now be of service to youth.[14]

These tours seemed to broaden and elevate the views of Fanning. Campbell's nearness seemed to give shape and tone to the high purposes which Tolbert had already marked out for his life. It is possible that the two men, both so committed to the liberalizing effect of a good education, discussed the need for a college operated by members of the church.

The rewarding experiences of these summers remained some of the most enriching memories of Fanning's life. There were many struggles ahead which he had no way to foresee. Some of them would involve the sage of Bethany himself. But Fanning came away from the summer convinced, as he ever afterward remained, that Campbell had accomplished a "greater work than any man alive."[15]

In addition to Stone and Campbell, Fanning studied under two others who guided his more serious development. The man who most convincingly instilled in Fanning an appreciation for the work of a teacher was Philip Lindsley. As president of the University of Nashville, he was one of the most talented and learned of American schoolmen.

Lindsley had received his A.M. degree from Princeton in 1807 and remained there for the next seventeen years in various capacities. In 1810, he was licensed to preach by the Presbytery of New Brunswick and in 1812 was promoted to senior tutorship at Princeton. He later was the college librarian. In 1817, he was elected vice-president and from 1811 to 1823 served as acting president. Lindsley turned down the opportunity to become president of Princeton, as well as similar offers from Transylvania University and Ohio University. He was approached by Cumberland College in Nashville (later to become the University of Nashville), and he at first refused their offer also. But the college in Nashville was persistent, and Lindsley was interested in making his life count to the fullest. Where else could he do this as well as on the rough frontier, helping pioneers to carve out guidelines which could shape the whole country for generations to come? He considered again and moved to Nashville.

In 1825, shortly after Lindsley arrived in Nashville, he raised the standards for admission to the University. Now a prospective student was required to know Greek and Latin, to have an acquaintance with Caesar's Commentaries, Cicero's orations, Virgil, and to be familiar too with the Greek New Testament. Also listed as entrance requirements were English grammar, arithmetic, and geography.

When Fanning entered the University, the hours of study were from sunrise to breakfast, from nine to twelve noon, and from two until five in the afternoon. During the winter session the period from eight until bedtime was likewise devoted to study. During the study hours students were required to remain in their rooms unless they were required to recite. It is significant too that each student was expected to attend worship services somewhere on Sunday and to be present for chapel twice daily during the week.

Fanning's association with Lindsley was very close. When Fanning married, Lindsley performed the ceremony. But there seem to be two areas where Fanning's association with President Lindsley had the most far-reaching effects. One involved education in particular. Lindsley's aim was to make available to all the people of the South a quality education. There was an idea prevalent in the minds of some people that colleges and universities were only for the rich. In addition, there was a common belief in many groups, though not unique to the South, that education had a corrupting influence at worst, or was useless at best, and this had contributed to a further aggravation of the tensions between the farmers, the universities, and the legislature in the state of Tennessee. Facing this discouraging situation, Lindsley once stated:

> Were it in my power, I would visit every farmer in Tennessee who is not already awake and endeavor to arouse him from his fatal lethargy. . . . and urge him to reclaim his abandoned rights and his lost dignity by giving to his sons that measure[of education] in the councils of the state and of the nation . . . Educate your son in the best manner possible, because you expect him to be a *man,* not a *horse* or an *ox.*[16]

It is not difficult to trace Lindsley's views in Fanning's later life. He was anxious for every young person, no matter what his financial ability or his plans for life, to have the opportunity to obtain a classical education.

In addition to this accent, Fanning evidently felt the impress of Lindsley's motto: "Let us aim at perfection." Although Nashville did not always respond to his challenge, it could never be quite the same after confronting Lindsley's exacting expectations. He planned for Nashville a university which would rival the best universities in Europe. He also dreamed of a medical school for the city. He called his plans "the grand experiment." Some of Fanning's mature plans many years later seem to revert back to this dream of Lindsley's.

Indelibly etching Fanning's profile further was the influence of still another professor at the university, Gerard Troost. As one of the most noted geologists in the world, Troost would have been pleased when Fanning also became noted for his interest in geology and mineralogy. It is obvious that these interests were nurtured in Fanning by Troost himself.

Born in Holland in 1776, Troost had studied with the French mineralogist, René Just Hany, and with the German geologist, Abraham Gottlob Werner. When he came to America, he helped form the American Academy of Natural Sciences in 1812. For some time he lived in Robert Owen's utopian experiment in New Harmony, Indiana and in 1827 moved to Nashville where he was appointed professor of geology, mineralogy, and chemistry at the university. About the time that Fanning became his student, Troost delivered an address before the state legislature on the natural resources of the state. The result was the legislative authorization of a geological survey with Troost serving as state geologist, mineralogist, and assayer. He did much to awaken the state to its natural resources and made studies which were very often carried in the leading scientific journals of the world. Some of Fanning's later editorial work dealt with geology and mineralogy and bears the unmistakable impress of Troost's influence.

Perhaps at the conclusion of Fanning's college years such men as Barton Stone, Alexander Campbell, Philip Lindsley, and Gerard Troost, largely accounted for outside impressions on his life. But certainly helping to climax this period of time was the coming of a new influence which was to grow stronger with the passing years. This was the influence of his wife, Charlotte.

Fanning was actually married twice. His first marriage came when, accompanied by B.F. Hall, he claimed the hand of his bride and in November, 1835, at Nicholasville, Kentucky, in the county of Jessamine, Tolbert was married to Miss Sarah Shreve. However, she lived only a short time.* After her death, Fanning filled his life with activity, perhaps pushing himself even more strenuously to crush his sense of tragedy and loss. First, he made a trip to his father's home in Tallahatchie County, Mississippi and returned with his younger brother, Andrew Jackson Fanning. A.J., as he was usually called, was now twelve years old and needed to be getting an education.

Up in Kentucky, among the people where his wife had lived and where he had cultivated a close acquaintance with John T. Johnson, members of the church were making plans to begin a college. They were searching for men to teach in the new school, and Fanning evidently gave some indication that he would be available for a position.

Then, as the year 1836 drew to a close, Fanning determined to end it on an optimistic note laden with themes of the future, rather than the past. On December 21, he and Charlotte Fall were issued a marriage license in Nashville,

---

* I have not been able to locate any more information about Miss Shreve—where Fanning met her or the cause of her death. In all of his writings Fanning never mentions her, though on one occasion in later life he mentions visiting with his "kinfolks" in Nicholasville, Kentucky while on a tour.

The records for Nicholasville for 1831 show that her father, William Shreve, was among the 110 residents who paid taxes that year (for owning one of the forty dogs in town). The records also reveal that he authorized the clerk to issue a marriage license for Sarah and Tolbert in 1835. Beyond this, there is at present, only silence. Who was Sarah Shreve? How long did Fanning live with her and where? What was the cause of her death? Did her death account for the fact that Fanning did not teach in the new Bacon College in Kentucky? Is there any particular reason why Fanning never did mention her? This is one of the areas of agonizing silence which has always made it difficult to write about the personal life of Tolbert Fanning.

and the next day the wedding was solemnized by Fanning's friend and teacher, Philip Lindsley.

Fanning's acquaintance with Charlotte had come while she was a teacher at the famous Nashville Female Academy. Her brother was P.S. Fall, leader in the church in Nashville at two crucial times during its existence: when it ceased using the name "Baptist" and voted a resolution of nondenominational discipleship, and later when it was wracked with dissension over doctrinal and personal controversy. On both occasions he demonstrated a maturity which was redemptive to the group.

Charlotte was born near London on April 10, 1809 and led a very sheltered life in childhood in a well-to-do family of England's aristocracy. Her grandfather and grandmother, Jonathan and Elizabeth Slater Fall, were painted by the noted Sir Joshua Reynolds after their presentation at court. Her father, after having lost and won several fortunes, brought his family of ten children across the Atlantic to Logan County, Kentucky in 1817 to try to remake his most recently lost fortune. Charlotte's mother died shortly after they arrived in America. Her father soon followed, but not before he had given a final admonition to his eldest son: "Philip, if you forsake my children, God will forsake you." Philip soon went to Louisville to teach, but he always provided for the other children. When he married, he took all of them, including Charlotte, into his own home.

Charlotte Fall was educated in her brother's private academy, and, among other accomplishments, was able to read five languages: Hebrew, Greek, Latin, French, and German. She especially enjoyed reading her Greek New Testament. Together with Tolbert, Charlotte represented in the church an element interested in education which was to be tragically lacking toward the end of the century. (Certainly a part of the tragedy of the Civil War was the alienation of the South from northern cultural influence and its determination to live alone, even if this meant living without the benefits of the northern universities.)

At the Nashville Female Academy Charlotte had taught French, although when she first came to Nashville she was employed as a private teacher in the home of a Mr. Foster. The Female Academy, like Nashville University, was nourished by a religious atmosphere. While not a sectarian school, its administration at one time boasted "that there have been in the last five years more conversions in the academy than in any church in the city, if not in all put together." Whatever fame Nashville later attained as the educational center of the South, it was due mainly to the work of Nashville University and the Female Academy. These were models for the other schools in the city and were widely copied throughout the region. Especially through Tolbert and Charlotte Fanning they were to have tremendous influence, for these two young people invested their lives in the educational circles of the state.

Not only was Charlotte scholarly, she was also selfless in character. One of her students reminisced, "There was not a negro cabin within her reach that she did not visit on ministrations of kindness. She visited them when sick, ministered to their needs, and taught them the love of the Savior and their duties to God."[17] At the request of her neighbors, her epitaph in stone read, "I was sick and you visited me."

Her liberality was proverbial. One Christmas she gave her own cake to the poor woman who "hadn't seen such a cake in many a day." She educated fourteen boys and girls herself, even teaching them during the summer months to expedite their education. Several were Negro youths who later became leaders among their people. She gave Aunt Easter, a Negro servant, an acre of land on which to build her own home. When the weather was cold, she would trudge out across the field to see if Aunt Easter had enough wood for the night, and she would not return until she was certain that her supply was ample.

It is obvious that in Charlotte Fall, Tolbert had made a wise choice. One of their students recalled how their talents were both compatible and complimentary: she could teach all day, and then at night do the ironing . . . He could preach, she could sing; he could argue, she could persuade."[18]

Fanning was twenty-six and Charlotte was twenty-seven when they were married. After almost ten years together Fanning returned home from one of his many preaching tours and wrote of coming back "to my humble, but sweet home, much rejoiced, and . . . no little refreshed with the reflection it was not good 'for man to be alone,' and that in the future, if I travelled abroad to preach the Gospel, I would endeavor to have 'an help mete' along."[19]

The author of a history of the county where they worked together for so long pictures the tremendous influence of Fanning in the area, but adds, "Tho' certainly a superior man, mentally and physically, we must record the fact that many of the achievements of Tolbert Fanning are due to the energy and ability, the devotion and coöperation, of her whom he delighted to call wife."[20]

Feeling the impress of such mighty intellects as surrounded Fanning, and coming to know the fortune of a companion who was so capable and so inclined to help, Fanning honed a keen edge to his maturing ability. Gradually and deliberately he gained the confidence he pursued in order to stand before the world, bearing his message with the assurance that he could handle any situation.

To understand everything that brings a man to the moment when he suddenly realizes that there are not only outside forces, but one from within as well—the keen awareness that he is frighteningly responsible for his own life—is an extremely difficult undertaking. Though he remains aware of the myriad influences which have shaped him, he also senses his responsibility for conscious, purposeful commitment. A man grasps the most important things of life out of this sobering awareness by throwing his total love and muscle decisively against his environment. No being is ever truly in God's image until at least once in his life he has consciously exercised his ability to change his environment. The eighth day of creation belongs to man.

Fanning encountered the die and cast his life against it. There were risks involved in such a decision. But then the stakes involved the victory or death of a destiny, and the risks suddenly loomed worthwhile.

As Fanning contemplated his early education, the tingling of his intellectual awakening, the capacities of his giant physical strength, and the challenge of being simply a Christian in a sectarian atmosphere, he recalled the moment of his decision. It had been made without reservation. There could be no honorable abandonment of his life voyage in mid-ocean. He declared, "We have set our lives upon a cast and we will stand the hazard of the die. On the treasure of God's knowledge we have fixed our hearts and victory or death is our watchword."[21]

CHAPTER 3

THE TRUTH
IS PREVAILING

EARLY EDUCATIONAL
ACTIVITIES

"The cause is prospering . . . The truth is prevailing."

Tolbert Fanning

MARTIN VAN BUREN was the Democratic candidate for president in 1836. But the people went to the polls to vote for the retiring Andrew Jackson, just finishing his second term, and through the magic of Jackson's name, Van Buren won the election. Jackson waited to watch the new president's inauguration, and then turned to bid his final adieu to Washington and go home at last. The journey home was a triumphal procession and a few days later, pale and pain-wracked, Jackson arrived back at the Hermitage near Nashville.

Andrew Jackson's controversial personality had provided a source of vital strength to the nation, and he has justly come to represent much that is best in the American democratic tradition. But the controversy over nullification and states' rights was still brewing. To be sure, many believed that Henry Clay's instinct for compromise could preserve the Union and prevent Civil War, and he was affectionately called the "Great Pacificator." But a more candid observer in South Carolina reminded the nation, "Nullification is not dead, but sleepeth; the grand object is disunion, and it will be attempted again."[1]

Jacksonian democracy, with its emphasis on the "common man," had its counterpart in the religion of the frontier, where there was a growing group of people committed to restoring the priesthood of all believers so characteristic of primitive Christianity. Fanning numbered the followers in this group at over one hundred thousand in the year of Jackson's retirement. While a place in history was now secure for Andrew Jackson, another of Tennessee's sons was approaching his most productive years. Tolbert Fanning, now twenty-six, moved with his new bride to the town of Franklin, eighteen miles south of Nashville, to open a Female Academy. It was January, 1837.[2]

As college students, Fanning and Absalom Adams had started the church in Franklin. Alexander Graham, also an able preacher, was now an elder there, but the church still had no permanent place to worship and its membership remained small. While Fanning was anxious first to develop a dynamic congregation, the town also needed a teacher to help train its girls, and it was this twofold mission which drew the newly married Fannings to Franklin.

At first the church often met in the Fannings' home, though Fanning occasionally preached at the Masonic Hall when it was not in use. Prejudice against their work was great when they moved to Franklin, but after some time, it began to subside because of the many friends which they made in the community. The church eventually grew to about sixty members.

The girls academy was opened immediately with sixty day students and a few boarders. The number soon increased to one hundred, and the newly-wed couple toiled day and night for the success of their school and its students. During the vacations from school work, they traveled together, conducting meetings in the surrounding communities. Tolbert did the preaching, and his wife led the singing.

But Fanning, reared in the country, was a farmer at heart. Even when deeply involved in his first school work, he was also busy with his livestock, and his wife sensed that he would never be satisfied with life in town. Through three years of satisfying labor invested in Franklin, Fanning's longing for the country continued to grow until one day in October, 1839, he rode the eighteen miles into Nashville for a meeting with several other men who were interested in agriculture. As a representative from Williamson County, he was attending the meeting to discuss the formation of a state agricultural society. The men met twice on Monday to hear the report of the constitution committee, and then again at 7 a.m. the next morning. On Wednesday they adopted the constitution for the Tennessee Agricultural Society, and Fanning was elected the recording secretary for the coming year. He was also selected to be one of the editors of the new organ of the Society, *The Agriculturist.*

Everything seemed to point toward a move, and Fanning had already laid the groundwork. When he moved to Franklin, he had purchased four lots for $1,700. Now he sold them for $1,600 and bought a good farm five miles southwest of Nashville on the Couchville Pike near its intersection with the Nashville-Murfreesboro road.

This was the last move which Fanning made. As the years passed, the city of Nashville grew dearer to him. It was always a warm experience to return from an extensive preaching tour to the city into which he poured so much of himself during the thirty-five years that he was its citizen. When he moved there, on January 1, 1840, Nashville was a thriving, active little city of seven or eight thousand people (not including Negroes). Already it had become a great emporium of trade, literature, religion and fashion for the state. Visitors almost always lauded it as a handsome city, and its citizens were usually fanatically loyal. Even then it was being compared to Athens because of its educational accomplishments, and someone observed, "it certainly cannot be said, there is a more church going place anywhere."[3]

When Fanning rode into town as the editor of the new *Agriculturist* magazine, he could count four banks and about forty wholesale and retail stores. There were several excellent hardware stores and a number of shoe establishments. However, he felt that Nashville needed to develop more manufacturing. The geographic location was ideal, and at the time most of the manufactured goods were of foreign origin.

Bacon was selling for seven and eight cents per pound and prime beef for five cents a pound. Cotton was available for five or six cents a pound, and a bushel of potatoes cost fifty cents.

Other things made Nashville a center of interest that year, including a great political convention. Since it was election time again, the city waited for the inevitable eruption of political excitement in the fall. Such ado about nothing was usually quite irritating to Fanning. For him there were more important things, such as a meeting of the Tennessee Silk Society which he called to coincide with the political convention. In the spring of that year, Fanning was encouraged to see twenty-six baptized into Christ in Nashville during a series of meetings. The preacher was B. F. Hall, from whose lips Fanning himself heard the gospel when he was a lad.

Fanning's farm was situated in the midst of mature forest groves, and his property eventually amounted to some three hundred acres. The buildings stood on an elevated plateau which extended east and west with a gentle slope to the north and south. The air was very pure and after much rain readily recovered its usual dry and elastic atmosphere. The tree most prominent in the locality was the fragrant and beautiful magnolia tree. To the north of the buildings there was a craggy limestone bluff where a good supply of water flowed from several clear springs. Shading the springs were large, towering red elm trees. While surveying this scene Fanning tried out the name, "Elm Crag," and the name stuck.

In the same month that the Fannings moved to Elm Crag, they opened a school for girls similar to their school in Franklin. Having taught in a girls school even before she married Tolbert, Charlotte could hardly have had a complete life now without her work with young girls. The school was advertised in the *Agriculturist* "under the direction of T. Fanning and Lady." Music was taught by C. F. Shultz, and Professor H. Masson gave instruction in French. The school continued for two years.

Fanning soon began to use his new editorial pen, urging the state agricultural society to take the initiative in establishing an agricultural school in the vicinity. At the same time he began carrying in the paper articles on the education of farmers. Failing to secure enough cooperation from others, he decided to start the school through his own private enterprise. Since his health had been bad, he decided to take time first to regain his strength and so planned an interim tour through the Southern states and a subsequent period of recuperation. Then he began to lay plans for the opening of the agricultural school.

The school began in January of 1843 with twelve students, although Fanning received more applications than that. There were seven young men and five younger boys willing to pay the charge of $100. About four of these planned to preach; so charges to them amounted only to fifty dollars. The second session, beginning in July, witnessed the arrival of twenty pupils for classes, and at the session beginning on January 1, 1844, there were twenty-four.

The school did not lack adequate organization and routine. Each student was given his own section of the six acres devoted to teaching the boys agriculture. This was called the student's "plantation," and he was responsible for the experimenting and harvesting to be done on his plot. The boys were out of bed each morning at five and worked in their garden until eight, except for the time they spent eating breakfast. Some plowed, some hoed, and some raked. Others planted, budded, spaded, or cared for livestock. They also worked in the garden from five in the evening until dark. From twelve to two in the afternoon the boys could choose either recreation or books, and the remainder of their time was given to study and recitation. Concerning his efforts Fanning explained, "It is my object to teach the students everything necessary to the improvement of land, and the best modes of cultivating and saving crops. It could not be expected our operations in manual exercises would be profitable to the proprietor. Many are city boys!"[4]

With such rigorous plans outlined for the young men, it is not difficult to understand that Fanning could close out the year by boasting that he had experienced no discipline problems. He doubted however if this could have been true if the school had been located in the city.

Besides his work with the school, Fanning traveled extensively, always alert to what other farmers were doing and anxious to be effective as the editor of the *Agriculturist*. In the fall of 1841, for instance, he made a trip to the summer fair at Gallatin. On his way, he passed by the Hermitage where Andrew Jackson had retired. It was located only a few miles from Fanning's farm. He commended Jackson for not planting too much cotton (Fanning always maintained that the South would never attain economic maturity until it stopped depending altogether on cotton. However, he never indicated any appreciation for the role of northern capital in keeping the south a one-crop economy and virtually a mercantile colony of northern bankers.). Traveling on along the Cumberland River, to the fair, "mounted on a fine charger," he stopped to chat with his neighboring farmers and to gather what bits of news he could for the *Agriculturist*. He was especially looking forward to seeing the thoroughbred stallions at Gallatin and talking with their owners. The leaves were changing color, and all in all, it was great to be alive and doing what he enjoyed!

But agriculture was obviously not all that occupied Fanning at this time. In about 1841 or 1842, his father paid him a visit. Fanning felt a deep burden for his father's spiritual well-being, and they sat and talked earnestly about religious matters. Fanning was never able to reach his father with the precepts which to him had seemed so simple, refreshing, and pure when he first heard them. But he was reaching others. In December 1842, he wrote to John R. Howard, editor of the *Bible Advocate:*

> The cause is prospering in Middle Tennessee. An express arrived for me this evening to go to the aid of brother Jones at Lebanon, where the gospel is, for the first time, making a favorable impression. Some 10 or 12 have obeyed. Several of Mr. Howell's Baptists have recently united in Nashville. The truth is prevailing.
> Your brother in Christ, T. Fanning[5]

Fanning's efforts were as varied as life itself. He explored each facet without reservation. Yet each had a common focus. The truth was prevailing.

CHAPTER 4

PAINT ME AS I AM
PERSONAL CHARACTER TRAITS

"He was always ambitious to do all the good he could in this world."
— David Lipscomb

TO KNOW Tolbert Fanning is difficult, if possible at all. The countenance of the face, the inflection of the voice, or the attitude of bearing can so decidedly color and completely renovate the impact of cold print. Yet no one now alive can remember Fanning.

That Tolbert Fanning was controversial, even to the church of the mid-1800s, none has ever denied. But one of the enigmas, even to his contemporaries, was the disparity between the reflection mirrored in the writings and the quite different image which emerged when he was confronted in person. Without some discussion of this personality, much that he said and did would lose its relevance and meaning, especially for us, a century removed from his world. On the other hand, when he is encountered in the flesh, a man with weaknesses and strengths, with battles to fight and virtues to exhibit, the value and power of his influence springs to life and he is extremely near to each of us in his struggles.

Fanning was a physical giant—six feet six inches tall. David Lipscomb, his student, said, "He was as tall, well-muscled, and active a specimen of lithe, vigorous manhood as is often seen. He gradually grew more portly, and at forty to sixty was one of the finest specimens of majestic and graceful manhood to be seen anywhere."[1] When J. W. McGarvey met him for the first time he was immediately reminded of Saul, son of Kish, who stood head and shoulders above his people. His handsomeness reminded McGarvey of Absalom, only without Absalom's vanity.[2]

If one should expect from Fanning's physical stature that he loved physical work, he would measure the man correctly. He scorned idleness whenever he encountered it. One of the scenes he most despised was the picture of inactivity which he often faced when he came into town to transact business and found so many farmers sitting and talking the hours away when they could have been working and developing their land. As for Fanning himself, he confessed that if he were able to have someone else do his "headwork" for him, he would prefer to spend all of his time spading! He often was at work long before daybreak, getting the farm ready for the day and preparing for classes in the college. He would gallop off, cyclone style on a fine stallion, to Murfreesboro or elsewhere to preach and be back at the college by candle-lighting for the evening devotions. He would then labor until one or two o'clock in the morning in his study, only to repeat the same staggering schedule the next day. He was known as a man of "all work—never idle—at work with his fine stock, in his garden, writing for publication, reading his Bible, or preparing for his sermons."[3] Through the uneven struggles of an era of sober decision and spiritual battle he was often found digging into the soil and working with his stock, finding there the calm and even pace for which he was also known.

Productive activity was more than mere personal taste. For Fanning there were moral implications as well. In fact, he believed that "idleness—indolence—aimlessness—laziness—sloth—indifference—carelessness and forgetfulness were very closely allied to the unpardonable sin."[4] To argue otherwise was to deny the demonstrations of history:

> It cannot be doubted that the physical condition of any people generally indicates also the intellectual and moral status. In barbarous nations we see manifested feebleness in muscular strength, deficiency of bone, lack of well developed brain, and great want of every element essential to a progressive and great people. In all communities deficient in physical power, the standard of intelligence and moral energy is low. It is a well-known fact, youths brought up too tenderly to endure the

toils of labor—are generally incompetent, physically and intellectually, to bear the labor necessary to make scholars or useful citizens.[5]

Occasionally Fanning would tell his students that it was a sin to be sick. God had authored the laws of nature as well as those of the spiritual realm, and anyone who broke them not only suffered, but demonstrated a lack of reverence for their author.

Always somewhat impatient with incompetency, Fanning's watchword was "improvement." He scoffed at "bad luck," replying that "misfortunes" and accidents are frequently the result of incompetency in the sufferer. Persons, he would point out, "attempt labor for which they possess not the requisite qualifications, and success in such instances should scarcely be anticipated."[6] No one could fail to achieve success, he added, if he had the independence to labor where he was best fitted.

Rather characteristic of Fanning was his advice to the farmers of Tennessee. To better their farms by improving their stock they should knock "in the head all their scrub cattle, sheep, and hogs." Fanning had little use for scrubs of any kind—least of all among those creatures whom God had chosen to be little lower than the angels.

Some who knew him best thought that Fanning's most outstanding characteristic was "the intensity of feeling and purpose that pervaded all he did."[7] In fact, his self-assertion and determination to succeed sometimes created unpleasant friction. Of his plans for Franklin College, one student recalls, "He may from time to time have done some things that the board of trustees and the faculty did not approve, but neither ever did anything that he did not approve."[8] Some even considered him to be stubborn and selfish—even tyrannical. Fanning admitted there were weaknesses in that direction. In describing his first youthful experience with reading the Bible he recalled, "Had a catechism, or any denominational book been put in our hands, it is more than likely we would have swallowed the very first system presented, and from our stubborn nature, we would likely have followed it through life."9

It is probably true, however, that some judged Fanning too much from his writings and too little from actual association with him. From such evidence it would not be difficult to misunderstand Fanning's nature. McGarvey supports this when he writes, "I had expected, from his severe morals and the effectiveness in the warfare against sin and sectarianism for which he was noted, to see in him a man of harshness, if not of some rudeness." But then McGarvey concludes, "I was therefore most agreeably surprised by a courtesy in his manner scarcely equalled by any speaker present, and by a silvery voice quite superior to that of any other."10

That Fanning was lacking in many of the personal elements which draw people close to a man is undeniable. But Lipscomb always felt that those who draw easily are often easily drawn. Whether or not one agrees with this judgment, many today are thankful that Fanning was not one who was easily drawn.

By economy and industry he was able to obtain more than an average financial competence. His friend, E. G. Sewell, wrote that he "struggled" so much with the world" that some thought his heart was set too much on money. He remembered at the same time that Fanning was "liberal with his means where he thought he could accomplish good. He always did these things unostentatiously, and few beyond the receivers knew anything of his benefactions."11

In answer to the critics Fanning's own reply was that he could not possibly have initiated his college or his other endeavors for the benefit of others were it not for some degree of financial adequacy.

Another dominant emotion, easily aroused, was Fanning's contempt for deceit and sham. His would have surely been the same advice which Oliver Cromwell gave to his portrait painter, "Conceal not my defects, hide not my scars and wrinkles; paint me as I am."

To accompany his contempt for hypocrisy and pride, he

had the rare ability "to see over, under, all around, and square through both men and boys. When undecided he always gave the benefit of the doubt, but he was seldom in doubt. Fanning claimed that he could sit on the first floor of the college building and discern the character of a young man by hearing him walk the hallway on the third floor. He said that "a bigoted, self-important fellow always took long strides, lighting on the heels of his boots, making as much noise as an ass with his hoofs shod."[12]

Fanning was not without his moments of humor. When David Lipscomb was a student in his classes, he heard Fanning ask a question just as he was dozing off to sleep. Fanning asked the other members of the class for the answer but none of them could respond satisfactorily. When he called on Lipscomb, he gave the right answer, waking up just as he heard his name. To the delight of the class Fanning suggested that they all go to sleep!

When Fanning Elssler, a celebrated French dancer, came to the United States, she set the fashion for large numbers of Northern ladies. In Fanning's paper, the *Agriculturist,* one finds an announcement of her plans to spend the winter in the South, with the plea appended, "We pray her to let the Southwest escape, till our fashionable ladies' poor husbands get out of debt."[13]

Sometimes his humor was more obvious and intentional. One day he promised the boys at Franklin College a date with the young ladies who were in Mrs. Fanning's classes. When the boys had exhausted the day shaving, bathing and excitedly planning for the evening, they met with great surprise when they were finally ushered in and seated in the parlor. They found their companions to be the little eight and ten year old girls instead of the young ladies their own age. After a few seconds of embarrassed silence, one boy suddenly jumped up and all followed him hurriedly out of the house, all to the delight of the older girls who had been forewarned by Fanning and were watching from above. The boys realized too late that it was the first day of April!

At other times his humor was dry and subtle. Traveling in the upper Cumberland country one time, Fanning stopped at a church building around which were clustered several horses and buggies. Finding a "church trial" in progress, he took a seat quietly at the back of the audience. A new member, a Mr. Jackson, had been found guilty of a terrible sin—fox hunting. The man apologized and asked for the forgiveness and the prayers of his brethren that he might overcome his weakness. He reminded them that he was only a recent convert. However, he requested the privilege of keeping his foxhounds. After some debate, the congregation finally agreed to grant his request, inasmuch as the hounds were good watchdogs, were company for his family, and kept the "varmints" away from his chickens. But he was on probation and must not surrender again to the temptation to take his hounds fox hunting!

With the trial over, the chairman recognized Fanning and asked him to preach to them. Fanning replied that he had a long journey ahead and could not stay. He would have left sooner, he added, but he had been anxious to know their decision regarding the foxhounds. He concluded, "Since fox hunting is my own favorite sport, I thought if you were going to make Brother Jackson dispose of his hounds I would like to have them myself. I thought I had fortunately fallen upon a chance to increase and improve my pack."[14] More than once Fanning used his tongue-in-cheek humor to nudge the ribs of the self-righteous and to question their Puritan-pinched provincialism.

Though he could be stern, he was also warm and sympathetic. Becoming preoccupied with his controversial writings, some have failed completely to see Fanning as a man of tender love and genuine humility. Yet his papers are filled with articles from his own pen, urging such characteristics as love, humility, meekness, and benevolence as the real measure of spiritual validity. He never wearied of reminding his brethren that in the early years of Christianity, their neighbors watched the disciples of Christ and said, "See how these Christians love one another!" Upon many occasions he called attention to the truth that "the law and the prophets hang upon the two commandments—love of God, and love of the brethren."

Especially typical of his ideals were Fanning's achievements in agricultural and scientific improvement. For instance, in 1840, with most of the nation interested in politics, Fanning noticed one of the nation's statesmen too, but for a different reason. "Andrew Jackson," he wrote, "the seventh President, is a farmer in our immediate neighborhood. His Hermitage plantation is one of the most beautiful situations in the United States." Then Fanning concluded, "Were he to quit cotton, read agricultural papers a little more, and study carefully the improvements nature suggests in this country, his indefatigable exertions even in his old age would make him a first rate farmer."[15]

Fanning had little doubt that "great men are generally farmers."[16] When he assumed responsibility as one of the editors of the *Agriculturist,* his efforts were complemented by John Shelby, president of the society, and Gerard Troost, Fanning's old professor who now served as state geologist. But Fanning did most of the work on the journal, and much of the material came either from his pen or was copied from other noted journals of a scientific or agricultural nature. By encouraging chemical analysis of soils, experiments in manuring, rotation of crops, and the improvement of livestock, the editors aimed at improving farming throughout the area. They were especially anxious to see the farmer hold his head erect and escape the ruts of ignorance. Farming, they hoped, would grow more respectable and its leaders more professional. The paper also carried many articles on horticulture, floriculture, and household affairs for the farmer's wife. The editors admitted from the beginning that they desired to place the farmer in a more independent position materially and to help him escape poverty and covetousness. The paper also carried suggested home remedies for various sicknesses.

Fanning was fond of good stock and was quite successful in improving strains of hogs, cattle, horses, and sheep. Oc-

casionally he advertised his stock in the *Agriculturist,* never
hesitating to point out in regard to a fine Berkshire Boar,
"I cannot believe there is a better or his equal in the
county."

Fanning's love of good stock is clearly illustrated in one
of his letters, addressed to W. C. Huffman:

Franklin College
May 25, 1868

Brother Huffman:

It is said "we are twice a child, but once a man."
I love fine animals, fine people, fine horses, fine cattle,
fine sheep, fine dogs, and fine hogs. Now I am at the
point. Have you the growing birkshires [sic] that are all
right in shape? If so, I want some two sows and a boar
if I can get them. I would like a young sow that will
have pigs toward fall, and then a pair or two of pigs.
Have you got them? Tell me exactly what you can
spare, young or old and the prices. If you have not
birkshires, [sic] who has the genuine? Health good.
Would like to hold a meeting with you. Write.

Truly,
T. Fanning[17]

Fanning especially found delight in raising thoroughbred
horses. Admirers of the walking horse still remember him
as one who originally introduced the Morgan strain into
Tennessee. One of his most famous horses was Vermont Boy,
a Morgan stallion which he imported from Vermont in
1858. Two others who were especially famous were Bullet,
an ancestor of the illustrious Roam Allen, and Chicamauga.
Both of these strongly endure in the pedigrees of most
Tennessee walking horses and trotters today.

Fanning's friends remembered that if he met a man and
a horse, he might not recognize the man (though this was
rare), but he never forgot the horse. He even had a track
on his farm to train his horses to harness, and members
of the church often criticized him for the associations fostered by his fondness for horses. For the most part, he
seems to have remained as indifferent to their criticisms
as the limestone rocks of Elm Crag.

Silk was an area of agriculture which became especially demanding of Fanning's attention for several years. Convinced that the South needed to diversify and produce more manufactured goods, he argued that King Cotton would someday be the downfall of the South if her citizens did not follow his advice. These efforts toward diversification led to his great silk enthusiasm.

> While the multitudes are holding up their hands, and sighing, and hoping for better times, and looking up to government to pay their debts and give them wealth, the individual who will purchase enough mulberry trees while they are cheap to plant a few acres and begin to feed silk worms, may make his fortune and retire before Presidents or statesmen either can bring relief. Hard work will make everything flourish—nothing else will.[18]

At the same time he was advertising that he had fifty thousand buds of the mulberry bush for sale, as well as eggs of the silkworm. On August 18, 1840, when few others were interested in silk, because of a large political convention which was being held in Nashville, Fanning and a few others, including the mayor, gathered in the basement of the Presbyterian church building to form the new Silk Society. Fanning himself served on the constitution committee. But enthusiasm for silk never took deep root, and after a while Fanning himself lost his ardor for it.

Fanning never lost his great ardor for fairs. The local papers often carried notices of the prizes which he won for his stock at the state fair. He explained his interest by showing how fairs could advance the farming interests of the state. By periodically coming together, farmers could be encouraged to return home better informed about their work and motivated toward perfecting their profession.

Fairs also gave him ample opportunity to express his pride in his own stock. The state fair in 1841 is a good example. Fanning spent most of his time in town on October 14 and 15. The temperature rose to the mid-sixties both days, and he could be found, in the crisp autumn air, either at the fair, looking over his first place cups, or in session with a meeting of the state agricultural society. He won first place cups for his heifer calf and his bull calf, as well as his stallion—Cleveland Bay. He won second place in the boars one year old and over and sows one year old and over. In two other classes, however, Giles Jones won first place, although it may not be significant that Fanning served on a committee to investigate the age of a first place hog belonging to Jones. The exact outcome of the investigation is not clear, although just before the society adjourned, after hearing the report of "the committee on Jones' pig," the minutes state, "It appeared that Mr. Jones was under a mistake with regard to the age of the animal, and was therefore acquitted."

For Fanning, the awarding of prizes at fairs was not in the same category as gambling, as some of his critics in the church, including several preachers, often claimed. For him this was simply a form of giving honor to men who were improving the lot of mankind. Money was due to them in return for their harder work. Still, throughout his life, there were many who urged him to give up his support of fairs because they tainted his influence for good.

Closely related to Fanning's determination to continue his activities in spite of his critics was his lack of sympathy for the opposite number of the fairs—the moral societies which in his day tried to reform people by force. In an article on "Worldly Amusements," he took note of the concern of many regarding whiskey, dancing, and other amusements, and concluded,

> A single congregation of the Lord, walking in the light of the Spirit, would exert more influence for good than all the missionary societies, anti-whiskey societies, and anti-amusement societies of earth. When the church comes back to the light, humble fishermen and carpenters will again convert thousands at a single hearing. Brethren, let the world dance and hop along to satiety till we can show our friends the better way. Our fail-

ures are in ourselves, much more than in the amusements of society. Indeed, amusements are generally the
most innocent and hopeful exercises of the world.[19]

While Fanning never completely severed his ties with fairs
and similar "amusements" of society, he did have anxious
moments about his influence. In a letter from William
Lipscomb to W. C. Huffman, Lipscomb suggested:

> Brother Fanning has been much engaged in stock
> business but I hope he is pretty well through. I think
> an occasional word of admonition from abroad might
> be of service in calling his thoughts to more important
> matters. And I trust now he will labor abroad more
> than he has done. The cause I know demands his
> service and I think the brethren ought to be more ur-
> gent upon him to devote his time to the work.[20]

Fanning finally concluded, "Whilst, therefore, we admit
nothing necessarily sinful in fairs and can say much to encourage them, and while we believe they have been, and
will be of great service to the country, we see, as we think,
adequate reasons for giving them less of our attention in
the future." He admitted that "the minister of truth is possibly in best condition to serve others the less time he gives
to worldly associations."[21]

No doubt Fanning would have been happy with the less
supercilious attitude of most church members in later years.
But he finally resigned his "honorable offices in Agricultural
associations," even though he served at the time in official
capacities with both the county and state organizations and
received a great deal of satisfaction and enjoyment from his
work with them. The conscience of his fellow Christians
was of great concern to him, and the worth of his influence
on them was without a purchase price.

Tolbert Fanning was also an outstanding friend of science.
Toward the close of 1845, after almost six years as editor
for the *Agriculturist,* he announced plans to alter the paper.
While he was certain that the journal was accomplishing
much good, he was not satisfied with the arrangement
which prevented his seeing the proofs on the paper before

it went to press. Believing that his lack of close contact cost the paper a needed spirit and accuracy, he determined to change its form, its name, its style, and its place of publication. Since Fanning was just getting under way with the first term of his newly founded Franklin College, he announced that it would be published thereafter at the campus, located on his farm. The magazine would have four departments with a competent editor at the head of each. These were to include Natural History, Scientific and Practical Agriculture and Horticulture, Education, and Miscellaneous (in practice the fourth division turned out to be literary).

So on January 1, 1846, there appeared the first number of *The Naturalist,* a monthly journal with forty-eight pages. Professor I. N. Loomis, on Fanning's faculty at Franklin College, was the editor of the Scientific Department. This section contained articles on geology, chemistry, and related subjects and decidedly belonged on the scholar's shelf.

Fanning himself edited the section on Agriculture. Perhaps reflecting his herculean tasks at the time, reprints from the earlier numbers of the *Agriculturist* often appear. At any rate the articles demonstrated a continuing interest in the field of agriculture.

The educational department was ably edited by J. S. Fowler, another professor at Franklin College, and the Literary department was under the careful eye of young John Eichbaum, son of W. A. Eichbaum, one of the elders of the Nashville church. John Eichbaum had recently graduated from the University of Nashville before joining the faculty at Franklin College, and his literary department reviewed current books of merit. It reflected a great deal of meticulous study and capable research.

The whole production was a scholarly journal of the highest rank. Eichbaum also included articles on such themes as the Affinities of Language, Egyptian Hieroglyphics, and the Origin of the English Language. Typical articles in the Scientific section of the journal treated the geology of Palestine, the Egyptian delta, and fossils and geology in Tennessee.

It is not difficult to understand why the *Naturalist* did not enjoy a long life. Tennessee farmers were evidently not too concerned with Fanning's dissertations on the place of carbon, oxygen, and nitrogen in their work. The farmers thought it was "too theoretical, and perhaps a little too scientific." It was better designed for the college professor than for the common reader; so its fate was decreed, and Fanning temporarily abandoned the venture. Three years later, however, in January of 1850, a second *Naturalist* appeared with another Volume I, No. 1. Charles Foster helped with the editing, and each issue contained twenty-four pages. It was by far the most attractive periodical which Fanning ever edited (in all, he edited five, embracing three religious periodicals). Numerous pictures were used. Included too were articles from William Strickland, the architect. Strickland, architect of Washington's sarcophagus and father of the Greek revival in American architecture, was in Nashville working on the state Capitol building. He included an artist's conception of the completed edifice.

The second version of the *Naturalist* was not destined for a healthier fate than its forerunner. At the close of the first volume, Fanning confessed that his work at Franklin College was simply too great and ill health compelled him to make a change in the publication. Its successor would be *The Southern Agriculturist,* to be edited by a close friend and former schoolmate of Fanning, Dr. Richard O. Currey, of Nashville.

Even without contemplating his far-reaching religious influence, Fanning appears as a man of influence upon his community and upon the state. Though he was a man of many talents and varied interests, they all were brought to focus, in Fanning's mind at least, on the same noble aim— *the improvement of mankind.* After carefully observing his life from a close vantage point, David Lipscomb said, "He was always ambitious to do all the good he could in this world."

CHAPTER 5

OUR DANGERS ARE GREATLY AUGMENTING

EARLY RELIGIOUS EDITORIAL EFFORTS

> *"It may be prudent to intimate, that from the fact that schools and colleges are multiplying amongst us, it becomes apparent that our responsibilities increase, and our dangers are greatly augmenting."*
>
> — *Tolbert Fanning*

IN MANY WAYS 1844 was a watershed year. Late in the fall Tolbert Fanning was looking through his mail when he picked up his copy of *The Christian Messenger* which had just arrived from Illinois. From the cover where they were scribbled in the handwriting of its junior editor, D. P. Henderson, several words leaped to Fanning's attention: "Please say to Mr. Fanning, that B. W. Stone sleeps in Jesus." The one who, in Fanning's estimation, had first plead for a full return to primitive Christianity on American soil had at last sheathed his sword. Barton W. Stone was dead.

Other changes were materializing that year. Fanning made one of his tours up into the eastern states, spending some time in Boston, Massachusetts, before returning through Ohio and Kentucky. In Boston he met with members of a Second Advent Church (Millerites) who were praying for and expecting the end of the world "in a few hours." The year 1844 had been set for the final hour. Back in his hotel room he sat down to write for his readers and noted that in Boston he found only five members of the Church of Christ.

When he arrived in Cincinnati, however, there were five congregations, all of them flourishing. There he met D. S. Burnet who was preaching at Sycamore Street church, James Challen on Lower Vine Street, and J. J. Moses in Jefferson Hall on Upper Vine.

He also noticed that the churches in Kentucky were growing. He was especially impressed by a rather "tall and showy" steeple which crowned a very fine meeting house in Lexington, where between four hundred and five hundred of the eight thousand citizens were members of the church. In Harrodsburg he stayed in the home of Bacon College's President Shannon, the college having recently been moved there from Georgetown. He also met a young Lutheran clergyman named McChesney, who had been converted while listening to the Campbell-Rice debate. Fanning preached once in Nicholasville and visited with friends and relatives in the little village where he had met his first wife. While in 1836 Fanning had estimated the strength of the Churches of Christ to be about 100,000, he now placed the figure at closer to 300,000 in the U.S. and Canada.

Such was the progress of 1844. But other signs did not appear so encouraging to Fanning. While he was heartened with the church's growth in Cincinnati, he thought he detected there a "disposition to seek popular preaching, and rather an 'itching of the ears' of many, for false eloquence." Also, since this was election year again, he encountered political excitement wherever he went and was compelled to ask, "Can Christians put *'coon tails'* in their hats, or carry *'poke stalks'* to convince the sovereign people who should be President, and act agreeably to their sacred profession?" Fanning was convinced that they could not![1]

The year 1844 engaged the special attention of Fanning for another reason. It marked the beginning of the *Christian Review* and thus of his long career as a religious editor. Fanning's most successful publication, the *Gospel Advocate,* to be started a decade later, in 1855, certainly reflected the valuable experience of his first contribution to a field already boasting over a dozen religious journals. John R. Howard was editing a paper which he had started in 1836, calling it first the *Christian Reformer,* then from 1842 the *Bible Advocate.* He was having serious financial difficulties with the publication when a group of men met at Rock Springs, in Rutherford County, on September 18, 1843. Those present unanimously decided to begin a periodical in Middle Tennessee to advocate "the interests of the church of Christ." They scheduled its formal debut for January of the next year.

One month earlier than the meeting, Jacob Creath, Jr., living in Palmyra, Missouri, had received a letter from Fanning:

> Elm Crag near
> Nashville
> Au. 18th 1843

Dear Bro. Creath,

The brethren of this country are making arrangements for publishing a paper in Nashville, on the plan following. Viz. To have some 8 or 10 Editors, one from each state, and a kind of Safety-valve committee at the place of publication for the purpose of reviewing everything of doubtful character before it goes to the press. It is thought a work nearly or quite [sic] as the Harbinger can be published at one dollar per annu, and that upon the plan the circulation will be extensive, and the means of doing good very considerable. It is supposed the publishers will be able to pay Editors postage, for paper & c, but cannot offer a salary. Mesrs Cameron & Fall in Nash- offer their services as publishers. So far as we have heard from the brethren the project received favor, and this work will evidently be a medium of communication unknown before amongst the disciples of the Savior in this vast country. We suppose, if the work is successful, we can increase its size to a large magazine or review.

It is our wish that your state be represented, and the object of this letter is to ascertain, if you will become one of the Editors. We wish to send out a Prospectus, next month, and we hope that you will not only lend

your aid, but that you will inform us of your willingness
to take this responsibility as soon as possible. Very
sincerely,

T. Fanning[2]

The first issue of the *Christian Review,* as the paper was
called, appeared on schedule in January of 1844. Its editors
were Tolbert Fanning, W. H. Wharton and H. T. Anderson.
The other representative editors were to include Jacob Creath,
Jr. of Missouri; M. Winans, of Ohio; W. W. Stevenson of
Little Rock, Arkansas; John R. Howard of West Tennessee
and W. D. Carnes of East Tennessee. At first Howard was
offended when he received the prospectus for the *Christian
Review.* He was afraid that it would cut into the subscription
list of his own ailing journal. But Fanning responded with
a kind letter indicating that the new journal represented the
desire of brethren in Middle Tennessee to have a periodical
for their own area.

In the first issue of the paper there were numerous reports
of the Campbell-Rice debate which had just been concluded
in Lexington, Kentucky. The Presbyterians were claiming
victory, although the discussion was causing them to lose
a conspicuous number of members, according to the reports.

Although it began with three editors, in reality the *Christian Review* was Fanning's paper, and the lion's share of
copy was from his pen. An article on page one of the first
issue focused on the proposed policy, giving four reasons for
the magazine's inception. First of all, because of the many
opposing journals which filled the mails, it was felt that the
general public entertained distorted views about what the
churches were teaching. Secondly, the editors were convinced
that no party practiced the Christian religion fully. The
periodical was hopefully designed to lead men toward the
perfect pattern. In the third place, "the churches of Christ"
were not "as a whole, as intelligent, spiritual, and zealous"
as they should be. Finally, its corresponding editors, spread
over the country, provided better equipment than its sister
journals for reporting religious news from every section.

That year, Calvin Curlee spent most of his time preaching in Franklin County, Tennessee. Already a close friend of Fanning, he took some time along with his other work to help Fanning get together the first subscription list for the *Review*. Fanning and Curlee had already invested much time together in evangelistic efforts. Curlee lived near Woodbury, in Cannon County, and started preaching with the Baptists when he was fifteen years old. When Campbell came to Nashville, Curlee heard him, and after some disturbing days of study and reappraisal, he embraced Campbell's reform ideas. Perhaps one reason he and Fanning were such close friends was their mutual love for good horses. He was able to amass some wealth through his industrious efforts in farming and also fashioned one of the largest congregations in Middle Tennessee on his own farm (Brawley's Fork). So, with the aid of Calvin Curlee and others, the *Christian Review* began with every promise of good health and long life.

Fanning's policy, through more than thirty years of religious journalism, was to grant to others the right to be heard. While the opposition did not always extend this same courtesy to Fanning, he persisted in doing so himself. In his first issue of the new paper he stated, "We seek and invite investigation on every topic connected with man's salvation and therefore, we say to Jews, Catholics, Protestants, and the world, our pages will always be open for discussion." He promised this freedom, "provided that all articles be written in respectful manner, are short, and bear the author's real name." Fanning concluded, "We are for fair sailing."

The *Christian Review* was an immediate success. After two years, Fanning moved it to Franklin College since he had been able to secure his own press and type and was anxious to provide his students with opportunities to work in the print shop. He also wanted to give the paper closer personal attention.

In the second year he was aided in his editorial work by Jesse B. Ferguson, a young preacher up in Maryland who had preached with good success in a series of meetings in

Nashville. Passing unnoticed that year, 1845, was an article by Ferguson in which he indicated his belief in a second chance after death for those not hearing the gospel of Christ in this life. While Alexander Campbell was to drive Ferguson from the editorial field ten years later because of this conviction, it received no evident notice here.[3]

By the end of 1845, Fanning felt compelled to apologize for his lack of space. He wrote, "It has been my misfortune not to be able to publish one half the communication which should be before the public." To remedy the situation he increased the size from twenty-four to thirty-six pages in 1847. While every paper which Fanning edited was a success when measured in terms of circulation, his paucity of time doggedly curtailed the attention which he always planned to invest in his editorial efforts.

The tremendous influence which his writings had throughout the Churches of Christ demands a closer consideration of several miscellaneous items here, though several salient teachings will be discussed more fully later.

Man's means for obtaining knowledge was of basic importance to Fanning's views and the tremendous number of articles dealing with epistemology are indicative of the accent he placed in that area. While he realized that the language of philosophy was not very practical to many of his readers, circumstances convinced him that he should give more than cursory attention to metaphysical scrutiny. As shall be evident later, Jesse B. Ferguson led away almost the whole Church of Christ in Nashville partly as a result of the influence of transcendentalism and a belief in direct intuitive enlightenment from God to man.

Fanning also believed that German rationalism loomed as a cloud ominous for coming generations. At a time when few in the Church of Christ were even aware of its existence, he was already trying to inoculate the members. In 1856 he noticed, "We moreover suggest that we think we see clouds, thick and lowering, gathering in various sections. It may be prudent to intimate, that from the fact that schools and colleges are multiplying amongst us, it becomes apparent that our responsibilities increase, and our dangers are greatly augmenting."[4]

To challenge the transcendentalism of Strauss, Descartes, Spinoza, and Kant, Fanning placed the Bible on a pedestal as a "book of authority . . . with the pure life required as the only condition of eternal life."[5]

> Kant employed the word Transcendent, to denote what is wholly beyond experience, what is without condition, and transcends every category of thought. He used it to signify necessary cognitions which transcend the sphere of the conditioned . . . All knowledge which is original or primary—or all absolute truth, is by Kant classed as Transcendental. This necessarily excludes knowledge from observation, or the Baconian philosophy, and all revelations through the Bible. It is the knowledge, *a priori,* or that which springs spontaneously from the divine essence in man—the god within the soul.[6]

Fanning not only denied direct enlightenment from God, but he also denied the availability of knowledge through mere reflection upon nature (from effect to cause—*a posteriori*). In an exposition of Romans 1:19, 20, he stated,

> . . . we ask if Paul's language is stronger than David's (Ps. 19:1, 2) where he says, "The heavens declare the glory of God, and the firmament showeth his handiwork." Does the Psalmist mean to say that the heavens *reveal* God's attributes—his power and divinity? Or did he intend to teach that the world was originally enlightened by revelation, and until the minds of men became darkened by philosophy, they could see *reflections* of Jehovah's power and majesty by contemplating the heavens? Place men in a room destitute of the rays of light, or without eyes, and although there may be thousands of objects of exquisite beauty, they see them not. But let the light fall upon them, and they will not only see but admire the wonderful genius of man. In our view also the works of God in nature reveal neither their Author, his power, or divinity, to the unenlightened mind; but only let the dark veil that rests upon universal nature be lifted by the light of revelation, and we see God's power, divinity, and surpassing wisdom, in all his works. If we are correct in these conclusions, the world is inexcusable, not on the ground that men

fail to see God through nature, but because they ob-
scure the light which Heaven has given in revelation,
by means of which, as a lighted torch, we can read
nature, and look up through nature to nature's God.[7]

To bolster his cause he quoted from Alexander Campbell:
"I boldly assert here, and I court objection to the assertion,
that every principle of sound reasoning, and all facts and
documents in the annals of time, compel us to the conclusion, that the *idea* and *name* of God first entered the
human family by revelation."[8]

That the best men since the establishment of the Christian
religion have maintained that the Bible, fairly translated into
the various languages of earth, is the only safe guide in all
spiritual investigations, was one of the main theses of a
sixty-five page booklet which Fanning wrote on Bible study.[9]
In a sermon delivered in 1857 at Ebenezer Church, he further
illustrated his point:

Are we deceived when we say that in our words and
example we exert all the good or bad influence in our
power? When a friend whom we know writes to us that
dear ones of earth are dead, although we see no spirit
of resolution our hearts sink within us and the scalding
tears flow freely. This is *moral* force. We think we are
prepared to conclude on this point by stating that we
know of no spiritual or moral influence which acts
chemically or directly on the organs of body or soul;
but God approaches man through his *mind,* his *understanding,* his *thinking self,* and in this manner only does
he control the world spiritually. Hence his employment
of words, ideas, and ordinances (are) easily understood
and believed.[10]

Fanning became convinced, by arduous study and searching, that all of the boasted light of science and philosophy
on the part of nineteenth century scholars with reference to
God, and heaven, man's origin and destiny, consisted of a
few straggling rays of light stolen from the Bible. Without
the words and ideas of the Bible, men could neither think
nor talk on spiritual subjects.

Thus positioned at the root of all knowledge, the Bible
became for Fanning the sole and sufficient guide in spiritual

matters. This conviction was a polar star throughout his life. It is impossible to assay to what degree this conviction was the result of his earliest impressions, when, as a young man, he spent many months with only the Bible to guide him. But one thing is certain: Fanning related every teaching to this major premise. Beside it he tested every position. What could not be reconciled to it, he rejected.

As an editor, Tolbert Fanning quite often saw the need to write about religious sectarianism. None could accuse him of encouraging denominationalism. He declared, "We profess to be anti-sectarian, anti-partisan—anti-denominational, in our belief and practices. Courting denominational favors, we forfeit all our self respect."[11] He noticed that young people seemed to prefer open infidelity to the Babel of a Christianity torn into sectarian groups, but concluded, *"our motto is, Union and peace on the Bible alone:* but for our lives, we can unite on no other system."[12]

While Fanning continually censored division, he was not prepared to deny that there were Christians in the denominations which he saw around him. "That there are Christians in confusion," he said, "we doubt not," and then later he wrote, "While we could cheerfully fellowship all who are pure and of good report in the denominations, should we admit the divine origin of any sect, this fact alone would certainly afford unmistakable evidence of insincerity."[13] Fanning finally summed up, "I would not hesitate to say, there are many sincere and devoted persons under sectarian governments, as well as some evil and ungodly sectarists, that profess to take the Bible alone in religion; but these are exceptions."[14] Fanning would most certainly agree with his brethren who were fond of saying, "Though we are not the only Christians, we are Christians only."

A question inevitably related to the recognition of Christians in denominational bodies involved the validity of "sectarian baptism." In some sections of the movement there early set in a tendency to draw the boundaries of fellowship with an ever decreasing circumference, and after Fanning's lifetime, this continued even more rapidly. The tendency was expressed most often in the refusal of some to accept the validity of baptism at the hands of a preacher who was not a member of the Restoration Movement itself. Fanning and his associates, unlike their Baptist neighbors who commanded baptism "because of" the remission of sins, believed that immersion was necessary to salvation. Still, it was often the practice of preachers in the Churches of Christ to receive members into fellowship from the Baptist Church without rebaptism, even though the Baptists generally taught that salvation followed faith with baptism a subsequent event. Evidence of this general acceptance of Baptist baptism is abundant in the pages of Fanning's *Gospel Advocate* where one may read many evangelistic reports such as these: "We received two *additions from the sects without baptism,* seven by baptism, one restored, and one confession [to be baptized later]."[15] Or again, "The result of our meeting is nineteen additions to the cause of Primitive Christianity, four of whom were from the Baptists, and fifteen were immersed."[16]

Realizing the difficulty involved, Fanning emphasized that it was just as necessary for the person immersed to understand that his immersion was "for the remission of sins" as it was necessary for him to worship with understanding. He concluded, "We teach the Baptist the Christian religion, and after understanding the great facts, if they are satisfied with their baptism, *I know of no brother who would not fellowship them.*"[17]

Twenty years later, in an article on "Unprofitable Questions," he closed his discussion by warning, "This is a subject about which little can be said, and many words darken counsel."[18] After Fanning's death, this problem caused a great deal of difficulty, and everyone evidently did not agree that "little can be said" with profit about the question. For many years, notable especially in the *Firm Foundation* in Texas, edited by Austin McGary, and in David Lipscomb's *Gospel Advocate,* the question was debated heatedly. It would appear that most members of Churches of Christ have usually agreed with a stand very similar to or identical to that which Fanning emphasized in the beginning, even though the distance between his people and their Baptist friends has tended to grow wider in subsequent years.

Another important subject to which Fanning gave editorial notice was the Holy Spirit. From his strong conviction against direct intuitive knowledge, it might be supposed that he belittled the work of the Holy Spirit in the lives of Christians. On the contrary, when J. M. Hackworth, a minister who subscribed to Fanning's magazine, suggested to Fanning that the Holy Spirit was the word of God, Fanning replied, "Although the word of God is spiritual, or spirit, it is not the same as *the Spirit* of which it is said to be the sword . . . if the Bible is true, God has a spirit which dwells in the bodies of his saints, as literally so as the breath was breathed into Adam's nostrils when he became a living soul."[19]

An additional subject, noticed only briefly by Fanning as an editor, was the subject of prophecy. After the Civil War, when the *Gospel Advocate* began publication again, he initiated a series of articles on "The Signs of the Times." While admitting that he did not have any revolutionary light to share with his readers, he declared, "This is a rich field for examination, and we invite attention to the subject, in the firm confidence that our readers will be pleased and much profited by the investigation."[20]

Fanning, along with others, wondered if the time had come in the movement to give prophecy a thorough study. Campbell and Stone had served other purposes, and that was all very well. But did they not need now to make commensurate progress in their study of prophecy? Probably two quotations capture the extent of Fanning's thinking at this time:

> Our reading has led us to the conclusion that Christianity really exists on this earth; that Christ has a spiritual Church; that it is at war with the powers of earth; that the subjects of Christ's kingdom will really subjugate, overcome and put down, by the Gospel of peace, all of Satan's subjects that can be saved; and afterwards the Lord will reign with his people a thou-

sand years. At the end of the thousand years Satan is to be loosed for a little season, just long enough to collect his forces around the Saints, when the Lord will send down fire to destroy the King's enemies, the judgment will take place, the righteous will be saved, the wicked damned, and God's government will be approved.[21]

Since this is the most lucid of Fanning's statements regarding prophecy, it becomes obvious that his eschatology was very general, lacking the minute details of depth study. His statements carry the reluctance of exploration rather than the attitude of conviction which emerges from thorough investigation. Although he challenged the church to give more thought to such areas, he decidedly denied the expectations of a future generation of premillennial Fundamentalists:

Touching the speculation of all second adventists, who look for the Savior to restore fleshly Israel to Palestine. . . . The doctrine not only carnalizes the Christian religion, but really denies that the Lord has a spiritual empire on the earth, and what is promised is not a spiritual institution, but a bloody one, little, if any better than the old Jewish yoke.[22]

Churches of Christ became embroiled in controversy over instrumental music in worship toward the close of Fanning's lifetime, although the heat of the friction was greatest and division actually came after his death. The first instrument to become a permanent fixture was evidently at Midway, Kentucky, introduced about 1860 or a little before. But small incidents had threatened to burst ablaze even prior to this. It was not until after the Civil War however, that the controversy reached maturity, and as a result, Fanning said very little about it.

Most of the earliest objections to instruments of music in worship, like Fanning's sole reference to it, were made in conjunction with objections to other innovations such as choirs, fashionable church buildings, and "hired" preachers. Fanning's single comment came in 1856, too early to betray any mature and seasoned position. He wrote, "It is scarcely necessary for us to say to *our* readers, that we regard the organ and violin worship, and even the fashionable choir singing of our country as mockery of all that is sacred." He continued, "It is a piece with 'hiring out' the teaching, admonishing and prayers of the saints."[23]

During the second half of the century, as instruments were introduced more widely, the various arguments for and against their use became both more sophisticated and crystalized, and with the crystalization of theology came also a greater crystalizing of division. Finally, after 1900, the U.S. Census listed the two groups separately: non-instrumental churches as Churches of Christ and other churches as Disciples of Christ.

As an editor interested in both religion and science, and as an outstanding student of both geology and the Bible, Fanning's contributions regarding geology and the Bible are especially significant. They are even more important since they preceded by half a century the Fundamentalist-Liberal controversy over evolution and are not freighted with the biases which attended that period of time. Having studied under the famous Gerard Troost at the University of Nashville, Fanning annually conducted geological excursions with his own students from Franklin College. Difficulties between science and the Bible, he acknowledged, were the result of biased and unfounded statements from both geologists and preachers. In an article entitled, "Geology and the Bible," Fanning affirmed that the six days mentioned in the first chapter of Genesis referred to God's *preparation* of the world *for human habitation* and have nothing to do with original creation. This, according to Fanning, was covered in the first verse and was the original act "anterior to the six days of creation." Fanning pointed out that fossil remains demonstrated that "races of animals lived and became extinct" many years before man appeared on earth. He expressed concern that many disbelieved the Bible because they had heard that it teaches that the earth was created only six thousand years ago. He compares this situation, later to be aggravated by some self-styled fundamental defenders of the Bible, to Galileo who was labelled an infidel because he said the sun and not the earth was the center of the universe. It is interesting also to notice that Fanning held the flood to be local, rather than geographically universal. He believed that all of the human race, however, lived in the area of earth affected by the flood. [24]

Tolbert Fanning also found room in his editorial pages to consider many miscellaneous problems of lesser importance. One of these was Masonry. His associate, Jacob Creath, Jr., was a dedicated Mason as well as a preacher. Creath thought that Masons did much good, especially during the Civil War. Fanning, while not obsessed with a radical position, never could feel that a Christian could glorify God through such organizations. Upon one occasion, while on a preaching trip with B. F. Hall and S. E. Jones, the Masons permitted the latter two men to preach in their hall but refused the courtesy to Fanning. (Interestingly enough, this was in Franklin, Tennessee, the very place where Fanning had preached regularly in the Masonic Hall for three years while living there.) They had become convinced that he was against the working man because of some statements made in the *Agriculturist* in regard to high and low wages. Later, on the same trip, he did preach in the Masonic Hall in Columbia. A few days afterward he wrote, "Forbearance is a virtue, and, therefore, I will not permit myself to speak unkindly of these good friends. Masonry is a pretty good institution, but there is no room for it in the precincts of Christ's kingdom." He also urged, "However useful these associations may be to the world, we have never seen the propriety of Christians having anything to do with them."[25]

All of this again highlights Fanning's emphasis on the all-sufficiency of the organized church in God's plans for doing good among men. If the Bible as the only source of divine light was the major point of reference for Fanning, and it most certainly was, a second guiding landmark, emanating from the first, was the "all-sufficiency of the church" to do good work among men. He believed that if the kingdom was given its proper place in the Christian's activities, there would be no need for multiplying human benevolent institutions. His work in education (noted in a later chapter) was the result, in his mind, of his being an individual citizen in God's kingdom, more than as a citizen of a civil government. Fanning's criticism of organizations should certainly be accepted against its historical background, inasmuch as he lived in a time of the proliferation of reform societies, from temperance and feminist movements to various types of moral societies designed to crusade forcefully for moral reforms. Many of these were aimed at social injustices, such as prison and asylum practices, while others, like the mission and Bible societies, as well as the Sunday school movement, were designed to accomplish less tangible improvements in the realm of spiritual advance.

Fanning's response to the many societies within and without organized religions again underscores Fanning's concept of his own work, especially since many would have pointed out that even his own religious journals, as well as his schools, were certainly separate institutions. He seems to have viewed his journalism as an extension of his influence as an individual Christian. Had he limited himself to activity as an editor, he would indeed have wielded extensive influence. *The Christian Review,* featured in this chapter, was only his first effort in the field of religious journalism. In addition to this journal and his *Gospel Advocate,* started in 1855 and still continuing today, there was his last paper, the *Religious Historian,* started in 1872. In each of these he reveals keen perception of the intellectual drift of his times as well as a concerned knowledge of the practical needs in the church. In the face of a greater emphasis on education among the members (which emphasis he heartily encouraged), he saw clearly the need to know current philosophy and to communicate the message of Christ in a relevant way to his own day.

With infatuation for German rationalism growing among younger preachers, he warned, "Our dangers are greatly augmenting." But he also saw this as a challenging opportunity for positive, enlightened teaching. Had more of his contemporaries been in touch with the intellectual pulse of their day it is probable that the subsequent direction of the Churches of Christ would have been far different. And how can one better know the tragedy and the wasted potential of the division of the period, than to call the roll of the many who owed so much to the clear, sure voice of Tolbert Fanning.

CHAPTER 6

GREATER THAN STORMING A CASTLE

FRANKLIN COLLEGE

"Happy are they who get the mastery over themselves. The conquest is greater than that of storming a castle, or even taking a city."

— *Tolbert Fanning*

AS HE NEARED his thirty-fifth year, Tolbert Fanning could not have known that his life was more than half over. Yet there was an apparent urgency about the way he leaned into his efforts. He was already editing two papers, the *Agriculturist* and the *Christian Review,* and both were doing well. He had been conducting a small agricultural school while also executing extensive farming operations. In addition to this he was engaged in some of the most enterprising evangelistic efforts of his life, debating, starting new churches, and strengthening older ones.

As if all of this were not enough to deplete his six foot six inch reserve of strength, he approached the state legislature in January, 1844, to secure a charter for the founding of a college. Fanning had been saving, dreaming, and planning for his own school ever since he graduated from the University of Nashville back in 1836, and besides, thirteen of the students who enrolled the previous year in Alexander Campbell's Bethany College in Virginia were from Fanning's own state of Tennessee. After the charter was issued, the trustees were immediately called together in the office of the *Agriculturist* to lay further plans for the opening of the school.

One of the significant aspects of the charter was its silence about religion. Fanning was anxious to teach the Bible, but he was just as anxious that the school not be considered denominational. While most of the faculty and trustees were members of the Churches of Christ, the charter did not require it. The school was to be named for Benjamin Franklin, who, as a practical philosopher, had captured the admiration of Fanning.

Before the school opened its doors to the first young men, much was required to prepare for their arrival, and the carpenter's tools soon disturbed the slumbering slopes of Elm Crag. The main college building, three stories high, was one hundred twenty feet by forty feet, built with an "L" shaped floor plan. It contained a large hall, provision for the literary societies, rooms for recitation, and fifty rooms for students' quarters. Two years later Fanning added a commodious building for the Preparatory department where younger students were placed under the care of some teacher until they were ready to enter the college. In addition to these buildings there was Fanning's residence, a spring house over the perennial fountain of water which issued from the limestone crag, and a baptistry which was erected later not far from the springs. Stretching out before the buildings extended a wide lawn of richly carpeted bluegrass, adorned with shrubbery and shaded by clusters of majestic trees. Around the springs was an abundant growth of tall peppermint, luxuriant sods of bluegrass, and a shaggy willow here and there among the elms. Charlotte's love for flowers was evident from the garden in front of her house where hyacinths, French lilacs, spider lilies, white chrysanthemums, roses, buttercups and daffodils splashed an accent of color on the surrounding greenery.

In addition to Bethany College in Virginia, members of the Church of Christ were also continuing Bacon College in Kentucky, which had collected $50,000 at the beginning and was still asking for permanent endowment. Bethany had received $25,000 in gifts and was asking for an additional $75,000 to confirm its endowment. Since the time of his own graduation from college, Fanning had deprived himself of many comforts to secure funds necessary to establish

Franklin College, and he was anxious to be as independent as possible, having determined to endure without endowments. Helping him in his work was Bowling Embry, who invested his savings in the venture along with Fanning's money. Throughout 1844 Fanning traveled to every village and city where he could obtain an audience, but he succeeded in raising only about $2,000 for the new school. By the time the school was ready to open, Fanning and Embry had invested about $15,000 and there was still an urgent need for another four or five thousand dollars.

After two and one half years of operation, Fanning had spent about $24,000 and still was $6,000 in debt for the enterprise. One method he proposed to make up this difference was through the sale of scholarships. For one thousand dollars the trustees would grant the perennial privilege of sending one student to school free of cost for board and tuition. For five hundred dollars, the donor would have the privilege forever to send a student to the college tuition free. Fanning also would accept gifts or would sell stock in the school. The daily journal which he kept during these early years[1] indicates that several accepted his offer for the lifetime scholarship privileges at $1,000 each.

A call for gifts of books and equipment was also issued. Among those responding was Alexander Campbell, who sent the second series and volume one of the third series of his *Millennial Harbinger,* a family testament, and several copies of the *Christian Baptist, Christian System,* and *Infidelity Refuted.*

The courses offered at Franklin College were divided into three broad departments: Juvenile, accepting boys from five to twelve years of age; Preparatory, taking boys above twelve years and preparing them for college; and the college proper which involved a four-year course of study.

The Juvenile class received instruction in spelling, reading, writing, arithmetic, and grammar, as well as geography, history, music and a study of the Scriptures. The Preparatory class studied Latin, Greek, mathematics (algebra to quadratic equations), and history (history included "Sacred

Literature"). Not until his sophomore year did the student begin chemistry, and in his junior year he commenced his study of geology. By his senior year he was ready for mineralogy as well as mental and moral philosophy (which included rhetoric, logic, political economy, and history). During each year the student studied Latin, Greek and Mathematics. While there were no "Bible" courses in name, the areas of sacred history and sacred literature covered this, as well as a four-year study of Greek.

Fanning always emphasized that the church at Franklin College and not the school itself was responsible for training young men to preach. He was convinced, however, that any effort in learning, no matter in what area, was of "doubtful" value if it did not have Christianity as its basis. He also believed that the study of metaphysics was calculated to encourage skepticism and produce infidels unless the teachers were careful to show its true place in the course of education. Thus he taught philosophy to give his students a fuller "knowledge of the speculations of men of renown." He also observed, "Those who know us best, flatter us that no institution West has done more than Franklin College in Chemistry, Natural Science and Natural philosophy." He continued, "We have seen but one institution with a better cabinet for the purposes, and in our laboratory we have the best means for investigation. True, we read no prosy borrowed lectures to our students, but we *work* with them in circumstances favorable for improvement."[2]

One student, T. B. Larimore, remembered that "Graduation at Franklin College meant something. It implied the completion of the announced curriculum without modification or variation. In no grade or department was shoddy, superficial work tolerated."[3]

The second year, 1846, began with ninety students. A month later the *Naturalist* indicated that one hundred students were enrolled and warned that no one should come expecting to gain entrance. By August of that year, however, the number had risen to one hundred and thirty-six, and for the next fifteen years remained near this number.

The cost for a ten month session was $160, which included board, room, tuition, fuel, and laundry. Half this amount was required for initial entrance, with the remainder to be paid later.

Campus life at Franklin College lacked neither variety nor demand. Fanning encouraged the students to earn funds through manual labor on the campus to help meet their own expenses. This took the place of athletics. When school was well under way he noticed that several of the students were paying for all of their expenses by working as carpenters. But he indicated a need for young men who could work as blacksmiths, coach makers, saddlers, shoemakers, tailors, and cabinet makers. Anyone willing to give four or five hours daily to one of these trades was assured of his tuition and board and possibly more. Fanning pointed out that any young man willing to work could secure as good an education as if he possessed millions.

Although the daily schedule was changed somewhat from time to time, it remained very similar to the original plan published in the *Naturalist* in 1846. The college bell announced the various activities of the day with a vigilant dependability, usually beginning a little before five. At five all assembled in the chapel for prayer. Several classes would recite before breakfast, usually reading, by paragraphs, a chapter from the New Testament. When the bell signaled that breakfast was ready, the students assembled in a line in front of one of the professors and marched in together. Each had his appointed seat. Fanning stood at the head of the table, and the teachers scattered themselves among the boys. They all stood while prayer was offered, and after sitting down to eat, no one talked except the boy selected to read to the others during the meal. "The meal was not epicurean," one student recalled, "but, as a rule, satisfied all who had been accustomed to plenty at home and who had been blessed with a good mother's training as to manners."[4]

From about seven in the morning until eight-thirty, they worked in the garden, each boy having his own plot to care for. By nine their rooms were to be in order and the bell called them to their first class. The boys had from noon until one o'clock for lunch and relaxation before classes began for the afternoon. From four to five all students studied music together, singing "by note" before going back to the garden for another hour and a half of physical work. About a half hour after supper the bell announced that it was time to study. This evening study period continued until 9:30, and by 10:30 the lights were extinguished for the night.

H. R. Moore described life there ten years later. By that time the original rigorous schedule had been relaxed somewhat, mainly by permitting more free time in the place of work in the garden. When David Lipscomb, who later continued Fanning's educational and editorial leadership among Southern Churches of Christ, first attended Franklin College, one of the things he immediately learned from the older boys was how to scrape the legs of his chair noisily along the floor in such a way as to make a great deal of commotion over the hall as the boys were being seated for meals.

Sundays were mainly occupied with activities connected with the congregation which met at Franklin College. Of worship on the campus, William Anderson remembered Charlotte and Tolbert Fanning:

> I could almost see her again, sitting in the old chapel, leading that grand old song ("Sorrows"). She was not afraid to open her mouth, and she could sing. I never heard a sweeter voice than hers in all my life.
> I can almost see him (Fanning) now as he used to stand in the old chapel on Sunday morning, with a song book in his hand, and say: "We will now sing 'Dundee,' on page 93:
> "Approach my soul, the mercy seat,
> Where Jesus answers prayer;
> And humbly fall before his feet,
> For none can perish there.' "

A warm evening might find the Fannings, with some of their neighbors from nearby farms, on the front porch singing to the accompaniment of Charlotte's guitar, while Fanning himself tossed one of the neighbor's children in his arms.

At the beginning of Franklin College it was Fanning's aim to make an education available to every young man, no matter what his financial position. He felt that his manual labor system would make this possible. He was also convinced that the mind itself was more alert when each day was seasoned with some manual labor. Then too, it gave opportunity for putting classroom theory into immediate practice. David Lipscomb, after fifty years' experience with schools, said that he had never seen a school which did better work, even in the literary and moral departments, than was accomplished at Franklin College during the time that the manual labor was continued. "The students were kept busily employed and were cheerful, contented, and studious." N. B. Smith, a student during the first year, made saddles which were carried throughout the country and sold during vacations.

In 1848, the manual labor department was discontinued, although Fanning always felt that it was the only true basis for proper education. The reasons for its demise were evidently twofold. First, the teachers failed to sympathize with Fanning in his plans. He felt that the teachers should work along with the students in order for the plan to be effective. He believed that if a farm hand were hired to work along with the boys, their estimation of manual labor would be lowered, whereas if the professors themselves worked, then the students' estimation of manual labor would be enhanced. It is likely that this imposed on the teachers too much labor in addition to their literary work. But Fanning himself was also to blame. He became involved in other pursuits and thus gave less attention to the manual program in later years.

Because his many travels permitted Fanning to learn so much about both land and people, he decided that travel would also be a good educational experience for his students. Accordingly, the vacations of most of the advanced stu-

dents were spent in making long tours to observe agricultural methods, geological and botanical phenomena, and
the patterns of life in different sections of the country. The
boys were usually divided into two or three companies. One
group might journey north to the Mammoth Cave in Kentucky, while another toured south into Alabama and Mississippi. The boys would camp out along the way, doing
their own cooking. Fanning and his wife usually went along
on one of the tours, and he preached along the way.

The summer tour of 1846 was typical.[5] The group left the
campus on Wednesday, June 17th, with three faculty members and about eighty students. Fanning was shocked by the
reluctance of some of the parents to consent to let their
sons take the trip. He wrote,

> Several mothers who were far too fond of their chil-
> dren for their good, attended at the college on the
> morning of starting to bid a *long* farewell to their
> tender boys. It required some degree of firmness, to
> carry our purposes into execution—our difficulties were
> not with the students, but with parents who had no
> means of appreciating such excursions.[6]

Finally on their way, the boys paused at the Hermitage
long enough to visit the grave of the late President, Andrew
Jackson, better known to some of them as the hero of New
Orleans. At Saunder's ferry, where they reached the river,
they required five hours to get all of the wagons across and
then were able to travel only about one mile further before
stopping for the night. Sandy E. Jones read a passage of
Scripture and after prayer the group retired for their first
night away from home.

The next morning they reached the Gallatin turnpike and
began preparation for a concert in Gallatin, since the band
members on the trip had their instruments along. However,
on discovering that "a wedding in high life would probably
attract all the elite," and being "unwilling to perform for
any other," they decided to continue their journey without
stopping in Gallatin. As they passed through the city, with
eight of the boys on their team of horses, and the others,

with raised flag, formed in companies behind them, they created such a stir that doors, windows and other places of observation were thronged with spectators, black and white. Several thought they were soldiers returning from the Mexican War in Texas and asked if they had "taken Mexico." Others inquired, "What is the latest news from the seat of war?" One old lady ran out into the street crying, "What is the matter gentlemen? What is to be done?" To all of these remarks, the boys made no reply, but marched on through town, stopping only to set up camp about four miles past the community. That night, however, they gave their concert after all, beside the river. For an audience they were encouraged by a large group of Negroes who gathered at a nearby bridge and danced to the music of the Franklin College band.

The next day the expedition stopped to explore a cave in which the band played their second concert. The following day they reached Scottsville, Kentucky. It was Saturday and they gave a concert that night. Fanning preached twice the next day, and in the afternoon they met with the Scottsville church to observe the Lord's Supper.

Two days later, when they reached Glasgow, Kentucky, the band gave another evening concert in the "Christian meeting house." An overflow audience was present. Returning to camp in the forest, Fanning sat down at the foot of a large oak to write his first report of the excursion for the readers of the *Christian Review*.

By June 24, a week after leaving home, they reached the Mammoth Cave and spent some time exploring and making notes of their findings. When the time for their return to Franklin College came, Professor Loomis remained behind with an artist and spent four more weeks making a complete study of the cave and gathering specimens for the college's future studies. All of this he fully reported in the *Naturalist* when he returned.

As they returned home the young men stopped in Dripping Springs, and then in Bowling Green, where the Methodists offered their building for a concert. However, a downpour of rain compelled them to cancel their plans, flee their tents, and seek lodging in houses of the community. At South Union, they stopped at a Shaker village, which usually did not lodge strangers. The Shakers, however, permitted "friend Fanning" to camp in their midst.

The company finally reached the campus on July 4. When Fanning sat down to write a complete resume of the tour, he included, in great detail, the progress reports from the churches in each place which they had visited. While geology, band concerts, and training in leadership were constantly on his mind, these all led into his supreme allegiance and interest in the cause of Christ.

Another tour, taken without Fanning, went south into Alabama and Mississippi with three younger professors overseeing the boys.[7] The professors, Fall, Loomis, and Cook, took the choice musicians with them, and when they reached Huntsville, Alabama, a committee of men from the town came out to their camp to notify them that they had arranged for their lodging in the two hotels in town. The young professors were introduced to the community's choicest young ladies. Since the students followed the example of their teachers, the city was "soon all aglow with promenades, flowers, and bouquets." Boys seemed to be "on stilts" and that night the courthouse was "jammed" for the concert. Flowers showered "like meteors" on the musicians. The next day was Sunday and J. M. Barnes preached a "big discourse." During the afternoon and evening the young men were to be seen "gallanting their lovely girls around Huntsville," planning to continue their excursion the next day. But the townspeople imposed upon them to remain for another concert that night, and "two courthouses" couldn't contain the audience. The musicians, of course, surpassed even their own expectations.

The next morning they were scheduled to leave early in order to reach a barbecue which had been scheduled for their benefit at Savannah, but the professors were determined to wait until their young ladies were up and about in order to say goodbye to them. "For some time the boys had no leader till young Carmack of Mississippi assumed the role and sent messengers over the city to find the professors." Having finally gathered their teachers, the boys had to quick step it in order to make the barbecue. One of the students, L. C. Chisholm, remembered that "from that time on, the interest in geology seemed to fag."

While these descriptions show that the trips were times of excitement for the boys, they demonstrate too that Fanning tried to make his college practical. He believed that the lessons of the classroom could best be retained and impressed with immediate application in the world, away from the sheltered atmosphere of the school itself.

Saturdays at Franklin College were devoted mainly to the activities of the two literary societies, the Appollonean and the Euphonean clubs. Each boy was required to join one of these groups, and the rivalry between the two societies as they acquired new members was heightened at the beginning of the new year. Each group had a well-furnished hall and a library of nearly a thousand volumes.

In their debates they usually discussed the question under consideration from two standpoints—one purely logical and the other "sentimental." The minutes of the Appollonean Society begin just six weeks after the school started. One of the first debates posed the question, "Which exerts a greater influence over man, the love of money or woman?" The secretary scribbled into the minutes that the affirmative won, but it is not plain which was in the affirmative! At the next meeting they discussed, "Whether it is right that the aborigines of this country should have been dispossessed of their lands in the way they were or not." The minutes usually reveal that "a heated discussion" followed the speeches.

From the topics one is impressed with Fanning's willingness for his own students to discuss the pressing issues of their day. And when one remembers the zealous and revolutionary sermons of Fanning in his own youth, it becomes obvious that he was still ready for students to attack the injustices of the institutions of their own society. Topics included: "Will the Republic share the same fate as others have?," "Should slavery be abolished in the U.S.?," (the affirmative won), "Which is the greatest passion—love or anger?," and "Is the present war with Mexico justifiable on the part of the U.S.?" Other areas approached were, "Resolved that Henry Clay would be the most suitable individual for the president of the United States," and "Should a female institution be established in the vicinity of Franklin College?"

In its early years the college had two sessions of about four months each, with a two-month vacation between each one. The first session, from January to early May, was followed by a vacation which lasted through early July. The second session continued through the middle of October. Later, however, the term began in the fall and finally was completed about the last of June, with commencement exercises on about July 4.

A typical commencement day witnessed carriages making their way early to the campus from every direction. The bell would sound to give notice for all to gather in the chapel with the faculty and senior class entering to take their places last of all. "Ole Boss" (as Fanning was affectionately called by many of the students) took his place in the center of the rostrum, behind the pulpit, flanked on either side by other members of the faculty. Fanning usually gave the invocation, and then there was music from the orchestra. Interspersed between the musical selections were the speeches, with the valedictory at the close. Fanning himself gave out the diplomas, an anthem was sung by everyone, and the meeting closed with a benediction. In the afternoon they would gather again in the chapel to hear an address by one of the alumni. Then in the evening, as one student reminisced,

Ole Boss, Mrs. Fanning, Professor Lipscomb and wife and others vie with each other in efforts to see that each "greeny" is properly introduced to harness

as a ladies' man. Now at last, the midnight bell is
tolling; goodbyes must be said; and tomorrow's sun will
find us all leaving the dear old college, with all the
hallowed associations connected with it.[8]

The first graduate of Franklin College was A. J. Fanning,
Tolbert Fanning's younger brother. He graduated in 1846,
at the close of the second year's term, with a Bachelor of
Arts degree. After leaving school, he traveled west to California with a group in search of gold. From San Francisco
he visited South America and Mexico, finally reaching Texas
where he taught school, first in Galveston, and then in
Austin. In 1852, he finally returned to Tennessee to become
a professor at Franklin College. There may not be any connection, but while his younger brother was traveling in
foreign countries, Fanning made the following remarks at a
Baccalaureate address in 1847:

> In the estimation of most youth it is not sentimental
> after finishing a college course, to content themselves in
> some steady business. New countries too often present
> bewitching charms, which seldom fail to reward with
> disappointment and poverty . . . It is impolitic and
> unwise for men of ability to seek the wilds of the West
> and the unpeopled regions . . . A thousand channels to
> wealth, honor, usefulness and happiness are found in
> densely populated countries, and particularly those ad-
> vanced in civilization, where one can be found in new
> and sparingly settled portions of earth. It is a desperate
> conclusion for a man of ability to gain his consent to
> spend the vigor of youth and prime of manhood in the
> toils of frontiers, where he will barely qualify himself
> for the refinements of life when his snowy locks begin
> to admonish him that his days on earth are well-nigh
> numbered. Our sincere advice, then, is to select at once
> the city or country most advanced in intelligence and
> improvement, and make a permanent settlement.[9]

The professors at Franklin College labored under a unique
system of financial remuneration. Fanning opposed salaries
to teachers, and so at the close of each year, the teachers

themselves were permitted to determine the comparative value of each one's service, and the settlements were made accordingly.

When he moved to the farm at Elm Crag, Fanning at first worshiped in Nashville. Later, a congregation was formed at Franklin College. This group, while it included many from the surrounding area, consisted primarily of the professors of the school, and, of course, when school was in session, the students attended also. By 1847, when a co-operation meeting representing some fifteen congregations was held there, the Franklin College church numbered about forty members. About ten years later it had two evangelists in the field, S. E. Jones and J. J. Trott. Following the established custom of the times, they met three times each Sunday. In the morning they gathered for Bible study. Then they gathered at two o'clock in the afternoon to partake of the Lord's Supper. This was a meeting completely separate from the other worship services of the day and non-members were not encouraged to attend. William Lipscomb, a teacher at the college, would hang a bag on the corner of the pulpit for the contributions. Some time during the afternoon the students were expected to memorize their Scriptures and recite a verse. At seven in the evening they gathered once again in the chapel to hear preaching, or a lecture of some sort, occasionally on a recent book. Fanning usually made a point, sometime near the beginning of each year, to preach a series of lessons on the first principles of Christianity. In many of the most active congregations the Sunday evening meetings were evangelistic in their purpose.

On Wednesday nights, there was a prayer meeting, usually conducted by the students, although the teachers sometimes officiated. Some of the earliest mission interests of the church at Franklin College were manifested when J. J. Trott was sent to the Cherokee Indians.

Two schools for girls were simultaneously operated near Franklin College. The first was operated by Mrs. Fanning and had actually started when the Fannings moved to Elm

Crag five years before Franklin College began. Students from Franklin College and Mrs. Fanning's girls school were carefully segregated, except upon rare occasions, although the senior classes in both institutions recited together to President Fanning when they had lessons in common. Otherwise the girls studied in Mrs. Fanning's schoolroom in the Fanning home. The room was furnished with sturdy desks which the young men made during the early manual labor days of the college.

In her school, Mrs. Fanning presided from eight until ten each morning and from two until four each afternoon. From ten until noon, one of the college professors came to teach mathematics, and at four the whole school stood up to spell a page from Webster's dictionary.

Charlotte Fanning wore hoops all of her life, whether they were in style or not. She usually wore a white or light-colored muslin dress with a black silk or lace mantel about her shoulders and black lace gloves. There was always a bow of ribbon at her throat.

With the last word from Webster out of the way, the girls came to her one by one to make their curtsies, and then left the room. After school hours, Charlotte usually accompanied the girls on long walks. When she did not go along, they were on their honor not to go beyond the far fence of the big wooded lot. If they happened to pass some of Mr. Fanning's young men, they were allowed to speak, but not to stop and visit. When going to worship together, they were not even allowed to speak.

The girls also helped with the chores in the garden or with Mrs. Fanning's chickens. When she visited the sick, Charlotte Fanning always took one of the girls along and on these occasions, she was never without her Bible.

Coeducation was something new when Fanning announced his plans for Franklin College. Even with his severe conditions of segregation, he sensed the need to defend his proposed endeavor. He pointed out that the boys, by their example and competition, would challenge the girls to do better. The girls' association would in turn help the boys learn to be gentlemanly and refined.

Even at Franklin College there were occasions, to be sure, when the two sexes had social contact. Besides worship together before breakfast each day and singing in the chapel after supper, there were semi-annual occasions when the young men were invited to spend an evening with Mrs. Fanning's girls. On May Day, for instance, there was a picnic in the woods, followed by the crowning of the Queen of May in the chapel. The other occasion was presented following commencement exercises when the young men were encouraged by the professors to get acquainted with the girls. While these opportunities were few, they were evidently sufficient to cultivate many a fine romance which blossomed and flourished, in spite of Fanning's unvarying custom, when a lad and lass fell in love, of expelling the girl and keeping the boy.

In April of 1848, in the *Christian Magazine,* edited by Jesse B. Ferguson as a successor to Fanning's *Christian Review,* there appeared announcement of the plans of Sandy E. Jones and his wife to open another girls school near Franklin College. It aspired to offer a thorough classical education equal to those given to the young men and to bestow appropriate degrees and honors. That fall the board of trustees, on which Fanning himself served, announced that the school would be called Minerva College and would be ready for the education of young ladies by January 1, 1849.

Minerva College consisted of a main edifice some fifty feet long, thirty-six feet wide, and three stories high, with a basement for the kitchen and dining room. The structure was built of substantial brick and was located about three hundred yards east of Franklin College itself. W. A. C. Jones, graduate of Franklin College and son of the superintendent of Minerva, served as the professor of mathematics. After the Civil War the Minerva College buildings were sold to the Fannings who subsequently operated a girls' school there.*

For some years before the war, Franklin College, Mrs. Fanning's girls school, and Minerva College provided a complete and competent college community. Scores of young people went forth from one of the finest educational backgrounds available to mold and shape the young nation.

The educational philosophy which guided Fanning's schools was developed through observation and tempered by experience. At the University of Nashville, he had originally intended to become a lawyer. Witnessing his tremendous success in preaching, most of his friends urged him to give all of his time to this. It is significant, however, that Fanning chose the training of young people as his major field of concern. After more than thirty years of such educational activity, he surveyed the handiwork of an eventful life and wrote, "Next to the church, schools are the most important institutions known, and it is a matter of doubt if they can be very well separated. We are, at least, well settled in the conviction that the best and only safe schools on earth are such as are under the direction of Christians."[10] During the same year he wrote, "At the outset, we are frank to admit that it is difficult if not impossible to place the line, with certainty, between Christianity and Education. They are so nearly related, indeed, that we are not sure that the wisest of the age can tell precisely where they pass the precincts of education into the dominion of spiritual power."[11]

---

* It was this structure which later served as Fanning Orphan School after Fanning's death. After the death of Charlotte Fanning, the property continued to be used to help homeless girls. When the land was sold in 1942 to make way for a modern airport to serve Nashville, a fund was set up so that the money could be used for Christian education. The Fanning School Trust Fund is still used today to provide a college education for about twenty needy girls attending several Christian colleges. Those serving on its board in 1965 were: M. N. Young, President; W. E. Fentress, Vice-president; I. C. Finley, Secy.-Treasurer; Dr. Fred Hall; James P. Neal; Jim Bill McInteer; J. B. Burton, and S. Franklin Young.

One should remember that these two quotations reflect Fanning's maturest educational philosophy. Since true education involves the whole man, how could one separate it from Christianity? In his earliest efforts, Fanning does not demonstrate such an emphasis on Christian education, even though he was dedicated to teaching. In Franklin College, he occasionally employed men who were not Christians (several were converted while teaching there). Even in later life some of his plans, as shall be seen, seem to emphasize a dominant and primary desire to initiate a first-rate school to teach agriculture and other practical pursuits in the atmosphere of the classics. Yet after seeing the course taken by other schools started by members of the Church of Christ (notably Bacon College which was lost completely to his brethren), Fanning seems to be searching for some means to couple completely his educational efforts with Christianity. However, he never developed any approach which was different from that of Franklin College. As indicated already, while the Bible was not mentioned in the title of any courses nor as a special department, it was taught to every student as a part of his classroom work. In addition, worship services were held daily as a part of each student's schedule. Furthermore, a congregation of the church met on the campus, spreading its influence into the lives of all who were members of the college community.

While Fanning's charter did not require his teachers to be members of the Church of Christ, there was never any doubt in anyone's mind that Fanning was a teacher because he was a Christian. As a Christian, he searched for channels of influence where he could be most effective in spreading the gospel of the kingdom. Obviously he was convinced that in the classroom of the college campus he could, as a Christian, exercise this individual responsibility both efficiently and consistently.

One of the best reflections of his philosophy is his criticism of the educational systems common to his day. For instance, he was convinced that education cost too much and consequently left many of the most deserving students untouched because they came from large families which could not bear the financial burden of a college education. Another shortcoming of education was its failure to provide for physical labor and discipline in addition to its design for educating the brain. For Fanning, men plagued by bad health were the inescapable result of such a system. They were burdens to themselves and to others.

Another great liability, he felt, was the practice of locating a school in a town or city "where every species of vice is inviting our most favored youths to partake of the forbidden fruit, 'whose moral taste' never fails to bring moral death."[12] While he realized the need for large centers of population to facilitate commerce, he remained convinced that they were not the proper matrix for educating the young. Perhaps closely related to this was Fanning's complaint that the current education had a pernicious influence on "dress, fashion, extravagance, and frolicking." Finally, he was sure that college students were given too much free time to engage in idleness and thus to acquire bad habits. He favored overcoming this by either supplying a fuller course of study, or by covering the same curriculum in a shorter amount of time.

Fanning was determined that Franklin College would surmount all of these shortcomings. One not only must admire his determination, but he must stand amazed at the degree of success he achieved in overcoming in his own educational efforts the weaknesses which he noted in others.

Fanning's insistence that physical fitness and development should be an essential support in any worthy education has become legendary. But there is ample evidence to substantiate the legend. He lacked no fuel from his personal habits for his convictions. Even his wife was noted for physical labor—in the garden, at the ironing board, visiting the sick, and carrying on a full load of teaching. Before her marriage, while she was teaching at the famous Nashville Female Academy, there were classes in calisthenics which were held in a large recreation hall as a required activity for all of the students at the Academy. Dancing, as a part of their regular activities, was introduced "for the sake of health, cheerfulness, and recreation, but at the same time 'in a manner consistent with the spirit of piety and devotion.' "[13]

Fanning's emphasis on physical training was closely related to his plans for providing an education for any who were genuinely willing to work. "Labor," he said, "is the best capital of a nation and the surest means of great achievements in individuals." He added, "To be brief, before education can be general—universal, the community must be convinced that it is better for the young to gain instruction by their own industry, than by the dollars of parents."[14] Fanning also demanded physical activity to enforce and extend the learning process of the classroom.

But beyond this there were moral implications: "If it be an object to have *honest* society, the proper plan is to form it on a working population; if we wish good morals, we must find people who live by industry." Otherwise, "all the sermons, lectures and papers of Christendom will fail to make an idle, luxurious and sport-loving community either wise, virtuous or happy."[15] Finally, Fanning indicated that physical labor brought good health, and it was a sin to be sick. He was quick to cast reproach upon the man who confined himself to his study so long that he grew feeble and fretful so "that it is not always advisable to approach him." Fanning joined many others who, about the same time, were urging manual labor schools for similar reasons. He remained convinced that, ". . . no system of education or religion can reform or permanently improve society unless industry—daily labor, is made the basis. This is God's order, and education and religion must fail in any organization of society where this plan of Heaven is not regarded."[16]

Fanning understandably had few discipline problems. He was accustomed to telling his students, "If I can get a boy to obey, I have him safe." A former student, R. Hannibal Gardner, after sixty-four years had passed, recalled being sent into Nashville to take a visiting lady to her home. "My instruction was to *go* and *come back* without *any* delay," he wrote. "When we got to her home, dinner was just ready. She persuaded me to eat with them. I did so, and got a flogging from Mr. Fanning for disobedience, which has done me good all of my life."[17] David Lipscomb remembered that the last "whipping" he ever received was from Fanning, for stealing a kiss from a "cherry-lipped Baptist lass" while he was a student at Franklin College.[18]

Mrs. Fanning occasionally punished one of her girls by assigning her a column from Webster's dictionary to memorize. The girl would be required to spell and define the words, always beginning with the word indicative of the offense for which she was being punished.

Tolbert Fanning loved to teach young people, and while he had no children of his own, he spent his life training and encouraging the children of others. With the parade of years has come a deepening appreciation for the lasting results of his work in the classroom. The host of young men and women, who in later years became outstanding leaders in the Churches of Christ in the Southern United States, must have been a constant source of inspiration and satisfaction to him. Fanning observed, "Franklin College has practically demonstrated the proposition that with a proper system, a young man can become a scholar without fortune and without debt. Labor and energy will furnish all the means." He added, "Indeed, we are not sure, but money, as useful as it may be, has been in more than half the instances that have come under our observation, a hindrance rather than a help in the cause of education."

No matter how one measures the success of Franklin College, Fanning must be commended for the efficiency of his work and respected for his lasting influence in the lives of others. The school was an outstanding institution in its own day. But, even more decidedly its success is obvious in the pattern it set for the dozen colleges now supported by members of the Churches of Christ.

When considering the success and longevity of Franklin College, one is naturally drawn to discuss Fanning's attitude toward endowing colleges. Shortly before opening the first session at the college, Fanning announced that it would not be an endowed institution. After it had been in operation for about two years, he saw no valid reason for changing his decision. To explain fully his attitude, he wrote,

Now we are aware that endowments are of some utility by way of rendering the faculty and board independent of the influence which money may exert upon them. Men acting in any responsible station should be left untrammelled, that they may perform their duty fearlessly. Men dependent on the community are liable to truckle to the opinions of the public. We will by no means urge all the reasons in favor of endowments, but state some opposed to them.

Every institution should depend on its own merits for support. The price paid to preserve any institution in existence, should be determined by the good it contributes to those who support it. The rule is correct in general, that the public estimate is correct, that men are themselves the best judges of what is best adapted to their condition, and hence support that from which they derive the most advantage. Hence we infer that an institution needs no other means of support, than that afforded by tuition fees. If one be more liberally patronized than another, it is an evidence that it is the most deserving. Again, most men when supported by a permanent salary, relax their efforts as they naturally recede from the arduous, to the easy task, well assured that their salary is constant whether their exertions are preserved or not. Endowments may perpetuate an institution, this is true; but they may perpetuate, as they have perpetuated, errors and long established usages in institutions after a community has risen above them which is the tendency of such a course. Besides they engender pride and arrogance in those upon whom a fat salary has been placed. Perpetuity is not dependent upon such causes. It depends upon the utility of the institutions which is the proper test of existence.[19]

Fanning's hesitancy to endow Franklin College was based upon three considerations. First, every institution should depend upon its own merits and thus, if the school deserved to continue, men who benefited from it would support it through the paying of tuition. If the school did not serve the people to the extent that they were willing to pay for its benefits, then it should not continue to exist.

Secondly, if the school were endowed, its teachers, assured of their salary, would not work as devotedly since they would not have to depend upon the effectiveness of their work for income.

Fanning's third objection to a heavy endowment was the school's temptation to perpetuate practices even after the people it served had outgrown the need for the specific practice. Thus, a teaching or practice designed to meet the needs of the community at the time that the school began, might continue in existence long after it was no longer relevant to the community. In this manner "errors" might actually be taught as a result of endowments. Since heavy endowments engendered pride, arrogance, and independence, the people for whom the school was originally built would have no way to show their displeasure at its course. Since their support would not then be needed, their voice would no longer be heard.

Standing in opposition to this concept, both Bacon College and Bethany College were calling for endowments totaling $100,000 between them. Naturally, Alexander Campbell felt called upon to defend his practice. He said, "Not a college in the world has existed one century without endowment; nor can they. This fact is worth a thousand lectures. Can any one name a college that has been one century without other funds than the fees of tuition?"[20]

Fanning was not as dogmatic in his objections to endowments as some have supposed. In answering Campbell, he expressed gratitude that at least Campbell had granted him a hundred years probation to see if Franklin College would last! Then he went on to say,

> . . . with my present views of education, I could not ask an endowment for Franklin College. . . . If the system should prove a blessing to the country, and it be ascertained that an endowment is necessary to support it, strong efforts will be made to secure it. In the meantime, I shall rejoice to see Bethany and Bacon spreading their benign influence through the country, and if either should do more than Franklin on account of an endowment to pay professors, I will exert myself to obtain a rich endowment for her, and if I should be out of place, no doubt others will do the same. . . . I hope my views of endowments will have no influence in preventing Bethany and Bacon from receiving each an endowment.[21]

Fanning left ample room for changing his own course of action in case conditions required him to do so, and, in fact, he did eventually seek endowments toward the close of his educational efforts. Were Fanning and Campbell to express their views today, it seems certain that neither would say that Franklin College, after one hundred years, is dead! The lives of a dozen schools provide ample progeny for its pride. It lives on in hundreds of lives. Fanning realized that genuine perpetuity is not always insured in perpetual institutions. It would also be interesting to learn of Campbell's thoughts in regard to the course of his own Bethany College after one hundred years.

The men who took up places of leadership in the Church of Christ after graduating from Franklin College were legion. There were men like F. M. Carmack, P. R. Runnels, David Lipscomb, William Lipscomb, N. S. Smith, James E. Scobey, P. R. Caldwell, K. M. Van Zandt and I. L. Van Zandt of Texas, H. R. Moore, E. G. Sewell, and T. B. Larimore, as well as a host of others whose names were prominent among their brethren in that day. Many of these were distinguished educators in their own right.

On October 17, 1849, a group of alumni who were on the campus for the fifth annual commencement exercises, formed the Alumni Society of the college. Several of the alumni taught in the college, including A. J. Fanning, F. M. Carmack, William Lipscomb, and N. B. Smith. T. B. Larimore, in addition to his strenuous preaching efforts, trained scores of young men at his own Mars' Hill Academy, where a Christian Academy is still operated today, in Florence, Alabama.

Perhaps more than any other of Fanning's students, David Lipscomb reflected the convictions and the aspirations of his teacher. Lipscomb had been baptized by Fanning shortly before he became a student at Franklin College, and for some years after his graduation these two men were coworkers in numerous enterprises. Lipscomb reflected and further developed Fanning's views on civil government. Together they reissued the *Gospel Advocate* after its interruption by the war. As noted already, Lipscomb continued Fanning's work of Christian education.

Fanning urged all to realize that life itself is a school which one enters at birth and leaves, with honor or disgrace, only at death. He always approached education as an endeavor which included improvement in every field of activity: physical, intellectual, and spiritual. For him, the purpose of education, as well as religion, was "to enable us to govern ourselves."

It is little wonder then, viewing education as an adventure with challenge, intrigue, romance, conquest, and satisfaction, that Fanning, even though busy with many things in life, was seldom far from the classroom. He exclaimed, "Happy are they who get the mastery over themselves. The conquest is greater than that of storming a castle, or even taking a city."[22]

CHAPTER 7

AS A GIANT FILLED WITH HIS THEME

TOLBERT FANNING AS A PREACHER

"He preached as if he believed the temporal and eternal salvation of the whole human race and all the holy angels depended upon that discourse as then and there delivered."
— *T. B. Larimore*

A HALF INCH of snow threw a gentle blanket of white over the shoulders of Elm Crag the last week in January, 1842. But the days were warm and the snow soon melted. Tolbert Fanning also felt his strength melting away. The girls school had been conducted for two years, and he had labored hard as the editor of the *Agriculturist*. All this was in addition to his anxiety for improving his land and his stock. Charlotte, always anxious to insure her husband's success, was also showing signs of stress. Both Tolbert and Charlotte, restless to elude the pressing demands of their toil for a while, agreed that they should visit Tolbert's boyhood scenes in Alabama, and then go on over into Mississippi, making opportunities along the way to encourage the cause of Christ. Also, Fanning was contemplating beginning his Agricultural school, and having suggested the project, he wanted to test the reaction of the farmers.

So, in a slender carriage drawn by Jacob Faithful, a thoroughbred Morgan stallion, the Fannings set out on their journey South. They stopped briefly at Columbia and Lawrenceburg, before pushing on to spend some time at

Cypress Creek with Fanning's old teacher, Ross Houston. Fanning could not help noticing the change which had occurred during the past twenty years. He was disturbed to see that the cotton yield had diminished by half since he worked on his father's land as a boy, and was certain that the South must find another crop, both for the survival of the soil, and the economic survival of the South.

But Fanning was probably not the only one aware of change. Many of his old friends must have detected quite a metamorphosis in his sermons, which were not nearly so embarrassing as ones they could remember.

On Monday, February 7, the Fannings crossed a long, substantial bridge across the Tennessee River and turned Jacob Faithful toward Tuscumbia, about five miles south of Florence, Alabama, where they spent about a week in the home of a Sister Cayce. Although she was not able to attend the meetings to hear Fanning preach, her son responded to his message, and Fanning hurried home to bring her the news. He later mused that her friends were astonished at her reaction—they had never heard a "Campbellite" (as they called her) *shout* glory to God.

After one Sunday in Tuscumbia, the Fannings left on Monday for Russellville, the county seat of Franklin County. Jacob Faithful generally made good time, except occasionally when they came to an especially steep hill. Then Fanning would get out and walk while the stallion pulled Charlotte to the top. About five miles out of Tuscumbia, the road stretched up and finally settled comfortably atop a three or four hundred foot summit. Fanning let Jacob Faithful rest while he looked back at the fifteen or twenty miles visible from the ridge. He could clearly see Tuscumbia and La Grange, and as he sat, entranced by the scene spreading out before him, he longed to be an artist and plead with time to stop, and let him stay. But, unable to stay longer, he wrenched himself from the spell and urged Jacob Faithful on his way once again. Fanning's zest was returning and he was anxious to confront the people of Russellville.

Fanning found the roads of Russellville to be of little credit to the local citizens, even in good weather, and now in addition, there had been an unusually rainy season. The mud was so deep, in fact, that Jacob Faithful found it extremely difficult to make much headway. Fanning had to admit that even for him, the whole situation was enough to "provoke the best saint of his Italian holiness." As both the Fannings and nightfall approached Russellville, the shadows crept in to cast their spell of slumber around a town that would awake to a vastly new life.

That first night, Fanning spoke to a small audience on, "The Importance of Searching the Scriptures." Among the three hundred people in the community he found so much prejudice that he climbed into his carriage the very next morning, convinced that his time would be spent better somewhere else.

With Jacob Faithful heading south toward Columbus, Mississippi, they struggled along through the mud. But when they had gone less than a mile one of the springs on the carriage broke. Together, Charlotte and Tolbert trudged through the mud back to Russellville to investigate the possibilities for having it repaired. When they learned that they would have to wait several days until a part could be shipped from another city, Fanning announced around town that there would be preaching each evening at candle lighting. Then he set out to visit the farmers and find out more about their agricultural pursuits.

Perhaps it was largely a credit to Fanning's ability to mingle with the people and intelligently discuss their farming interests that their prejudice began to subside and the number who came to hear him preach began to grow. By the time that the carriage was repaired, about forty people had been baptized, and Fanning couldn't leave. Within a month, he had baptized over one hundred persons. When he finally decided to continue his tour, leaving a town where he had found little interest and great prejudice, Fanning was able to leave a congregation consisting of more than two thirds of the heads of the families in the community! He would never declare that God broke his carriage spring though he occasionally mused that "the salvation of precious souls often depends upon what, to us, seems to be a very small matter." The most he ever admitted about the incident was that while he did not want to appear "superstitious," the incident certainly "seemed at least providential."[1]

On Tuesday, March 15, the Fannings started once again toward Columbus, Mississippi, a journey of about one hundred miles. It is not difficult to imagine what Tolbert and Charlotte said to each other as they passed the spot where their buggy had given way a few short weeks before.

On the first day out of Russellville, about a third of the way to their destination, they spent the night at the "Tollgate," a tavern owned by Mr. M. A. Price from Tennessee. After another night along the road, and another full day of travel, they sighted Columbus just at dusk. Though weary and travel-worn, they were refreshed by the sweet perfume of the yellow Jessamine along the water courses, and having reached the city, they proceeded to the home of the mayor, another old friend from Tennessee.

Columbus was a handsome city of about three thousand, located on the east bank of the Tombigbee River, three days from Mobile by steamboat. Fanning was especially interested to hear the talk around town about England's plans to grow its own cotton. Perhaps, he thought, the South would be *forced* to diversify its crop and develop its own industry.

But other concerns were in the air in Columbus besides cotton. A procession of letters had preceded Fanning to Columbus, telling of his success in Russellville. The anticipation in Columbus bordered on excitement. Many waited anxiously to hear the preacher who could kindle such interest in a community. The denominational preachers had warned their people not to attend, although few heeded their restrictions. What could be the harm in a man who simply called himself a Christian? Fanning found only one lady who was a member of the Church of Christ. The gospel, he was convinced, had never been preached here before, without sectarian dilution, and he began his preaching.

There was no response to his first sermons. But the people continued to come. Skepticism had been heightened since Columbus had recently experienced a thirteen-night discussion between a gentlemanly and courteous infidel, and an impatient and easily provoked Presbyterian. Many, contrasting the demeanor of the two, had decided that the position of the infidel was superior, and, it was in this preconditioned soil that Fanning began his patient work, convinced of the power of his simple message. The hours between the meetings were spent in searching the Scriptures to test the validity of Fanning's teachings. As he continued to preach, many who claimed to be infidels were transformed into serious listeners, along with members of the city's churches.

The first person to respond openly was a Mrs. Sarah Hatch, who was a Presbyterian. Others then began to follow, and Mr. Lyons, the Presbyterian preacher, feared that many would leave him. He began to speak out more freely, and finally, he and Fanning had a public debate. N. L. Rice, the Presbyterian preacher, who became famous because of his debate with Alexander Campbell, was noted for his bitterness and personal animosity in debate. Yet Charlotte Fanning remembered that Rice was far from being the equal of Mr. Lyons in sarcasm and in intellect. By comparison, Fanning's calm and intelligent approach reached many who were impressed not only with his message but with his manner. Soon the courthouse was overflowing every night. Men, women, and young people looked forward through the day to hearing Fanning, and his presence eventually dominated most conversations. He was able to baptize between eighty and ninety persons. Visitors who came to scoff remained to marvel at those who, though recently declaring disbelief in the Scriptures, now reverently read and sincerely bowed to pray. Soon, the small group provided itself with a house of worship, and was self-sufficient when Fanning left.

During their travels, the Fannings sometimes gained friends whose lives became inseparably woven with their own. In Columbus, for instance, they became personally acquainted with Cornelius and Agnes Carmack. Carmack had been subscribing to the *Agriculturist* for several years, although he had not met Fanning personally. He later sent two of his sons to Fanning's college. One of the sons, E. W. Carmack, sent four of his own Mississippi pupils back to his alma mater. One of these, H. R. Moore, wrote a sketch on the life of Fanning for the book, *Franklin College and Its Influences*. F. M. Carmack, the younger son, not only graduated from Franklin College but also became a professor there. In addition, he was an able writer for Fanning's *Gospel Advocate* before the war. What started in Columbus, incited by Fanning's nightly sermons in the courthouse, continued and expanded with the widening horizons of the coming years. One of the sons of F. M. Carmack, Edward Ward Carmack, later became a U.S. Senator from Tennessee.

After two and one-half months in Columbus, the Fannings continued their tour. In all, they were away from home about six months and witnessed about two hundred people confess their faith in Christ and submit to him in baptism. But when Fanning reached home, he was seriously ill and lingered near death for the next four months. When he finally began to regain his strength, he regained an even more determined purpose to pursue his goals, and by January of the next year, 1843, he was ready to open his agricultural school at Elm Crag.

The preaching tour between semesters was a familiar and essential part of Fanning's life. Scores of congregations were started. Like Paul, revisiting the cities where he had planted, Fanning periodically visited Russellville, Columbus, and a host of other churches to water and cultivate where he had originally found virgin soil.

Perhaps only eternity can adequately evaluate the materials with which Tolbert Fanning built. But with the educated eye of history, one is hardly presumptuous at least to begin the evaluation. One who often heard him preach remembered that he approached the pulpit "as a giant filled with his theme."

His mature ability as a preacher was assessed by many who were more than capable of making such evaluations. And if those who listened to him preach have preserved a true picture of his ability, it is not difficult to understand why he had such success, especially among the more thoughtful. One of the men who was baptized during his meeting in Russellville remembered, "As a public speaker, his style was simply inimitable. His voice was strong, and his articulation was distinct. As a preacher, he was always logical and scriptural. He appealed to the common understanding of his audience, holding it spellbound to his subject."[2]

While he was still a student, P. R. Runnels traveled often with Fanning, and over hundreds of miles and in dozens of communities, he listened to him preach. He sat through several of his debates and later became an outstanding young preacher himself. Runnels remembered that Fanning had but few equals as a debater. "As a preacher, I never knew his superior. I have heard him hold his hearers for three hours, and they were loath to leave."[3]

Another student, who also became an outstanding preacher, editor, and teacher, was E. G. Sewell. He wrote,

His utterance was clear and distinct, his person tall and commanding, his voice pleasant and clear, and blest with an almost perfect self possession, he seldom failed to command the undivided attention of his audience, whether they believed or disbelieved what he said. And in Tennessee, Alabama, and Mississippi, and in other states, there are perhaps hundreds of communities that are indebted to his public preaching for their first knowledge of the truth as it is in Jesus, and through which some thousands have been led into the kingdom of the Savior. As a speaker of pure English, we are sure we have never seen his superior. And as a reader, we are satisfied we have never met his equal. His pronunciation, accent, tone, and emphasis was [sic] superior to any we have ever heard, according to our judgement.[4]

Perhaps few men were in a better position than T. B. Larimore, himself noted as a graceful speaker, to evaluate Fanning as a preacher. Larimore wrote, "While at Franklin College, I heard him preach more than I have, in all my life, heard all other gospel preachers preach—school boy practices excepted . . . He preached as if he believed the temporal and eternal salvation of the whole human race and all the holy angels depended upon that discourse as then and there delivered."[5]

A. L. Johnson remembered an occasion when he was a student at Franklin College when one of the teachers was asked to speak at the Sunday evening gathering of students and faculty. The speaker, Professor Fowler, was a graduate of the University of Ohio and was quite capable in communication. His subject was, "Man Is Essentially Corrupt." Since he was extremely popular among the students, his lesson on total hereditary depravity had a very deep impact on the student body. After interviewing him, Fanning decided to speak the next Sunday at the 11 a.m. service on a subject designed to deal with Fowler's address. One student reproduced the scene with vivid detail:

When the hour came, the old chapel was filled with students and others. The grand man came in with his stately tread, a flush on his cheek, and, with the appearance of a giant, filled with his theme. Of all the discourses I ever listened to, in my estimation, that was the ablest. Could it have been taken down as delivered, I am sure it would rank as his best, and would, if in print, now stand, under severest criticism, in clearness, elegance of diction, strength, power, and pathos, unexcelled by any pulpit effort of the nineteenth century. We were all, young and old, held spellbound from 11 a.m. till 2 p.m. We took no note of time. Boys of fifteen years took in with deep-set interest every word. He concluded with an invitation. Prof. J.S. Fowler, who had begun to take notes close to me, and who soon dropped his pencil, pale and trembling, arose and went forward. I.N. Loomis, Professor Fowler, and S.R. Hay, all confessed their faith and were baptized that afternoon.[6]

But Fanning could have remembered days when he had not known such encouraging success. There was a rather amusing incident, for instance, involving a group of Negroes who had been stirred by emotional religionists in a series of meetings until "the nights were rendered hideous" by their "frightful screams." They were praying for the Holy Spirit, and it supposedly was being poured out on them in ample measure. Hoping to help them, Fanning announced a meeting for them and began to preach. Scarcely had he initiated his sermon when, being accustomed to the impassioned threats of hell-fire and deep damnation, they were fast asleep under Fanning's more reasoned efforts to enlighten them.[7] Upon another occasion he went to Lebanon to begin a series of meetings. It was Sunday morning, and according to his custom, he preached two or three hours, telling everyone assembled of their duty. Then, when no one accepted the invitation to come to Christ, he simply said, "You are not ready for a meeting," and dismissed the audience. He went home, resumed his work, and explained to his class the next day why the Lebanon meeting was so short.

Fanning saw the responsibilities of the preacher as manifold. First, he was to preach to sinners. Second, he was to hear their confession and baptize them into Christ, planting churches and "congregating the brethren." Next, he was to teach the new converts (an area which Fanning was convinced was much neglected in his day). He said the next responsibility was to "set in order the churches," and then "to ordain elders, or experienced members, in all the churches, to the bishop's office." Sixth, Fanning saw the need for evangelists to "supervise all the congregations of the Lord."[8] In this last area of responsibility he felt that it was their duty to guard against false teaching. But he always emphasized clearly that they did not have any authority over the churches, in the sense of a denominational pastor or bishop. He wrote,

> The brethren must not understand us as maintaining any special or official authority of evangelists over the churches, further than what springs from their *obligations* to the congregations they may address, either by word or letter. It is undeniably the duty of the preachers of the gospel to see that the churches are in order, and with this view the care of the congregations should rest with great weight upon their hearts. Further than a right and duty to endeavor to profit the churches by teaching, earnest exhortations and fervent prayers to the members, to cleave unto the Lord and the word of his grace, preachers possess no authority.[9]

While the preacher had a definite responsibility to those whom he fathered in the gospel, he should always remember that his first responsibility was to the unsaved. When T. Cash reported the cooperation meeting of April, 1847, in Livingston, Tennessee, he indicated that four men had "agreed to preach for the brethren" so that the congregations could be supplied with regular preaching. Fanning replied, "This is wrong: preaching should be to the world, and congregations should edify themselves."[10] Fanning never took the position that the evangelist could not address a group of Christians. To the contrary, the preacher was shirking his duty if he did not help them to grow. He often did so himself. But he often reminded them that members should not lean on the preacher to take charge of their worship and their Christian service. The members should soon be doing this for themselves. It not only freed the preacher to go to the unsaved, but also helped the members themselves, learning to stand alone, to grow faster and stronger.

Fanning was not always convinced that his fellow preachers had captured the proper attitude toward their work. Noted by his associates for his disdain for show and pretense in anyone, and most of all in preachers, he wrote, "Perhaps, there is no class of men in existence more envious than preachers; and none who are so unwilling to do justice to their fellow laborers." He continued, "Many have no heart to preach unless they can occupy the popular hours, and be considered the big preacher of the occasion."[11] One of the first qualifications for a preacher, in Fanning's mind, was an attitude of humility, love, and sincerity.

The attitude which Fanning so despised often found expression in the pulpit manner of the preacher. On the other hand, there was another attitude, that of compromise, which was just as much to be abhorred. Fanning drove many editorial paragraphs hard against these two extremes. In 1861 he wrote,

Amongst teachers of religion we are persuaded we have two dangerous extremes. In the first place, we have long been troubled with an inferior class of preachers, men of bad temper, self-willed, puffed up with the smallest amount of knowledge, and clothed with a large share of what they called official authority—whose highest ambition is to abuse the "sects," but who never advance beyond a very imperfect acquaintance with a part of the alphabet of Christianity. Another class, equally objectionable in our view, may be found[who] affect to have risen above first principles, profess very great regard for what they call "other denominations," endeavor to live on good and fraternal terms with all "orthodox Christians"—men they are who adopt the clerical style of the times, seek an early charge as pastors with such salaries as are offered and they talk in a melancholic mood about the heart and higher attainments in devotion, without laying the proper foundation for genuine godliness. These are always sickly, sentimental, ease loving, and frequently money loving preachers, who are never satisfied with getting, and never satisfy such as hope to govern by the pure milk of the word.[12]

Though widely commended as a speaker, Fanning appeared to be unaware and unaffected. Even some who disagreed with his positions openly recognized his ability as a preacher. J. W. McGarvey, with whom Fanning disagreed in regard to the missionary society, described him as having "a courtesy in his manner scarcely equalled by any speaker, and by a silver voice quite superior to that of any other."[13] But it is impossible to be with Fanning for long without bringing him into sharp contrast with some in his day who seemed to search for places of honor either as spiritual sharp-shooters out to draw the fastest Scripture in the performing art of debate, or, just as disgusting to Fanning, fawning over the shallow social amenities of the silk stocking set. Speaking to young men just beginning their preaching, Fanning warned against "cutting off the heads of the sects." Such "fighting preachers," as he called them, if they convert anyone at all, simply make converts who share their own bitter spirit. On the other hand, he advised the young students not to flatter sin in high places. Such preaching, he observed, may "wheedle" a few stragglers into the church, but these are "more difficult then to turn to righteousness than those who never heard of God or the kingdom of heaven."[14] Especially odious to Fanning were those preachers who tried to embellish their reading of the Bible with false eloquence consisting of "Chinese, clerical, or some other kind of tones, or grace notes, which they imagine give the highest value to the text."[15]

When he began preaching, Tolbert Fanning listened to the voices of his critics who believed that he was not capable of doing an adequate job. If anyone was in a position to offer advice to other preachers who needed improved attitudes

or more education, Fanning was the man. Instead of becoming bitter when he was criticized, he accepted the suggestions as indications that he needed more education. He
worked diligently and at great sacrifice to complete his work
at the University of Nashville. Too many young preachers,
he observed, did not take the time to store their minds and
hearts adequately, attacked the sects, and gained the flattery
of a few "ignorant old women, of giddy girls, and they have
concluded they are great men."[16] This compelled him to
urge the churches to take the initiative in searching for
young men who were especially fitted for preaching, helping
them to gain an education that they might be prepared to
go forth and represent the kingdom honorably. "The practice of men commissioning themselves," Fanning wrote, "is
a reproach on the good cause of our God."[17]

While placing tremendous emphasis on training preachers,
Fanning constantly reminded churches that the proper
method was for the church to be responsible for such training. In answering a letter, he warned against a ministerial
course in a theological seminary:

> 1. Theological departments in schools to make preach-
> ers, it seems to me, robs the church of much of her
> valuable service and honor.
> 2. It is making the impression, that there is a distinct
> class of men to take official responsibility in the
> churches.[18]

Fanning's life was dedicated to the education of youth.
Yet his emphasis upon the church as a training school for
preachers was completely consistent in his mind with his
emphasis and work with schools. Commenting on the plans
of the Kentucky Christian Education Society, he wrote, "Our
experience is unfavorable to educating men in the schools
with the view of making preachers of them. It is our duty
to the church and to the world to do all that is in our
power for the education of the youth of our country, but
we should not think of training men for the ministry but in

the church." In keeping with these views, Fanning urged that preachers should be acquainted with mathematics, psychology, history, science, chemistry, and the classics, as well as the Scriptures. But the church was responsible for their gaining aptitude in service. They were no different than any other member of the church. The church was the "seminary" for instructing *all* the members, and the preacher was simply filling one particular role in the function of the body.[19]

Fanning's announced attitude toward training preachers was not unique in his time. Alexander Campbell at one time wrote, "To train any young man, purposely to make him a teacher of Christianity, I am always ready to show, to be ridiculous and absurd; contrary to reason and revelation."[20]

Fanning no doubt looked at his own experience of preparation for service. For a year he had studied the Bible all alone, without the aid of a concordance, a commentary, or a religious paper. He went to college and secured a classical education, as everyone should do. During this time he continued to preach, thus learning, in the kingdom, his work as a preacher.

Fanning was an ardent supporter of Christian education. To him Christianity was the only true basis for proper education. The emphasis of his life and his writings were always in that direction. But at his Franklin College there was no preacher's course. Men planning to preach were permitted to enter his earliest agricultural school (1843-1844) at half price, yet it still remained an agricultural school! He would also point out that during the operation of Franklin College it was the congregation meeting on the campus which had the responsibility for training the young men to preach. At the services they were encouraged to take a public part. When Fanning made preaching trips, he took young men with him to observe and learn. While it must be remembered, in all justice to Fanning, that there was no ministerial course at Franklin College, one should also remember that from its classrooms went forth some of the most capable preachers of the period. But Fanning would be quick to point out that they had been trained and commissioned by the church. He further concluded that "Blacksmiths are made by hammering iron, and a preacher of Jesus Christ can be manufactured in no way but by laboring in the body and with the world."[21]

As a preacher, Fanning naturally was called upon occasionally to defend his beliefs in public debate with those who disagreed with his positions. Part and parcel of both the social and religious life of most communities, the religious debate was an event of major proportions. Like barn raisings, debates were welcome opportunities to get away from the lonesome drudgery of the farm and visit the neighbors. Many a romance first blossomed into life as a result of the young people introduced to the social amenities of courtship as a result of a debate. Many slept in their wagons during the course of the several days usually consumed by the debate.

Fanning was always ready to defend and declare what he conceived to be truth, but he soon became aware that many individuals used debating to bolster their pride. Others came for entertainment, observing the debate much as they would watch a sporting event—as spectators. Concerning religious controversy Fanning wrote,

> Should not all controversy be conducted with the reverence and solemnity which the Savior manifested when he wept over Jerusalem on account of the errors of its inhabitants?
> If this course were pursued, would not all persons desirous of knowing the truth of God, anxiously seek investigation for their own good?
> Is it not highly criminal for preachers to seek controversy for the purpose of exposing an opponent; to gratify pride; or for the purpose of acquiring fame as a debator?[22]

When he penned these words, he had just finished a year in which he took part in several debates which impressed him more than ever that some engaged in debating for selfish motives. In what was probably his first debate, Fanning encountered a Presbyterian named MacKnight, although it is not certain just when or where this took place. When he was on his first trip with Campbell in 1835, he had a debate in Perryville, Kentucky, with a Methodist named Rice (not N. L. Rice who later met Campbell). He held three debates with Edward McMillon, a Presbyterian. The first was in 1840, and another was in Moulton, Alabama, in June of 1843. Moulton was just a short distance from Russellville where the broken buggy spring had prefaced such a successful endeavor the previous year, and interest was understandably high. At the conclusion of the discussion, Fanning continued to preach each evening. After the first night's sermon, he reviewed the debate and asked if anyone present was ready to become a Christian. One of the most prominent lawyers in the state, David G. Ligon, arose immediately and said, "I believe it, sir, and I will obey it promptly." Many preachers of the day, being uneducated, used poor grammar and as a result appealed more to their own kind of people, occasionally even making a point of ridiculing their educated neighbors. Ligon later told Fanning that as he passed by the building where he was speaking, he heard Fanning pronounce a word as he had learned in college to pronounce it, rather than the way most preachers in his area mispronounced it. This one word caused him to stop to hear more, and he soon had developed a deep interest in the things being discussed. Encouraged by his obedience, fifty others followed his example, and the church in Moulton was started. Ligon, a State Supreme Court judge, had previously scoffed at Christianity. Now he began to preach and became quite eloquent in its cause. Not only did he lead many in his state to follow his example, but he later served as a member of the board of trustees at Franklin College.[23]

Fanning returned home and wrote, "I rejoice in such triumphs no little . . . Oh, Lord, to THEE, and thy precious work, I am indebted for all that I have witnessed in Moulton. The brethren are strong in numbers, talent, and influence, and I pray God they may be kept humble." Observers could not help noticing the contrast between the attitude of Fanning's opponents in Moulton (who were boasting victory) and the attitude of Fanning himself.[24]

Though he often desired rest from his preaching, Tolbert Fanning seldom could find it. He returned home from his debate in Moulton to begin the second session of his agricultural school. The boys began to arrive on July 4, which was Sunday, and the schoolmaster settled them in their rooms. The next morning at four o'clock the bell rang and in fifteen minutes they were called together to read two chapters in the Old Testament. After straightening their rooms and eating breakfast, they were ready for the morning chores in the field before classes.

By the end of July, things were running smoothly and one day, as Fanning was with the boys in the classroom, Mr. Wharton, one of the elders from the Nashville church, arrived and called Fanning out of the room. When he returned, after a brief conference with Wharton, he placed the class in the care of A. J. Fanning and hurried into town. The next morning he told the boys he had agreed to debate the Presbyterian preacher, Nathan L. Rice, and that he would make arrangements for them to attend if they desired.

The debate was held in the Presbyterian church building in Nashville, and the meetings found Rice pouring out his ablest sarcasm and bitterness. Fanning always regretted meeting Rice on this occasion, not because he felt his cause had suffered, but because he later became convinced that Rice had lured him into the discussion simply to gain practice for his coming debate with Alexander Campbell in Lexington, Kentucky.

In December, 1850, the Baptists in Lebanon, Tennessee, sent for Fanning and asked him to come to hold a discussion with a Mr. Chapman, a Methodist preacher who had been challenging all in that section to meet him in debate. Fanning accepted, and the debate covered the mode and the subjects of baptism. The discussion lasted five days, closing on Saturday evening. Thus, even if his Baptist friends called on him, Fanning was ready to do what he could to search mutually for enlightenment.

In debate, Fanning's style was "assertive rather than argumentative. . . . His statements were clear and pointed, stated with force, and he greatly left the point thus stated to vindicate itself."[25] He never stooped to sarcasm and humor at the expense of his opponent, but remained stubbornly with the facts in hand and courteously called upon all present to give their attention to the Scriptures alone.

In one of his more noted encounters, Fanning was called to debate a Methodist preacher, and when he had given his first speech, the Methodist representative arose. He began by quoting the lines of Alexander Seikirk:

> I am monarch of all I survey.
>   My right there is none to dispute,
> From the center, all round to the sea,
>   I am the lord of the fowl and the brute.

When he pronounced the word, "brute," he defiantly pointed to Fanning, and the uncultured portion of the audience, as if they were attending a sideshow and believing that the act was smart, laughed heartily. Fanning, along with the more intelligent part of the audience, felt that the man was a braggadocio of questionable worth. He calmly arose from his chair and walked out without any comment. The debate ended there. Fanning was convinced that sacred things were to be reverenced upon every occasion, and for a Christian, this was the only course of action. Wise men agreed with him, and his position won a decisive victory in their minds.

T. B. Larimore admired his teacher not only for his work in the classroom, but for his life as a preacher. He wrote of Fanning,

> I have never fallen at the feet of orators or worshipped at the shrine of oratory, but I have always loved to linger there. In all my life I have heard but one orator whom I deem it admissible to compare with

Tolbert Fanning. That man was the great and gifted lawyer and statesman, Daniel Voorhees, "the tall sycamore of the Wabash," whose oratory thrilled the greatest nation on the globe. As I heard him plead with power and pathos for the life, liberty, reputation, and honor of a prominent prisoner in the prime of life, . . . I could almost see Tolbert Fanning, and hear his melodious, stentorian voice, as, in faultless English and perfectly rounded periods, he preached as no other man I have ever heard could preach the gospel, "the power of God unto salvation." Wonderful men were they![26]

CHAPTER 8

NO ROOM FOR REPENTANCE

NASHVILLE AND JESSE B. FERGUSON

> —"*The error committed cannot be corrected*— *'there is no room for repentance.'* *But we would gladly shroud the past in impenetrable night.*"
> —*Tolbert Fanning*

NASHVILLE MOVED out of the "fitful forties" and into the "fabulous fifties" in grand style. On a summer evening the streets would be crowded with people—some on horses, some in expensive carriages, and some in buggies. But all were well dressed in what was fast becoming the "Athens of the South." Visitors were seldom unimpressed by the high fashion and apparent luxury. One observer announced, "There is as much fashion here as in New York, and the ladies dress far more than anywhere else I have been."[1]

Nashville had its conscience, too. The self-righteous were condemning the habit of reading novels. To some it was "the most dreadful and most to be feared of any calamity that ever has or ever will oppress our nation!"

By 1847, when a group of churches sent messengers to the cooperation meeting at the Franklin College congregation, the Church of Christ in Nashville numbered five hundred, although it was destined to suffer such violent convulsions ten years later that it would be reduced to shambles, and Fanning's hopes for it would be all but demolished. But none dreamed of such foreboding events in 1847.

Another strong congregation had developed at Woodbury in Cannon County where there were two hundred fifty members. J. J. Trott was working with them as an evangelist. Cripple Creek had one hundred forty-four members, and Robinson's Fork reported one hundred fifty. Fanning had helped to establish a congregation at Robinson's Fork when he was a college student, and now it was one of the most outstanding congregations in the area. The group there had sent out from its own membership three "colonies" of Christians to Missouri and Texas to start new congregations. One of these consisted of twenty members and one preacher, another of twenty-five members and two preachers (trained in the church there), and a smaller colony which had gone to Texas was reported doing well. Robinson's Fork was in Giles County, and together with the other four congregations there had selected the same messenger to represent them at the meeting at Franklin College. The church which met on the campus numbered forty.

By 1850, Tennessee had one hundred thirty-five Churches of Christ, ninety-three in the Middle Tennessee district. Total membership in the state probably reached twelve thousand by the close of the decade. But there was still much to be done and Fanning pressed the churches to be more regular in their meetings. Too often they waited for the random visits of a traveling preacher before they assembled for worship. Fanning reminded them that mere preaching does not make strong and pure churches.

About this time Nashville was enjoying a building boom which was primarily produced by the announced intentions in the state legislature to erect a new capitol building. William Strickland, the architect, had designed eighteen buildings in Philadelphia, including the steeple on Independence Hall, had worked with Latrobe on the capitol building in Washington, and had designed Washington's tomb. He was offered $2,500 per year to come to Nashville and although he estimated the cost of the completed capitol structure (using prison labor) to be about $180,000, it actually cost over three times that amount. (It will be remembered that Strickland, while working on the capitol building, submitted for Fanning's *Naturalist* magazine in 1850 several articles in which he discussed the architecture of the building. While the capitol building in Nashville was under construction, he died and was buried in its wall).

Much of the territorial growth of the United States came during this period since it was the time when Americans were fond of speaking of their "manifest destiny" to extend their borders to the Pacific, and, some even dared to dream of a nation which included the whole North American continent! In 1848 the Treaty of Guadalupe Hidalgo concluded the Mexican War and gave the U.S. clear title to Texas, New Mexico, and Upper California. The Gadsden Purchase in 1853 added another small strip of Mexican territory. Near the middle of the decade, several prominent statesmen died, including James Polk, Zachary Taylor, John C. Calhoun, Henry Clay, and Daniel Webster.

Evidently this was also one of the most encouraging and active times for Tolbert Fanning as well. When he opened Franklin College in 1845, he was still editing the *Christian Review* and the *Agriculturist*. He loved his work with the young men at Franklin College, his farm at Elm Crag was doing well, and the Church of Christ in Tennessee was working and growing with harmony. These were happy times for Tolbert Fanning, now in his thirties. Little did he dream how such a wonderful time could be so suddenly enshrouded in darkness. Nor did he suspect that the foreboding clouds were stealthily building on a horizon where he least expected them to develop.

Onto this stage came Jesse B. Ferguson, one of the most promising young men in the church. Almost immediately he took his cue and moved to the front and center. Born in Philadelphia in 1819, Ferguson moved to Virginia with his parents. When he was eleven he entered the Fair View Academy. But young Jesse was destined to suffer a whole series of disappointments. Just when he was ready to follow his brothers' footsteps to William and Mary College, his father experienced financial setbacks and he could not send him to college. Ferguson was then apprenticed to a printer but his employer soon went bankrupt and Ferguson then went to Baltimore to be employed by a book concern.

After a few weeks there he became ill. The sickness, called "white swelling," left him ill for several months and caused him to be a cripple for life.

Among relatives in Kentucky, Ferguson came in contact with the plea to restore New Testament Christianity and later he began preaching. One of his first reports was sent to the *Millennial Harbinger* in 1838. In the report he urged, "If the brethren would avoid *'foolish questions'* and attend to the living oracles, truth must and will prevail." He never could countenance "foolish questions" among people who claimed to be like Christ.

Almost overnight Ferguson became one of the most popular preachers in the area. At the age of twenty-two he was asked to co-edit a religious periodical called the *Heretic Detector!* In 1842, only four years after he began preaching, he was invited to Nashville to preach in a series of meetings. The meetings were a tremendous success, and Nashville was, to say the least, quite impressed by this eloquent and gifted young man. The members held a consultation meeting that year and, having been without a full-time preacher for more than ten years, decided they needed a man like Ferguson to work with them. Fanning pointed out that they had grown to five hundred members without a paid worker, but they decided to hire one anyway. When they insisted that Ferguson should come, he at first refused. In 1844, he returned for an even more successful meeting than before. The church continued to urge him to move to Nashville. Finally he consented and arrived to begin work on February 24, 1846. He labored with them for a year without his family. When the request that he remain permanently was unanimous, he moved his family to the "rock city," and Tolbert Fanning, even though he had urged the Nashville church to continue without a "hired" preacher, nevertheless placed great confidence in young Ferguson. And Ferguson spoke highly of his elder brother in Christ.

When Ferguson moved to Nashville, the church consisted of about two hundred sixty-five white members and about the same number of Negro members. These lived in harmony and the world, according to Fanning, exclaimed, "Behold! how these people love each other."

Ferguson was a tireless worker. He visited at regular intervals in each of the homes of the members of the large congregation and was in great demand as a speaker at functions other than those of the church. He soon came to be the most popular preacher in the whole city of Nashville. During 1849 there were seventy-three additions bringing the total membership to five hundred forty-six. The church was meeting three times on Sunday, with the Lord's Supper at a separate service in the afternoon. W. A. Eichbaum, one of the elders, was still in charge of Bible classes among both the white and Negro members, with one hundred sixty-five among the former group and some one hundred twenty-five among the latter.

Ferguson's popularity continued to soar, especially among those who were not members of the Church of Christ. He attracted both the dregs of society and Nashville's social butterflies as well. He also rose in the church. "Never was man so honored and caressed by the disciples of Christ in the Southwest," one writer remembered. He was made the chief agent for evangelizing by the Churches of Christ in the state, through their Tennessee State Evangelizing Association. Fanning selected him to serve on the Board of Trustees at Franklin College when he was only thirty-one years of age.

Although the actual membership of the Church of Christ in Nashville did not increase too noticeably during Ferguson's stay, the attendance at the worship assemblies grew to such an extent that a new building became imperative. W. A. Eichbaum was selected to superintend the erection of the building. While most of the money for the work was subscribed from the congregation, the other citizens of Nashville also donated money to help. The paper subscribing the money stated that it was for "the people known in Nashville as the disciples of Christ or Christians, and who regard the Sacred Scriptures as the only rule of their faith and practice."

The cost of the building and the two lots which it covered reached about $30,000. The old building was sold to the Presbyterians for about one-fourth of this amount. The new building was designed by J.H. Hughes and was Greek Corinthian in its architectural style. The front door was approached by way of a flight of stairs to a portico, which was in turn surmounted by a belfry and a finely proportioned spire rising one hundred fifty feet into the Nashville sky. The building itself was ninety feet long and sixty feet wide. Inside it had a cross gallery supported by Corinthian columns, and was lighted by eight windows, each shaded by venetian blinds. The one hundred fifty white walnut pews could seat about one thousand two hundred people and were finely cushioned with red crimson.

Inside the building, the walls and ceiling were stuccoed with ornate frescoes and lighted by a massive gas chandelier of bronze with twelve lights. On the frescoed alcove at the front where the pulpit was, there stood two fluted Grecian columns which sustained the pediment. A table at the front, styled like a Greek altar, was built on four blocks supporting four brass candelabra, all of purest Parian white. The building also had a complete and well arranged basement.

The new structure was dedicated about the last of May, 1852, at which time Ferguson preached on the ten virgins of Matthew 25:1-10. The sermon lasted about an hour and a half. Present was a Dr. Fowlkes, from Memphis, a member of the state legislature who always came to hear Ferguson when the legislature was in session. Of the speaker on this occasion he wrote in the *Daily Union* of Nashville, "The gentleman is yet in manhood. A bright future lures him on in his sacred mission and beckons him to its fruition." The *Memphis Express* wrote about Ferguson, "He is a ripe and finished scholar, a chaste, beautiful, eloquent, and logical pulpit orator. . . . We love and reverence all such men as this reverend divine."[2]

That most members of the church did not take any public leadership in the worship services at this time had begun to trouble Fanning. He later wrote, "The preaching, the exhortations, the singing, the breaking of the loaf, the prayers, the thanksgivings, the visiting the fatherless and widows, and indeed most of the service 'was let' to persons, the most conspicuous of whom were not even members of the church."[3]

Even before Ferguson reached the greatest heights of his popularity, others were also expressing concern about his direction. They could not deny that he attracted large crowds, "But," they declared, "the stage and the opera please many of the same persons quite as well." The stage, the opera, the dance, fairs, and various other kinds of entertainment were almost always found in the same sentence with reading novels and all were classified as belonging too much to this world.[4] Some of the older members even dared to point out that Christ and the apostles had not enjoyed such success with men in the flesh.

Ferguson's most formidable and extensive influence probably issued through his pen. As the editor of a religious journal, an instrument supplied to him by Tolbert Fanning, his position of leadership became more expansive. It will be remembered that Fanning, along with several others, determined in 1843 that Middle Tennessee needed its own religious paper, and with the January, 1844 issue, had launched the *Christian Review*. With the able help of a carefully selected corps of correspondents, the paper enjoyed wide circulation almost from the beginning and soon was a familiar item in hundreds of Christian homes.

From the first year of the paper, Fanning printed occasional selections by Ferguson. As assistant editor of the *Heretic Detector,* his pen had become one of the most capable in the brotherhood, although its spirit did not carry out the theme one might expect from the name of the paper! His ability to use language was superb, and he immediately became a favored writer.

Shortly after Ferguson moved to Nashville, Fanning was searching for some way to ease the burden of his many interests. Before starting Franklin College, he devoted several months to travel in order to raise funds and secure interest in the school. Among the results was his growing neglect of the *Christian Review*. Although he assured his readers, at the beginning of 1845, that this would be different in the future, he continued to watch helplessly as his responsibilities only increased.

Finally, toward the close of 1847, it became apparent that he would be compelled to make other arrangements for the paper. To begin with, he needed to be out of town quite a bit during November and December. He left B. F. Hall (who had recently moved his dental practice to Nashville because of his health) and Ferguson in charge of the paper with instructions for his correspondence to be directed to Lexington, Kentucky, until the close of the year.

Then, in the November issue, while Fanning was away, there appeared an article by Ferguson announcing plans for a new paper, to be edited by himself and Hall. On the same page Fanning announced his plans to cease publishing the *Review* and commended the new work to his readers. The same subscription list would be used for mailing unless subscribers expressed other desires.

Even the closing issues of the *Christian Review* gave fore-tastes of the type of journalism that Ferguson had in mind. For instance the *Review* carried an article by the governor, N. S. Brown, and Ferguson commented on the executive's magnanimous feelings. He further expressed pride at his election and called for prayers on behalf of his administration. Such a flavor was certainly not characteristic of Fanning.

With the birth of the new year, 1848, came the appearance of the *Christian Magazine,* as Ferguson called it. The magazine was much more attractive in format than its predecessor, had larger pages with two columns, cost twice as much, and was decidedly Ferguson's paper, although Hall and Fanning were at first listed as co-editors. Ferguson introduced the new venture to his readers and immediately displayed his plans for its policy:

> We need a work suited to the times in size, spirit and matter. We have been often and earnestly solicited

to commence such a work; but until recently, owing to the fact that we have so many publications, but meagerly sustained, we have hesitated and declined. But in our present enterprise this difficulty is removed; we enlarge and seek to improve an existing periodical, while we have thrown around us increased facilities for making a paper such as we desire . . . the liberality and generosity for which they are becoming proverbial, will not be appealed to in vain by us when we ask that a publication free from sectarian bias and party bickering and exclusively devoted to the spread of religious knowledge, may be patronized and sustained.[5]

The following month the Nashville newspapers, as well as the *Tennessee Baptist,* editorially welcomed the publication's arrival. To the *Tennessee Baptist* Ferguson responded, "We love pleasant and amicable relations, and shall be most happy to reciprocate the favor of our polite and Christian fellow-citizen."[6]

The success of the magazine was immediate. Ferguson was surprised when, after one year, it paid for itself. Eventually it began to show a profit. With the third volume it became the property of the Christian Publication Society of Tennessee, and thus a formal organ of the Churches of Christ in the state. A Publication Committee which was formed to supervise the periodical made regular reports to the annual meetings of the Society until the close of volume five.

Though Fanning's name at first appeared as one of the editors, he did not actually serve in that capacity. The first volume of the paper finds his name mentioned only three times, and he contributed only six articles during the whole lifetime of the paper.

For a while young John Eichbaum helped Ferguson edit the *Christian Magazine* and at the beginning of 1852, the name of John R. Howard appeared as Ferguson's co-editor. The printing was done by J. T. S. Fall, book and job printers in the Ben Franklin office on College Street. These same printers contracted the printing for several of the early papers and publications by members of the Church of Christ.[7]

The *Christian Magazine* carried a well-balanced selection of essays, poems, sermons, and letters. The more than occasional use of quotations and essays from such leading literary figures as Henry Ward Beecher, Orville Dewey, William Innes, and Henry Ware, Jr., help to gauge the admiration which Ferguson entertained toward them.

From the beginning it was Ferguson's policy to refuse religious controversy. While seeking to speak the truth on every subject positively, he went the last mile in shielding his readers from the bitterness and sarcasm which were in vogue in contemporary journals, both religious and secular. In addition, he often indicated a spirit of fraternity toward other religious bodies, especially in his later volumes. Mentioning a new Presbyterian publication, he offered his "best wishes of success." He also announced a new book entitled *Heavenly Talking,* which was described as, "A talk with a deceased friend through a clairvoyant." Of the editorial organ of the Methodist Churches of the South he wrote, "The energy exhibited by its conductors entitles them to a large share of patronage." Thus christened amid scenes of optimism, the *Christian Magazine* continued to grow in popularity.

Then came the year 1852, and the serenity was shattered. In an earlier article in the *Christian Review* in 1845 entitled "Another State of Probation," Ferguson had raised the question, "What will become of the ignorant but honest heathen who have died without hearing the saving truths of the Gospel?" He answered, "Who knows but that with reference to such there may be another state of probation. There is at least as much authority for this as for the sweeping conclusion that covers them over with the impenetrable veil of everlasting oblivion."[8] This article passed without editorial notice, either in the *Christian Review* or elsewhere. But no such destiny awaited an ill-fated essay which assumed essentially the same position and appeared seven years later in 1852 in the *Christian Magazine.* Several letters had come to the desk of Ferguson asking about the teaching of 1 Peter 3:18-20 and 1 Peter 4:1-3. Admitting that his views were "novel," he acknowledged that he had held them for some eight years though he had expressed them to only a few personal friends. He then continued,

> It is clear to our mind that the language of the Apostle conveys the idea that Christ by his spiritual nature, or by the Spirit, did preach to the Spirits of the invisible world. And as if to include all, the Apostle refers to those who died in disobedience in the days of Noah, which would make his language equivalent to all the dead; which he afterwards confirms by declaring that in order that Jesus Christ might be the judge of the dead and living, the "gospel was preached to the dead"—to those now dead—not "in the flesh," "now in prison."[9]

To Ferguson this interpretation seemed to fit the language most perfectly. It seemed absurd that "the dead" referred to the spiritually dead since it was contrasted to men "in the flesh." Finally, he suggested, his position was in general accord with the Scriptures as a whole. Christ was to reconcile all things, *in heaven* as well as on earth. The church was to make known the wisdom of God even to the principalities and powers in heavenly regions.

> Ranks and hosts of these spread themselves throughout the spiritual world, like beings of different grades in this, and under Christ carry on the scheme of his Redemption for the benefit of millions, who either by age, or tyranny, or imbecility could never hear of him while in the flesh.[10]

Ferguson said that to view the passage otherwise was earthly and selfish. Perdition for those not having an opportunity to know the gospel was "revolting to every just conception of God, of Christ or the benevolent purposes of life." He concluded,

> We never commit the body of a single human being to the grave, for whom it is not a pleasure for us to know, that his soul has already entered where the

knowledge of Christ *may yet* be his; and if at last condemned, it will not be for anything that was unavoid-
able in his outward circumstances on earth. And should
we be so happy as to become a part of Christ's sancti-
fied host in the invisible world, our happiness, we ap-
prehend, will consist in giving knowledge to all to whose
capacity and advancement we may be there as here,
adapted.[11]

It would be hard to believe that Ferguson realized what
an explosive controversy he was igniting when he locked
this issue of the magazine in the press. At about the same
time that Alexander Campbell's copy of the magazine arrived at the post office in Bethany, Campbell was making
plans for a trip to Memphis, Tennessee, to attend a Bible
Revision Convention, held by many who believed that the
King James Version was not adequate for the needs of contemporary language. About two-thirds of those present at
the Memphis meeting were Baptists, but also present to help
form a Bible Revision Association were several members
of the Churches of Christ, including President Shannon of
Bacon College, James Challen, and Tolbert Fanning. Ferguson did not identify the man, but he later said that a
friend of Campbell had come back from the meeting to tell
him (Ferguson) that an attack on his article had been planned
while the men were in Memphis. Ferguson awaited an
editorial review of his position. But he was totally unprepared for the storm which swept down from Bethany to
engulf him.

The first controversial article appeared in April, 1852,
and Ferguson ran another in June, entitled, "The Rewards
and Punishments of the Life to Come." Alexander Campbell,
in his own magazine, the *Millennial Harbinger,* labeled
Ferguson's position the "post mortem gospel" and initiated
a relentless and well-planned attack against it. Until August,
his opponent refused to reciprocate. Finally Ferguson gave
his first editorial notice of the "Attack of the *Millennial
Harbinger* upon the *Christian Magazine* and its Editor."
From that time on the battle became increasingly bitter.

Campbell, the experienced debater, skillfully planned his

strategy. He published Ferguson's first article and labeled it, "A New Discovery," condemning the exposition with his own. He put Ferguson in bad company by identifying his views with those of Universalists. Accusing Ferguson of heresy, he demanded that he make a public and formal renunciation. He further declared that the publication of the view was the "funeral knell to the man that obtruded it" upon the church.[12]

Campbell also published letters from many influential preachers, including Samuel Church, John T. Johnson, John Rogers, and Isaac Errett. Church's letter read, "I am sorry to see that Bro. Ferguson has got a maggot in his brain. This will destroy his usefulness and influence, and probably end in his becoming a wandering star." He continued, "If there be a 'damnable heresy' this is unquestionably one. I can see in it a perfect Pandora Box." Campbell called upon all of the brotherhood to repudiate Ferguson. He wrote, "I have in common with every intelligent brother that I have either seen or heard from in the union, bewailed this blighting dogmatism, this leprous spot, this gangrene, which I have from its first utterance regarded as a funeral knell."

Setting Ferguson in opposition to all of orthodox Protestantism, Campbell called upon the church in Nashville to repudiate him or suffer the displeasure of the Lord. Campbell insisted that his reviews of Ferguson's essays be published in the *Christian Magazine,* but Ferguson refused on the grounds that the paper actually belonged to the Tennessee Publication Society, and was an organ of the Churches of Christ in Tennessee.

At one point, Ferguson wrote, ". . . and there is no Methodist Conference, Presbyterian Synod, or Episcopal Convention, that I would not prefer to the one Editor Court."[13] Campbell pictured this as a "personal attack" by Ferguson, stating that he had never before been so assailed and misrepresented by any man calling him a Christian brother, young or old, learned or unlearned. Campbell also attributed the new views to John R. Howard since he was

an editor of the *Christian Magazine*. Howard was thus con-
strained to write to the *Harbinger* and, before the brotherhood, repudiate any sympathy with Ferguson's position.
Finally, since the *Christian Magazine* was purportedly owned
by the Churches of Christ in Tennessee (about twenty-five
congregations actually cooperated in the Society responsible
for its publication), Campbell wrote that the views expressed
would "be regarded as the approved views of the churches
of that State," so long as they were not rebuked and dis-
owned by them. With powerful force Campbell drew the
whole brotherhood into the battle and made it necessary for
members everywhere publicly to divest themselves for any
sympathy with Ferguson in order to retain respectability.

Most of this situation developed before the brotherhood
heard one word of defense from Ferguson himself. While
he must have sensed early that his course against Campbell
was a lost cause, he nevertheless threw himself into the
battle with his whole heart once he decided to reply. Though
his methods were vastly different than Campbells, Ferguson
was equal to the occasion as he played well the role of a
martyr who had dared to cross the "bishop" of the brotherhood in Bethany. His first step was one of refusal to stoop
to the war of words. He simply refused to answer. He
claimed that the first thing to be decided was not the
validity of his exegesis of 1 Peter, but whether or not
Christian brethren had the right to differ with other members
of the church without being ostracized. He emphatically
denied any tendencies toward Universalism. He expressed
wonder that one like Campbell, who himself had so often
suffered from misrepresentation, should stoop to such misrepresentation of another without giving him a chance to
speak for himself.

Following Campbell's example, Ferguson likewise claimed
that the attacks made on him were personal. He added, "If
it be decided in advance that we are unsound in the faith,
nothing we can say can be heard impartially by those who
thus decide." As further proof that Campbell's attack was

personal, Ferguson called attention to a number of expressions which Campbell had used: "brainless and heartless translation," "tongue and pen devoted to error and schism," "irresponsible editors, just out of the shell," "cosmic scribes," "infant sages," "incompetency to teach religion," and "very amiable" with "neither the understanding nor education."[14]

At one point, Ferguson hinted that Campbell's vindictive attitude was due to some reason which remained beneath the surface. Of the anathema pronounced against him he said, "It was ready before my opinions were published." He also wrote, "We have been made to feel that Brother Campbell had somewhat against us. What it was or wherefore, we could not divine." To Ferguson this judgment seemed apparent since Campbell had made no effort to destroy him in the eyes of the brotherhood when he first published these same views in 1845.

Throughout the discussion, Ferguson maintained that his expressed views were in the realm of opinion. To him, the question to be decided first was his right to hold opinions different from Campbell's. His opinion was, "That men who have not heard the gospel will hear it before they are condemned by it." This was essentially the opinion which, on the Western Reserve (later Ohio) back in the 1830s, had been held by another young preacher, Aylette Raines.

Since Alexander Campbell had encountered this doubt before, the way in which he reacted on the two occasions provides an interesting case study. Aylette Raines believed that all men would eventually be saved, though he never preached this in public. Only when some one asked him privately if this were his opinion did he commit himself. When some in the Mahoning Association, a cooperative organization of Baptist churches of the Western Reserve, wanted to disfellowship him, Alexander Campbell preached on the distinction between faith and opinion and plead for charity toward the young preacher. Recalling the incident, Raines later wrote,

I was dealt with, and my case managed by Bro. Campbell and all the chief brethren in very great kindness and wisdom. Had they attempted to brow-beat me I might have been ruined forever. But treating me kindly, at the same time that they convinced me that my opinion, whether true or false, dwindled into nothingness in comparison with the faith of the gospel, redeemed me.[15]

Why was it that Campbell had reacted to Ferguson's situation so differently than he had responded to Aylette Raines? Did he feel that Raines was young and inexperienced and humble enough to accept guidance, whereas Ferguson was mature enough to have known better? Did he fear what might happen to the church if a paper with wide circulation was permitted to instill this teaching in the hearts of many others? Did he know that Ferguson harbored other ideas which needed to be exposed? Or, as Ferguson intimates, was there something else beneath the surface which would have further explained Campbell's almost frantic reaction? That he acted differently toward Ferguson than he had toward Raines is a matter of record. It is also a matter involving a perennial problem in the Restoration Movement—the realm of opinion. The problem may never be solved to the satisfaction of very many. And perhaps one shall never know exactly why Campbell saw this particular case as such a threat. Maybe, on the other hand, he knew more about Ferguson's real convictions than he at first admitted.

Campbell's attitude and approach drove Ferguson to write,

No wonder we lose our preachers. No man of any independence of mind and reputation worth preserving, would place either where the mere suggestions of some offended or impudent man from Texas or Maine may induce the Editor of the Harbinger to hold him up to contempt, at his pleasure. Our views of gospel liberty and Christian morals were learned in another school. . . . But if he or any may decide for us what we must believe, or conceive that our liberty either of speech, pen or press is committed to their keeping, we beg to leave us say, and we would say it very respectfully,

Brethren, we were free born and have preserved our
liberty at a great price.[16]

Needless to say, the whole city of Nashville, both in the
Church of Christ and out, was stirred by these events. Most,
having no real understanding of the issues being discussed,
saw their citizen and popular pastor as a helpless and blame-
less martyr. Perhaps their attitude, as onlookers, is best
illustrated by the comment of one who was not a member of
the Church of Christ:

> The ire of the Old Man of Bethany was fully aroused
> and he decided to put on his Christian harness, to un-
> sheath the sword of righteousness, and to enter the
> field in defense of true scriptural religion. With an
> editorial fanfare he announced a declaration of war
> and called for help from all the orthodox brethren. The
> Church Campbellite had become the church bellicose.[17]

No matter how much he denied it, it soon became apparent that Ferguson was steeped in Universalism. A Mr.
Quinby, editor of a Universalist paper, visited Ferguson in
Nashville and was invited to fill Ferguson's pulpit for him.
Soon Ferguson began to display his Universalist colors
editorially. He pointed out to his readers that he had no
"selfish heaven nor hopelessly imploring hell." When some of
the members ceased meeting with him and later expressed
a desire to return to their building, he told them that if
they could not meet together as "Christians," then they
could meet together as men. Man was not made, he said,
to be subservient to religious systems and therefore should
cast them aside when they destroy the feeling of brotherhood among all men. He concluded his sermon by declaring,

> I know then, religiously, but one connection, and
> that is as broadcast as infinitude. The world of intel-
> ligences, created by the same God, is my church; the
> human race are its membership, whether in the body
> or angelized in spiritual bodies; and its only ordinances
> are the rights of the heart. Spiritually I recognize no
> other church.[18]

In another address Ferguson said that he had not attempted to establish a Unitarian Church, but went ahead to say that he recognized the true Christian Church as a "Church of Humanity, Christ-like in spirit and administration; free and just in its acknowledgement of the rights of every soul that God had formed." "This then," he concluded, "is a Humanitarian Church."[19]

Campbell continued his attack on Ferguson. As some in the church in Nashville began to leave him, he moved even further from his former position. In an extra issue of the *Christian Magazine,* published in December, 1852, to answer all that Campbell had written until that time, Ferguson denied any sympathy with Spiritualism. However, two years later, he published a book entitled, *Spirit Communion,* in which he admitted having had his first experience with spirit communion as early as 1849. His book purported to be, "A record of communications from the Spirit-spheres with incontestable evidence of personal identity, presented to the public with explanatory observations."[20] By the time that he published the book, his wife had become one of the mediums for the Spiritualists in Nashville. When Alexander Campbell came to town that year, Ferguson claimed that the spirit of William Ellery Channing had admonished him not to see Campbell. In his book he also revealed his attitude toward the Bible:

> The Bible is a collection of Spiritual communications of unequal character, varying in the degree of their light and help according to the capacity of the individuals through whom they were made, and the necessities of the age that received them. . . . It should be remembered that the Bible nowhere purports to be a final revelation from God.
>
> . . . .
>
> The Bible is a record of spiritual communications made through departed human Spirits . . . called angels.[21]

So Jesse B. Ferguson, the eloquent young man in whom his friends had placed such great confidence and influence, was swept along to final shipwreck in the church by the intellectual fads of his day, influenced by the brilliant minds who fostered the Universalism which, in New England, was reacting to the narrow exclusivism of Puritan Calvinism. Perhaps unsatisfied by the cold, mechanical formalities of his own religious surroundings, as the Calvinist fathers had been unsatisfied, he became the prey of Spiritualism's promise of ecstatic fulfillment.

Tolbert Fanning was editorially silent as the first thunderbolts knifed down upon the church in Nashville to lay waste, almost overnight, much of what he had labored so long to build. Everything which Fanning or others said to criticize Ferguson was taken by most of the people in Nashville to be persecution of a fine man.

The episode had far-reaching effects in the lives of other leaders as well. W. H. Wharton, who had been an elder in Nashville for eleven years, resigned his work. Several young preachers, admirers of Ferguson, wrestled with their faith. One was young John Eichbaum. Twenty-seven years old, he was the son of one of the elders in Nashville, W. A. Eichbaum, and had graduated from the University of Nashville before joining the faculty at Franklin College. He had begun to preach before he was twenty and traveled some with Fanning on his preaching trips. He served with J. J. Trott as the state evangelist for churches in Tennessee for three years and served on the Board of Directors of the Christian Evangelizing Association of Tennessee for 1852 and 1853. Resigning as state evangelist, he became, with Jesse Ferguson, co-editor of the *Christian Magazine*. All of his life Eichbaum was characterized by a self-denying spirit, and an inclination toward asceticism. When Ferguson turned to Spiritualism, Eichbaum, who admired Ferguson so deeply, was influenced in that direction also. While he was able to overcome the initial shock of Ferguson's defection and of his own sense of alienation to the extent that he retained a position of leadership in the church, the experience seemed to rob him of much of his former decisiveness.

Another young man who at first staggered under the blow was David Lipscomb. Lipscomb, like young Eichbaum, held

Ferguson in high esteem. When Ferguson left the Church of Christ, Lipscomb was deeply shaken. He began to doubt his own faith and seriously considered turning to the Baptist Church, the religion of his grandparents. After a thorough reappraisal and study of his position, he decided that he was right in staying where he was. His only mistake had been in placing too much faith in a man. Those who stand in his line of influence must be grateful for another influence on young Lipscomb. The steadying, humble, dependable faith of his teacher, Tolbert Fanning, was a sure foundation in the difficult and puzzling time of trouble.

After Ferguson published the extra of the *Christian Magazine* at the close of 1852, he left Nashville and went to New Orleans to regain his strength and recover his health. He turned over the paper to the Publication Society, and Fanning made a motion that they accept his resignation as editor and offer him their thanks for his "gratuitous labor." Upon his return to Nashville, a few weeks later, they had not been able to secure a new editor so he began publishing the magazine again, as his own personal property. The 1853 volume contained articles on such themes as "Autumn" and "Time." The January issue was delayed four months, but all twelve issues appeared before the end of the year. His only mention of his controversy with Campbell was to say that he was through with it.

Ferguson continued to preach in the new church building in Nashville, although many who regularly attended were not members of the Church of Christ. At the end of the year there was an election in the church to decide whether or not he would be asked to stay, and Ferguson published some correspondence which asked him to remain. One of the letters was signed by two hundred ten residents of Nashville, including the governor, two U. S. Senators, the mayor, two bank presidents, the editors of two local newspapers, and a score of physicians. The timely publication came just before the election. Many did not know of the election, and some who did know stayed away. Ninety-six asked him to stay. The documents recording the meeting do not state how many wanted him to leave. Not long after this he pointed out that no matter what the brotherhood felt, only twenty-five of the members in Nashville were against him, and ever since the church there had left the Concord Baptist Association, it had been independent of outside control.

Ferguson thus retained control of the beautiful new building. When some suggested that P. S. Fall should be asked to return, only five people voted for him. When Alexander Campbell visited the city in 1855, he was publicly scoffed at by Ferguson's party, and even respected members of the church would not speak to him on the street or come to hear him preach.

The few who remained faithful to their original convictions secured the use of their old building while they tried to regain the use of the new building which they had erected. Toward the close of 1855, Ferguson asked the congregation if they wanted him to leave, and he read a letter asking him to stay. Of the five men who signed it, none of them was a member of the Church of Christ. Finally, four of the five elders asked Ferguson to leave. His reply stated that since he controlled the building he would continue to preach until forced to vacate. Several months earlier, when the opposing members left, one of the lots on which the structure stood was still not paid for. The sheriff had turned over the keys to the owner who in turn had given them to Ferguson. Since the faithful members actually owned half the building, they decided to take their case to court.

On June 1, 1856, Ferguson finally resigned, and by the end of the year a decree in favor of the opposing original members was handed down, although it was not immediately effective.

In April of 1857, the *Gospel Advocate* came from the press announcing in big, bold, black letters that the church building in Nashville had burned! It had been discovered to be on fire early on April 8, shortly after the members had regained complete control. The beautiful structure, with its pure white Corinthian columns, exquisite furnishings, and fine chandelier, burned completely before anyone could do anything to save it. Many were convinced that it was the work of the Ferguson party.

Tolbert Fanning sat down to prepare the *Gospel Advocate* for the press, and wrote, "The building is a mass of ruins." One can almost sense that his thoughts, running back over the past horrible months, reminded him that much more than a building of wood and tapestry had become "a mass of ruins."

The members of the Nashville church again began to meet in their old building and P. S. Fall was invited to return to work with them. His return was a wise decision since he had not been in Nashville when the troubled waters were boiling. As a result, no one connected Fall with either Ferguson or with Ferguson's "persecutors." Fall returned to find that of over five hundred members who had been there when he moved away, only fifty-seven now remained. By 1860, James Challen visited the city and wrote to Campbell that after Fall had been there for two years, about two hundred members were present on the Sunday of his visit. While this was less than half what it had been when Fall moved away from Nashville almost thirty years earlier, it was at least an encouraging effort to rebuild over the blackened ruins which awaited his return.

Ferguson, in the meantime, was preaching in a public theatre without much success. He eventually quit preaching, went to Mississippi, then on to New Orleans for awhile, turned to politics, and finally returned to lead a secluded life in Nashville. When he died on September 3, 1870, Lipscomb wrote in the *Gospel Advocate,*

> It may be a matter of sad interest to our readers to know the fate of this once honored but erratic man. He was the most popular preacher in the Southern country at one time. He was almost worshipped by his admirers in this city. He had not that humility of soul and strength of character to stand flattery and adulation heaped upon him. . . . Once no citizen of Nashville but felt it an honor to be recognized by him. In later years he was scarcely recognized by his former ac-

quaintances even of the world when met on the streets. The contrast was too painful to be borne by one so ambitious of popular applause as he. So, although his family resided in the vicinity, of late years he was seldom upon the streets of Nashville.[22]

When he died, a Presbyterian preacher spoke at his funeral, and it is said that only three carriages followed his body to the Mt. Olivet cemetery where he was buried.[23]

Tolbert Fanning was heartsick. He solemnly wrote that Ferguson had "renounced the spiritual authority of the New Testament, and in so doing blasphemed against the Holy Spirit." He had "committed the sin for which God's people are forbidden to pray."[24] The body of Christ had suffered "irreparable loss from the influence of the flesh-serving, *over covetous,* fawning Ferguson."[25]

Grieving Fanning the most was the fact that he bore a large share of the blame for what had happened. Why was this grand man, so noted for his ability to "see over, under, and right through" other men, not able to detect the pride and vanity of young Ferguson soon enough? Ferguson was able to do most of his deadly work in gaining sympathy for his cause through his articles in the *Christian Magazine,* and this instrument was placed in his hands by Fanning himself!

Despondently, Fanning viewed the wreck which lay before him. Hundreds had been lost to the cause which he loved, not only in Nashville, but in many other surrounding communities as well. On the streets of Nashville, the tongue of the world had toyed with the story as a dirty bit of gossip. Fanning appeared penitently before his beloved brotherhood, poured his tears into his pen and confessed, "The error committed cannot be corrected—'there is no room for repentance.' But we would gladly shroud the past in impenetrable night."[26] Then he humbly gathered up his worn out tools and began to build again.

CHAPTER 9

REMEMBER NASHVILLE—AND LOT'S WIFE

PREACHERS AND CHURCH ORGANIZATION

"It was not till more than two centuries after the establishment of the church that set sermons, long, studied, systematic, prosy, and speculative harangues were substituted for the spiritual worship of the saints. Tell us not that any congregation can serve God by such means." . . . *"Remember Nashville—and Lot's Wife."*

— Tolbert Fanning

TOLBERT FANNING refused to divide the church into "officials and non-officials," either through designations or through work. Furthermore, he was convinced that the Restoration Movement needed to go on to perfection in its concept of church organization. Although he always believed that all Christians were capable of offering "spiritual sacrifice to God for themselves," his own views in maturity show a marked advance beyond his earliest writings. That he changed and developed his views all through his life is obvious. What may not be quite as obvious is the degree to which he was successful in convincing the church as a whole that its practice was immature.

In the early days of his work, when Fanning became satisfied that a congregation was mature enough, he formally ordained elders and deacons. He also believed that the "laying on of hands" was a necessary ingredient in appointing elders and evangelists. Toward the close of his life he modified this concept and began to teach that a man becomes an elder or overseer in the same way in which any other member of the body finds his particular place. Without any special ceremony the member finds his place in the body—the church—simply by practicing the work and growing into his role in the functioning of the body. He wrote:

> We know of no authority in the scriptures for concluding that an election or ordination is a necessary qualification for doing any work in the house of God. These never made a preacher, elder, bishop, deacon, or deaconess, and this is what the brethren have to learn, before they can be prepared to examine satisfactorily the subject of organization and cooperation.[1]

Fanning came to believe that the prayer, fasting, and imposition of hands at the selection of Paul and Barnabas in the thirteenth chapter of Acts, were simply indications that the emphasis of their work would subsequently be different than before. The ceremony served as a "recommendation." "They were neither made preachers nor authorized to do a single thing they had not done for fourteen years."

In Acts 14:23 and Titus 1:5, men were not *made* elders but simply "consecrated" to have their "entire time and energies" given to this work. Fanning believed that just as each member of the natural body is especially fitted to function in some special realm, so the members of Christ's body have places to fill which they find quite naturally. No ceremony can affect or change their *natural work* (office) in the body. In fact, it seemed to him that such procedures could actually bring harm just as much as if a mother tried to rearrange the members of the body of her child!

Admitting that his views were somewhat revolutionary to most people, Fanning wrote,

> We are as sure that the brethren have not generally studied these matters, as we are sure that the Bible is true. Upon a careful examination of the subject, it will be seen that men are seniors because of experience, bishops because of their work, deacons, or deaconesses, as sister Phebe in the church at Cenchreae, in consequence

of having ministered to the poor, and that a man is a preacher because of his labor.[2]

J. W. McGarvey discussed this point extensively with Fanning. While the latter was visiting in Kentucky in 1868, he had objected to the use of the term "organize" in describing the appointing of elders in churches. As a newborn baby is organized totally when he is born, so, he affirmed, is the spiritual body of Christ. God "set" members in the church as it pleased him. "I understand the Scriptures to teach," he continued, "that God has set the older men, as seniors, to perform certain work which is most suitable for them."[3] But in his objections to "ordaining" elders, Fanning really seems to be objecting to *making* a man an elder. Even with an election, he might not be qualified to serve as an overseer. Fanning wanted to evade the abuse of making young men "bishops" to oversee or "pastor" the work of the church. He stated, "God ordained that men of age and experience should do this work, and every effort to make boys or new converts overseers or pastors is mere mockery of the divine authority."[4]

Fanning did not understand the word "elder" to denote an officer, as such. "*Bishop* implies office, but *elder* never. True," he continued, "the word *elder* is often applied to a bishop, but it is indicative only of a qualification, and no more denotes bishop than the word lawyer implies a judge of the Supreme Court." Since not all older members were to be considered bishops, the word "elder" should not be considered as always synonymous with "bishop."[5]

Fanning was quick to disagree with Robert Milligan, another outstanding scholar in the movement, who suggested that since two of the apostles had no wives a man could certainly be a bishop without being married. Fanning replied that Paul not only lists the married state as a qualification, but also urges the government of a family as further evidence that a man is qualified. This again indicated to Fanning that not all "elders" can be "bishops." He seems never to have admitted that the word "elder" could be used in more than one sense in the Scriptures, as most people in the Restoration Movement have claimed.

As suggested earlier, Tolbert Fanning objected to dividing the church into "officials and non-officials." In his early years he quite freely referred to "officers" in a sense later to be rejected. The first year that he edited the *Christian Review,* he wrote, "The primitive churches were fully organized with government, officers, and obedient subjects. That *officers* were necessary for perfect organization may be learned from the Acts of Apostles and letters of Paul and Peter." He later continued, "Before dismissing this subject, I will state it as a fact hereafter to be proved, that a church of God was never formed and cannot be at this day, without either extraordinary or ordinary officers, and divine organization."[6]

But in the span of his closing years, Fanning rejected his early position. Although he first wrote of "officers" and "obedient subjects," he later denied that the idea of *authority* was inferred in the biblical word for "office."

> While the idea of civil or other *office* is in the mind of the brethren, they cannot see the truth. But it will be remembered that Paul speaks of each member in the body operating in its particular office, and thus must the members of the Church perform the *work,* or office, which God has ordained. The word office—in this, and I may say every other passage, means work, and never authority. Hence, Paul said, I magnify my office, labor, mission, or work. Again, Paul said, "If a man desire the office of a bishop, (business of overlooking) he desires a good work. This was not a *sinecure,* or *official* authority, so called, but certain labor that good men may desire to perform.[7]

In his discussion with Fanning, McGarvey defined an "officer" as "one who is appointed to the stated performance of some public duty." Fanning replied, "In my view of religion, there is not a single member in the church who is not qualified, called and consecrated of God to some stated, public duty." Thus there were no classes of members with one group *over* the church in a way differing from the service rendered by *every* member.

To grasp Fanning's intended thrust, one must appreciate the backdrop provided by his fear of the clergy-laity distinction. If members conceived of some individuals as *officials* with authority, they were ensnared in the misconception embodied in the creation of a special class, exclusively empowered to administer the ordinances (to baptize, etc.) because of official authority passed down from the apostles through the laying on of hands, or "ordination." Because of this danger Fanning skirted the temptation to divide Christians into "officials" and "non-officials." To him, every Christian was a living stone, a king, and a priest, capable of offering spiritual sacrifice to God for himself.

Clearly, as Fanning himself admitted, much of his discussion with McGarvey involved a definition of terms. Yet there was obviously more at stake than mere logic-chopping. Fanning was sure that he saw real dangers, if not in the use of language, then certainly in basic attitudes and concepts. He wanted to lead the church to view itself as a living organism in which each member feels vitally responsible for activity. To do this, he seemed to isolate three aspects of the problem which were significant. First, he was disturbed about the use of church elections to select men to oversee the church as bishops. While he was not too clear in defining specific alternatives, he was sure that an election was not the proper approach. Secondly, he could not feel secure while the members appointed young men to serve as "pastors" and attached to them the title "Elder" (a title carried over from the Baptists by most preachers who used it widely among Churches of Christ and Christian Churches much as others later were to use the title, Reverend). Finally, Fanning looked at the church in Nashville, both before and after its experience with one man selected to do most of the public work in the church. He believed that the concept of church "officials," performing "official work" in the church, would lead the members to lean on one man or on a special class of men. As a result they would not develop their own abilities, their own knowledge, and their own spiritual sufficiency. Then too, a schismatic like Ferguson could rise to a position of influence much easier in such a situation where strength was ephemeral at best. What might at first appear to be a strong church would actually turn out to be made of straw.

Related to his concern for individual development in the church was Fanning's attention to the role of preachers. He urged individual growth in the body of Christ sufficient enough to foredoom any impotence which would force members to lean on one "pastor" to carry on their work for them in the local church. Though he boldly underscored this emphasis throughout his entire life, he invested even more concern in it after the Ferguson defection in Nashville. The members in Nashville, before they decided to hire a man to work with them locally, had been urged by Fanning to supply their own teachers as they had been doing for ten years. They had accomplished much without the aid of a young man to serve as a "pastor," overseeing their work. There is little doubt that if Fanning had been faced with this experience again, he would have been more insistent. While his teachings in regard to the preacher in the local church were not essentially different in later life, they certainly received heavier affirmation after the Ferguson episode, and it is only in this atmosphere that Fanning's view can be properly understood, appreciated, and evaluated.

Several incidents serve to clarify Fanning's attitudes toward preachers and their work. In 1844, as he was traveling about to inform others of his plans for Franklin College, he made a summer tour north, visiting Kentucky and Ohio. In Cincinnati he noted that while the church had grown strong in numbers, he detected "a disposition to seek popular preaching, and rather an 'itching of the ears' of many, for false eloquence.[8] After two months of travel he started home. Leaving Scottsville, Kentucky, he rode horseback the last fifty-eight miles to Elm Crag, tired from his journey, and contemplative about the progress he had witnessed. The fellowship with men like John T. Johnson was always welcome and refreshing. But other impressions were disturbing. As he rode along, he must have thought back over his visit to Cincinnati. There was no doubt about the talents of James Challen and young D. S. Burnet, both gifted preachers. That Cincinnati now had five congregations of the Church of Christ was also impressive. Still, something in the situation there disturbed Fanning. At home he sat down to write, "It was said the preachers had made some discoveries on the subject, and had taken their *salaries* in proportion to their oratorical powers. If I am not mistaken, the present system of paying large salaries to men who declaim to congregations weekly, to keep them alive, is opposed to the practice of the Apostles, and the whole genius of the Christian institution." He continued, "After careful observation, I was almost irresistably led to the conclusion, the disciples as they get strength and influence, incline much to the corruptions of the age, and become too well satisfied with mere conversion."[9]

It will be remembered that Fanning considered preaching to the unsaved to be the first and foremost responsibility of the gospel preacher. When Christians were gathered in one place, the preacher was to encourage them and help them to find their true area of work in the body, but was not to continue indefinitely preaching to them. When churches in the first century reached this degree of maturity, "preachers were no longer needed, and they travelled abroad to plant other churches. These organized churches were able to go forward in improvement without a stationed evangelist or monthly preachers."[10]

Tolbert Fanning knew that church members were "fond of good preaching." But he doubted if what they smugly called "good preaching" could convert the world or produce strong and pure churches. "Starvation and sudden death," he said, "await all who attempt to live by listening to 'good preaching.'"[11] He believed that a man was truly devoted to God only when he would be "much more deeply affected at hearing the word of God read than at listening to the most eloquent displays of human wisdom."[12] As long as members of

the church tried to "feed on sermons," instead of "performing the service which the Head of the church has ordained
for the spiritual growth of his people," the church would
not accomplish much permanent good.[13]

On the preacher's part, too many were in the habit of
"nursing congregations to death" instead of encouraging them
to perform their own spiritual labor, and experience true
"Christian enjoyment." "This proxy service," wrote Fanning,
"either by preacher, bishop, [or] elder, tends to keep the
members idle, inactive, and, of course ignorant and spiritless, till the whole moral heart ceases to beat."[14]

The experience of churches in the Restoration Movement
appears to have underscored the honesty with which Fanning
discussed their weaknesses in his day. It was not uncommon
for a preacher to report to one of the periodicals that in a
community where an evangelist had baptized perhaps a
hundred people within only a few days, only 25 or 30 were
meeting for regular worship a year later. Fanning would
say, "The main cause of apostasy in so many of the
churches, and coldness and indifference in others, is a failure
of confidence in the ability of the members to serve God for
themselves."[15] Too often churches did not meet at all until
a traveling preacher came by to call them together.

Realizing that many members simply felt inadequate to
take a public part in the worship service, he held that the
presence of a man who was especially eloquent made the
other members look with too much disdain upon their own
humble efforts. But he encouraged them to feel confidence in
doing their best:

> The members of the church are not willing to exhort,
> unless they can be eloquent. This is the result of ig-
> norance and pride. The plain and sincere exhortation,
> is always well received, though delivered by the
> lowliest.[16]

To make his point stronger still, Fanning noted,

> It was not till more than two centuries after the es-

tablishment of the church that set sermons, long, studied, systematic, prosy, and speculative harangues were substituted for the spiritual worship of the saints. Tell us not that any congregation can serve God by such means. Whenever a people cease to perform their own praying, singing, admonishing, exhorting, and in a word, worship, private and public, they are to all intents and purposes apostate, and they constitute the greatest stumbling blocks of the age to infidels.[17]

Fanning, to be sure, did not insist that every male member should take part by "preaching" in the worship services. This, in fact, he clearly denied. He did insist that every Christian should do something, and thus partake of true "Christian enjoyment" and at the same time develop himself into a position of greater strength and usefulness.

Also involved in the role of preachers were questions about financial support. Fanning was keenly aware of the "humiliating" experience of preachers kept dependent on church members as though they were "beggars." He especially abhorred the Christian who was the owner of many slaves, yet slipped a quarter into the preacher's hand as if he were being charitable to a menial. Lamenting the fact that in 1844 only two full-time evangelists, J. J. Trott, and S. E. Jones, were being supported in his area, he reminded the churches in Tennessee, "Unless too, we support the teachers, they will continue to turn their attention to the professions of law, medicine, and agriculture."[18] Fanning even emphasized that bishops, if they spent all of their time in their work, should also be supported financially by the church.

However, Tolbert Fanning did not always agree with others concerning the manner in which support should be provided for preachers. He saw no need for a "bargain to be struck" between the preacher and his supporting congregation, and all of this life he maintained that a stipulated salary was both unwise and unscriptural, not only for the preacher, but for workers in any field.

Several reasons were offered to support opposition to prearranged salaries. To begin with, men should "plow in hope," walking by faith and not by sight. Secondly, Fanning was convinced that a man's work tends to be inefficient when his salary is guaranteed. Those assured of a certain amount of money were tempted to relax their efforts. Thus he wrote,

> All salaries are corrupting in their tendency. They stifle exertion, beget habits of luxury and idleness, enervate responsibility, and too often deprave the heart. No lawyer, physician, teacher, preacher, field or shop laborer, in my estimation, will execute with half the energy, when working by the day, or year, that he will when his reward depends upon his exertions.[19]

Perhaps the most disturbing thing to Fanning was his feeling that the salary system seemed "to bring into existence and foster a class of selfish, envious and mercenary ministers, who fail not to work much evil."[20] He later added, "Without lengthy details, we state that it is a system producing envy amongst preachers, and personal disparagement of each other." Furthermore, Fanning feared that large salaries too often were "raised by flattery, and especially by failures in preachers to point out sins of the subscribers."[21] He finally rested his case with the declaration that the first-century church did not pay salaries. "There was no such thing as a man calling himself a preacher traveling on his own responsibility, in pursuit of profitable labor, and in fact, hiring himself by the day, week, or year, to feed some starving flock as their pastor."[22]

A year after the Ferguson defection, and surely with Ferguson in mind, Fanning wrote that the salary system tended to make preachers mere flatterers of the flesh. He then added, "Remember Nashville and Lot's wife." Fanning betrayed a certain reticence to say too much about his convictions before Ferguson came to Nashville since his ideas were in opposition to the judgment of most of the other members of the church. Perhaps, he reasoned, he was wrong. He hated to enter into controversy. But later, filled with penitence and sorrow, he felt that he should have been more insistent. One thing became obvious. He would never again withhold his judgment when it was in his power to bestow sound counsel on those for whom he was concerned.

Churches did not always follow Fanning's advice. In 1844, when he revisited the churches in Russellville, Alabama, and Columbus, Mississippi, he noted,

> . . . for about a year the disciples met and attended to *their own* worship; but unfortunately, they finally employed preachers to worship for them a good portion of the time; since which time they have not done too well. The best preacher in the world, preaching three times on every Lord's day, to keep the saints alive, will kill them spiritually; and without great care, eternally.[23]

When Fanning started the *Gospel Advocate* in 1855, he wrote much about hiring preachers to serve as pastors and was encouraged when some followed his counsel. Four years later he was able to write,

> Perhaps no church in the state has done more to set forth the power of truth than at Hartsville. The brethren think not of employing, or even permitting others to perform their service for them; and yet, perhaps have more good preaching than any other congregation in the state.[24]

At the time the Hartsville congregation was making plans to send out its own evangelist, T. Stalker, to preach in areas where no churches existed.

Fanning's influence also had striking effects on his student, David Lipscomb. It must already appear evident that Lipscomb agreed wholeheartedly with his teacher's emphasis. Said Lipscomb, "His teaching is in harmony with the Scriptures and with the laws of God in the material world, and the practical workings of the churches confirm it."[25] To Lipscomb the example of the church in Nashville was always significant. Beginning in 1828, he would point out, all the members took part in the worship. Four years later, when Fanning moved there to go to college, all of the elders and many of the members were teachers at home and abroad. They planted churches in the surrounding area and also sustained two evangelists in the field (Tolbert Fanning and Absalom Adams) who began churches at Franklin and Leiper's Fork in Williamson County, at Murfreesboro and Rock Spring in Rutherford County, and in several other nearby communities. Lipscomb noted however, that after the Nashville church employed fully supported preachers, the evangelizing spirit died out, they were broken up by the apostasy of a one man "pastor," and even ten years after they were called together again by P. S. Fall, not a member would pray at the communion service in public worship.

Fanning's concepts also had tremendous influence among his students who went out to preach after graduation from Franklin College. They turned to teaching more than to any other profession as a means of earning a living. However, they often continued to preach also, though usually not receiving any financial support. Such was the natural result of Fanning's influence.

Fanning's ideas about mature church organization were originally born before he knew much about the rest of the brotherhood of which he was a part. They gradually matured through his own experiences in preaching, including contact with a number of self-seeking fellow preachers who too often lacked genuine motives, ample preparation, or humble attitudes. His concepts were strengthened and underscored when he emerged from the fiery trial of the Ferguson incident. Not until after the Civil War was his influence most severely tested. But these earlier experiences had to be mastered first, before adversaries were permitted to put forth their hands to touch all that he had.

CHAPTER 10

CONCERT OF ACTION

CHURCH COOPERATION
BEFORE 1849

"We have talent, learning, worldly means, and no doubt, piety and zeal; but much of our labor is lost for want of unity of action, and proper employment of our resources."
                    —*Tolbert Fanning*

THOSE COMMITTED to a New Testament pattern as a valid authority for contemporary religion have historically suffered fracture as often as any religious group. One area which has proved to be a source of great confusion with almost every fragment of the movement has been the search for acceptable channels of inter-congregational communication and activity. Some of these problems may be perennial— innate in the movement's basic methodology of biblical interpretation. But some believe that many of them are superfluous to those willing to attend to the instruction of history and the motive of love. Because of this, a thorough reappraisal of the missionary society controversy is more than justified. The reappraisal is especially relevant to those who are sincerely searching for a meaningful rapprochement with alienated Christian brethren.

The tragedy which ripped through the Restoration Movement as a result of the questions surrounding missionary societies was woven into the fabric of Tolbert Fanning's life. His views about church cooperation were not easily fashioned nor hastily crystalized. As one searches each year of his life, he begins to see an evolution in attitudes which season into maturity. This development, tied to the experience of the church, is closely related to contemporary problems. But only after one has constructed a large portion of Fanning's life, is one prepared to consider the problems of church cooperation as they are imbedded significantly in these larger events.

Too often history has been rewritten to benefit the interests of a particular party. As an example of this type of historical tampering, some types of church cooperation have recently been maligned by some who point to a mythical end to which, they claim, certain practices inevitably lead. Often a knowledge of the history of the church in America can illustrate that the very opposite is true. Also lending fuel to this has been the fact that Fanning's position has often been misunderstood. He was misunderstood even by many of his contemporaries, and some of his companions evidently suffered lapses in memory when they wrote about him half a century later. Fanning wrestled, long with the questions involved in church cooperation before finally developing his mature position, and one cannot possibly understand that final stand unless he first lives with Fanning through the years which produced it.

In 1849, members of the church from all over the nation convened in Cincinnati to discuss plans for a general cooperation involving all of the brotherhood which they represented. The result of the meeting was the birth of the American Christian Missionary Society. This historic occasion provides a natural watershed in the advance of events, and it marks the climax in a whole decade of uncertain attempts at cooperation.

After Restoration Movement churches were generally divorced from the Baptist Associations (i.e. Mahoning, Redstone), other attempts at congregational cooperation were attempted. Perhaps one of the earliest efforts, according to Jacob Creath, Jr., came in 1830 when he met with his uncle, Jacob Creath, Sr., James Challen, Alexander and Thomas Campbell and several others at Mayslick, Kentucky. Creath often spoke of the "good effects" of the meeting. There were no church "messengers," he remembered, no resolution, and no debate. He described it as "a revolutionary meeting, a cooperation meeting for the good of each other and the whole brotherhood."[1]

After the Mahoning Association in the Western Reserve territory was dissolved in 1830 (*against* the wishes of Alexander Campbell), Campbell urged the members in Ohio (Western Reserve became the state of Ohio) to continue their annual meetings for fellowship in preaching and studying. Accordingly, in their meeting in August of 1831, they discussed cooperation. These gatherings, sometimes called "anniversaries," and at other times "cooperation meetings," were very similar to what Churches of Christ have come to call "lectureships." Their lack of extensive permanent organization is mirrored in some of the "conventions" sponsored by independent Christian Churches today. Through the 1830s and 1840s, these "cooperation meetings" became quite prominent throughout the brotherhood. Their boundaries were usually determined by natural geography or by governmental districts such as counties and states. In Tennessee, for example, the Tennessee River makes a large dip, cutting across the state twice, thus dividing it easily into East, West, and Middle Tennessee. At one time, each of these three areas had its regular cooperation meeting.

Evidently the first cooperation meeting in Tennessee took place in January, 1842, in Nashville. A group of men, including Andrew Craig, Robert Foster, James C. Anderson, and Tolbert Fanning, called for the meeting and sent out letters from the Nashville church in December of 1841. The next month twenty-nine churches were represented at the gathering. Among those present were fourteen preachers. J.J. Trott, J.H. Anderson, and Tolbert Fanning were requested to draw up an agenda. Among the things to be discussed were "the gospel manner of deciding questions," qualifications of officers, and the matter of voting. Fanning later recalled that they also discussed "The teaching of the New Testament regarding Christian cooperation."

They studied together "seven days and nights," and in the beginning of their deliberations there was little harmony.

Yet, their final conclusions were "heartily believed to be true, and strife ceased with the brethren touching religious expedients." Fanning observed, "We endeavored to look at the Bible as if we had never seen it before." He came away from the meeting deeply impressed with the value of Christians gathering to study, whether they came from two or twenty congregations.[2]

These meetings continued for several years. The meeting at Rock Spring in 1845 was typical. Fanning addressed a letter to the meeting requesting that they cooperate to gather statistics about the churches in Tennessee. Albert G. Branham of Sumner was selected to travel among the churches during the following year to assemble the information for the pages of the *Christian Review*. Those attending decided that the next meeting would be on December 27, at Berea, in Marshall County. Significantly, churches were requested to send *messengers* who would be prepared to tell how much each church would be able to do in a financial way in evangelizing the area, in educating poor boys to become preachers, and in educating the children of those giving themselves to full time preaching in the state. (This was the first year of the operation of Franklin College.)

The next year no plans were made for a state meeting. But in March Fanning carried news of state meetings in both Missouri and Illinois, noting that Alexander Campbell and John Rogers both attended the Missouri meeting where about eighteen thousand members were represented. Then he used the opportunity to urge the Tennessee churches to similar action: "Will the disciples have a state meeting in Tennessee in 1846? What have the brethren of East and West Tennessee to say? I trust the teachers particularly will take the subject into consideration."[3]

By December nothing had been done to arrange the meeting, so Fanning took the initiative himself. In the *Christian Review* he suggested that Wharton, Eichbaum, and Ewing, all elders in Nashville, serve as a committee for making arrangements. He also suggested December 18 as the proper time—and Nashville as the best place. For some unknown reason, the arrangements could not be made, but there was not enough time to inform everyone of the difficulties. Many came to Nashville for the meeting, causing some embarrassment to Fanning. That same month however, he wrote,

> Brethren in Tennessee, and further south, we should have at least two meetings each year for the purpose of *devising means* [emphasis—Fanning] to bring the machinery the Lord has given us to bear upon the enemy. We have talent, learning, worldly means, and no doubt, piety and zeal; but much of our labor is lost for want of unity of action, and proper employment of our resources.
>
> On those matters we are much at fault, and this essay has been hastily written for the purpose of reminding you of what is most needed, that we may see our faults and improve.[4]

Fanning obviously was anxious that the resources of the brethren in the state be used more effectively through "unity of action." He did not delay in opening the way personally for this possibility. The next month, January, 1847, there appeared in the *Christian Review* a proposition for a meeting for "Consultation and cooperation (not for preaching)" to be held at Franklin College, beginning on the first Sunday in May. This meeting was being announced, said Fanning, with the consent of the church which met at the college. It was to "bring concert of action in evangelizing the state, education, and cooperation." The announcement suggested that churches be ready to state what they would do financially to support the evangelizing of the area. In the statement on cooperation, the announcement read, "The ordinances of the Gospel and the Christian government are settled questions; yet the children of God are required to exercise their worldly wisdom as to the manner of employing their resources to advance the cause of God." This announcement from the pen of Fanning is extremely significant as it illustrates his understanding that there existed an area for exercising "worldly wisdom," or human judgment in church cooperation.[5]

Each church in the state was requested to send one or two messengers to the meeting and Fanning assured everyone that accommodations at the college would be available for them. The meeting actually got under way on April 30 when J.J. Trott opened the first session and then yielded the proceedings to Fanning. Fanning said that the purpose of the meeting was, among other things, to develop "a more efficient system of cooperation" for general purposes, for education, and for progress reports.

One by one, the churches represented at the 1847 meeting gave their reports. J.M. Barnes was there, but he insisted that he was attending as an individual, and not as a messenger from his home congregation at Millersburg! The members at Millersburg, he said, were afraid that the meeting might produce something which their sectarian neighbors would construe as a creed. But this was the only note of opposition sounded against such meetings, and it did not come from Fanning. He called the meeting, encouraged its success for months, and as a main speaker urged that the work planned there should go forward! Fanning, along with two others, Hopwood and Wharton, served on a committee on consultation meetings. In giving their report, they urged churches to unite their efforts by holding regular meetings in each district and county. They also suggested state meetings "or general meetings of some kind, for the purpose of employing our resources upon a more extended scale."

As a result of this meeting, which was held because of Fanning's leadership and at which he played such a leading role, the Church of Christ in Nashville was asked to serve as an agent for other Churches of Christ in the state to "receive, manage and disburse all the funds that may be collected" for the purpose of evangelism. The elders, Wharton, Eichbaum, Norvell, and Ewing, along with J.B. Ferguson who was then preaching in Nashville, were selected to form a committee to address a letter to the churches of the state. This action was designed to "make use of all lawful means to secure the ends we contemplate, to correspond with and select faithful laborers, and to make an annual report of all monies received and expended, and how expended." This means of cooperation, it was pointed out, was being proposed, not to interfere with any of the local churches' arrangements to supply their own immediate areas with preaching, but rather to call together and profitably expend whatever could be collected for a "more extensive proclamation."[6]

So Fanning had urged that they use their "worldly wisdom" to "devise means" to bring about "a more efficient system of cooperation" through "concert of action." As a result, the Church of Christ in Nashville was selected to act as an agent for other congregations in receiving and disbursing funds for this purpose. That Fanning was in full agreement with the plan became even more evident later.

Through the Nashville elders, two preachers were immediately sent out by the churches. The reports of their work were carried on the pages of the new *Christian Magazine*. These preachers received a regular sum of money and everywhere they went to preach, at some time during their meeting, they would lay the plan before the church there and then send to the committee in Nashville whatever funds each group might desire to give. Since what they raised from their travels in no way affected their own income, there could be no charge of selfish motives in their work.

That Fanning approved of this arrangement is further illustrated by two facts. First, in 1849 he accepted an invitation to serve on the committee to receive and disburse the funds. He and several others who were not members of the Nashville Church of Christ were evidently selected to serve with the elders in Nashville to give a wider representation from over the state. A second indication of his approval is illustrated by his motion at the 1849 meeting, "that any church, whether in Tennessee or not, willing to cooperate with us in sustaining evangelists, be united with us by contributions to the committee of the Cooperation."[7]

(This arrangement with the church in Nashville was even more formalized for a brief period of time. It also continued for several years after the establishment of the American Christian Missionary Society in 1849).

A second cooperation meeting was held in 1847 on September 11. Significantly, the scene of this next gathering was the very church which had expressed some doubt in regard to the previous meeting. At this meeting, in Millersburg, an agenda was submitted by a committee composed of Dunn, Trott, and Fanning. It included the question, "Do the scriptures authorize the cooperation of churches?" If so, the committee was ready to ask further if it would not be well for churches in each county, as well as in the state, to cooperate. Then Fanning and the other two men put forward this proposition: "Is not the proposition of the church at Nashville a wise and benevolent arrangement, and would we not do well to approve and recommend it to the consideration of the churches and benevolent individuals?"[8]

After placing these questions before the assembly, Fanning, Trott, S. E. Jones, and J. M. Barnes each spoke at length, urging everyone to work with the church in Nashville. Fanning explained the proposition in some detail, and, along with Trott, spoke of the liberty of churches in their use of expedients to carry out the objects of Christianity. According to the report the speakers stated "that many brethren in their opposition to cooperation with *all* the brotherhood, were more factious than Christian in their course."

While admitting an area of opinion and human wisdom which involved questions of expediency, the men were also anxious to follow some Scriptural pattern insofar as such a pattern might be discovered in the Bible. They observed,

> That we have the example of the ancient Christians, for united efforts to spread the gospel, and administer to the temporal necessities of the brethren. When it was announced in Jerusalem that unto the Gentiles also was the Gospel preached, they rejoiced and sent Barnabas to the aid of the church at Antioch, who having made

Paul a co-laborer, taught many people—Jerusalem and
Antioch cooperating—of their spiritual abundance made
many to rejoice in hope of eternal life.—See Acts 11.
The churches of Galatia and Macedonia cooperated in
relieving the temporal wants of the churches of Judea.
See 1 Cor. 16; 2 Cor. 8th and 9th chapters.[9]

Tolbert Fanning thus took a leading part in the early
arrangements for church cooperation in Tennessee. A puzzling
statement, often quoted as representative of Fanning, was
made in 1855: "Whilst we believe that the brethren in no
State have gone further in cooperation than in Tennessee, we
are satisfied and have been from the beginning of our efforts, that they have been wrong."[10] Some have done injustice to Tolbert Fanning by taking this statement out of
its historical context. Certainly, at face value, it seems impossible to reconcile the statement with Fanning's earliest
efforts. Perhaps even more puzzling, however, is his statement in 1866, eleven years later: "Why this effort to make
us an enemy to missions and missionary societies? We never,
to the best of our recollection, wrote an essay on the subject, or delivered a discourse with reference to such matters
in our life. We have never made war upon them."[11] This
statement was made over ten years after he claimed to have
been against cooperation from the beginning! Here again,
reading the passage in its historical setting is extremely important, and events which were taking place then, as shall
be seen, help to evaluate the statement properly.

It is impossible to believe that Fanning had his earliest
efforts in mind when he said that he had opposed "cooperation" from the beginning. To assume such would be to accuse him of acting against his conscience and conviction.
It must be evident by now that such duplicity was hardly
characteristic of Fanning. One should remember that he not
only acquiesced in the early efforts, but he *led, encouraged,*
and *urged* them. Later, when Fanning spoke of being against
cooperation from the beginning, the term "cooperation" had
taken on a different tone of meaning to most church members. It was in this new sense that Fanning used it, though

he did not subsequently limit himself to this use of the term.

During the period before 1849, churches did not feel limited to one particular approach to scriptural cooperation, as can be seen in their variety of arrangements. Sometimes, for instance, they gave support directly. In 1845, Fanning used the pages of the *Christian Review* to call attention to a need for helping the struggling church in St. Louis, Missouri. There were about one hundred members there, but they had no building and were relatively poor. Though convinced that the church in Nashville alone was in a position to supply enough to meet the need, he appealed to others to help also. He wrote, "Those who are disposed to give anything, will address R. B. Fife, St. Louis, Missouri."

Besides this *direct support* from one congregation to another, churches often sent their evangelists to help other congregations, and Fanning always called this a form of "church cooperation." By way of example, the church at Franklin College had two evangelists in the field in 1845. Through their efforts about one hundred fifty had been added at Woodbury alone.

A third type of church cooperation was the utilization of a *forwarding agent or church* (like the Nashville congregation). Thus churches were simultaneously using many different approaches. At the 1847 meeting at Franklin College, called by Fanning to devise means for more formal cooperation, the committee on which he served reported,

> We would recommend the brethren to raise funds, in all parts of the State, for the purpose of sending the gospel to Indian tribes and distant lands. We would suggest that the funds be committed to the care of chosen agents at some convenient point who shall distribute them as in their judgment circumstances require.[12]

This suggestion, as noted already, resulted in the selection of the Nashville elders to receive and forward funds from other churches in the state.

While these efforts were being developed in Tennessee, another series of events paralleled them further North. When Alexander Campbell began editing the *Millennial Harbinger* in 1830, he was just witnessing the dissolution of the Mahoning Association and was anxious for his readers to consider seriously how they might scripturally cooperate on a wider scale. Back in 1823 he had written in his *Christian Baptist* of the churches of the first century:

> Their churches were not fractured into missionary societies, Bible societies, education societies; nor did they dream of organizing such in the world. . . . They knew nothing of the hobbies of modern times. In their church capacity alone they moved. They neither transformed themselves into any other kind of association, nor did they fracture and sever themselves into diverse societies.
> . . . They dare not transfer to a missionary society, or Bible society, or education society, a cent or a prayer, lest in so doing they should rob the church of its glory, and exalt the inventions of men above the wisdom of God. In their church capacity alone they moved.[13]

It should be remembered that opposition to missionary societies was not limited to Churches of Christ. There were strong feelings against the organizations among some Baptists and other groups as well. The opposition also reflected the general independent spirit of a nation which had only recently revolted against the political control of distant England, including one of the ever-present reminders of England's control, the English church and its religious aristocracy. In the years leading to independence, the clergy hid under the wing of the King and came to be associated with outside control in the colonies. In addition, the self-sufficiency demanded by the frontier gave added cultural and social justification to the extreme individualism and localism which have become so engrained in the American character.

But when Campbell began the *Millennial Harbinger*, he was in an entirely different mood from that which characterized his earlier efforts in the *Christian Baptist.* In fact, his early work of tearing down societies had been done so well that he found it difficult to convince some of his readers that the societies were, after all, scriptural and wise. The dissolving of the Mahoning Association in 1830 coincided with a climax in the tyranny of discipline exercised by the Baptist Associations in censoring individuals considered to be heretics. Campbell, not at all in agreement with the dissolution, urged the churches to continue meeting each year at least for exhortation and discussion. (These annual gatherings on the Western Reserve were used merely for making reports, and, upon occasion, for the ordination of officers. Primarily, they were an excuse for members of the church to gather in larger numbers than usual for fellowship and preaching services.)

In 1831, following the dissolution of the Mahoning Association and early in the life of the *Millennial Harbinger,* Campbell began a well-planned and expanding campaign to call the attention of the brotherhood to the subject of cooperation. He wrote, "A church can do what an individual disciple cannot, and so can a district of churches do what a single congregation cannot." He was anxious however, that his readers search the Scriptures for a plan to be used. He continued,

> But although reason and the nature of things make this apparent, it must pass for nothing as respects the conscience, if we cannot show that in the apostolic churches such cooperation existed, and that it was a part of the means adopted by the authority of the Lord for the furtherance of the gospel.[14]

During the next nineteen years Campbell gradually led the brethren toward a more formal arrangement for cooperation. He moved slowly, to be sure, making certain that he had the brotherhood with him as he progressed. Yet, for all practical purposes, he laid down in his first few articles the broad basis upon which all of his plans were to be built.

In his opening series of five essays on the subject, the first and fourth appear to be most significant for this particular discussion. In the first, after emphasizing that they should search for a scriptural pattern, he proceeded: "This we hope to make very apparent in stating and illustrating a few propositions: 1. The churches were *districted* in the age of the *Apostles."* Here Campbell gave as examples the churches of Galatia (1 Cor. 16:1), of Macedonia (2 Cor. 8:1), and of Judea (1 Cor. 16:19). "That they were so districted with reference to some object, or some cause," wrote Campbell, "must be obvious." The question then arose, "For what cause?" He answered with his next proposition:

2. The churches planted in those districts of country, because of some local and discriminating interest, as well as because of their cooperation for certain specific purposes, were denominated from the districts of country in which they lived.

That churches of certain districts had peculiar circumstances, is evinced on sundry occasions. Hence all the churches of the Gentiles gave thanks to Priscilla and Aquilla, because they hazarded their lives to save the life of Paul. The *Gentile* churches show in this their deep interest in Paul, because he was an Apostle.

Particular districts also cooperated in contributing to the necessities of those who lived in another district of country because of some consideration which called forth their peculiar energies, made it their duty more than others' to assist them. Hence Paul "gave orders to all the churches of Galatia, etc."

3. The primitive churches in certain districts did cooperate in *choosing* certain persons for the work of the Lord, and these persons when chosen were called the *"Messengers of the Churches."*

We are expressly told, 2 Cor. 8:19, that a certain person was chosen by the churches to accompany the Apostles in ministering to the saints; and that persons so chosen were messengers of the churches, who cooperated in employing them for certain purposes—and that these persons, chosen by the churches, of any district, were the messengers of the churches of that district. All

> that we infer from this is that we have good authority, when occasion requires, to go and do likewise.[15]

Pointing out that soil, climate, and government provide the most natural boundaries, he said churches must consider their location before making any effort to convert the world. Campbell urged churches in each county therefore to form cooperative arrangements to convert first the county. "The only question is, *how shall this be done to best advantage?*" This, in Campbell's mind, is where human wisdom should enter. The Bible could not cover this area without containing a universal atlas with directions varying according to geographic, political, pecuniary, and climatic considerations.

> Whether then, they shall all meet annually, semi-annually, or quarterly, in one place in each county; or whether they shall appoint persons to visit all the churches in the same bounds, and to call forth all their means to enlighten and reform society at large, are questions which their own discretion must decide.[16]

For Campbell these matters were in the same realm as decisions regarding the architecture of the church building and the choice of the hour of worship.

In the same year that Campbell began this series of articles on cooperation, district cooperations were initiated in his own state, around Wellsburgh. By 1836, such district cooperations were present in Illinois, and by 1839, a similar meeting appeared in Richmond, Virginia, representing twenty-five congregations. As already noticed, a general consultation meeting was held in Nashville in 1842, and Tolbert Fanning's efforts during the 1840s should be held against the backdrop of Campbell's simultaneous articles.

By 1849, plans were being laid to meet in one grand consultation meeting or "convention," and Campbell reminded his readers of the form that the national meeting should take:

> *How shall such convention be obtained, when shall it be held, and for what purposes?* These I cannot more

than *moot,* or propound. I must, however, to suggest considerations to our brethren, say that it should not be a convention of bookmakers, or of editors, to concoct a great book concern; but a convention of messengers of churches, selected and constituted such by the churches—one from every church, if possible—or if impossible, one from a district, or some definite number of churches. It is not to be composed of a few self-appointed messengers, or of messengers from one, two, or three districts, or states, but a *general* convention.[17]

Gradually, through almost two decades of writing and encouraging state cooperation meetings, the stage was carefully set for the national convention. Tolbert Fanning, along with most of the church, had been willingly engaged in the direction of events. Finally, from all over the nation scores of delegates began their journeys to Cincinnati with high expectations. But few could have foreseen the outcome or the far-reaching results of the momentous days in Cincinnati in 1849.

CHAPTER 11

IN THE MULTITUDE OF COUNSELORS

AMERICAN CHRISTIAN MISSIONARY SOCIETY

"Resolved that a missionary society as a means to concentrate and dispense the wealth and benevolence of the brethren of this reformation in an effort to convert the world, is both scriptural and expedient."

— John T. Johnson

THE LONG AWAITED Cincinnati meeting opened its first "general convention" on Tuesday evening, October 23, 1849. There were one hundred fifty-six delegates present, and Alexander Campbell was elected to serve as president. Since he did not attend the meeting, D. S. Burnet presided in his place.

Attempts at coordinated efforts larger than one local church were not new to D. S. Burnet. Three and one-half years earlier, in January of 1845, young Burnet, then preaching for one of the Churches of Christ in Cincinnati, had taken the lead in establishing a Bible Society. He asked the whole brotherhood to stand behind his efforts even though the society was initiated through the four congregations in Cincinnati. Campbell, believing the project to be premature, criticized it from the beginning.

To further appreciate Burnet's unyielding insistence on such projects, it is necessary to look at his life and personality before this time. He had suffered a life filled with frustration. His relatives, who were leading citizens among Cincinnati's elite, had turned against him when he was baptized into the Baptist Church. Before he was eighteen years of age he was one of the secretaries at the first session of the Ohio missionary convention. "The Bible and missionary causes," he recalled, "have lain near my heart from before that time to the present." "I was born into the missionary spirit," he later wrote, "and did not relinquish it when I associated myself with my present brethren."[1]

His biographer notices that after many disheartening defeats, Burnet finally found some amount of compensation among the Churches of Christ. But then extreme illness became the most frustrating obstacle of all. While a victim of disease and fever on his sickbed, he became more and more obsessed with the conviction that churches should utilize their great power by organizing on a larger scale than before. From his long illness he emerged into his most aggressive period of activity. His biographer comments, "He vowed to fight as he had never done before to bring some kind of unifying experience to those who preached unity so fervently. The struggle of aggressive action, even against some of his closest companions in the movement, if need be, would be necessary for the survival of the new reform movement."[2]

When Burnet formed the Bible Society in 1845, several others besides Campbell attacked his plans as either unscriptural or premature. Fanning, however, had already been supporting a movement for distributing copies of the Scriptures and when Burnet started his society, Fanning noted that some had suspicions. In an effort to allay these he wrote, "Although the society has not yet had the countenance of the brethren generally, it is devoutly to be hoped it will live down the prejudices against it, and that the brethren universally will unite to give the Bible in a cheap form to the world."[3]

It was not at all out of character for Fanning to stand behind Burnet in his venture. He had served on the Nashville committee in charge of receiving and disbursing funds from the Tennessee churches, and at the same time, he was serving as secretary of the newly formed State Publication Society. Nor was it unusual for him to wholeheartedly support Campbell's announced encouragement of the 1849 general convention. Fanning signed his name to the statement which appeared in the *Christian Magazine.*

> We believe in the necessity and propriety of such a meeting. We think Cincinnati the most eligible point for such meeting, and would make an effort to have the churches of our state represented there. We would be gratified that the meeting should take place so as to include the 4th Lord's day in October next. We are confident our State meeting, which will convene some ten days prior to that time, will make arrangements to be represented.[4]

At the Nashville meeting it was decided that time would not permit a representation in Cincinnati. However, the Tennessee churches exhibited a hearty sympathy for the meeting and expressed their anxious desire "that some plan may be devised by which to secure a general cooperation· among our brethren in the spread of the Bible, and the cultivation of the great missionary field at home and abroad." Thus, initiated by Campbell, encouraged by most, including Tolbert Fanning, and guided by D. S. Burnet, the convention got under way.

At the second session of the convention, on Wednesday morning, John T. Johnson, who had been very active in the organization of cooperative arrangements in Kentucky, pointed out that they were present to inquire into the expediency of forming a missionary society. He expressed concern that they seemed to be proceeding too slowly and wondered if they did not have all the right of expression on the subject. He urged that it be brought immediately to the floor for discussion.

Burnet tried to temper the situation, explaining that it was not generally understood by those who had come as delegates that they were specifically to organize a missionary society. It was simply a called convention of "messengers." But Johnson was not satisfied with Burnet's caution and wanted to get at the matter directly. During the noon hour, he prepared a resolution:

> Resolved that a missionary society, as a means to concentrate and dispense the wealth and benevolence of the brethren of this reformation in an effort to convert the world, is both scriptural and expedient.
>
> Resolved that a committee of seven be appointed to prepare a constitution for said society.[5]

Noel L. Keith, Burnet's biographer, suggests that the turn of events was really not what either Burnet or Campbell had in mind. But by Wednesday evening, the direction of events was becoming more evident if not inevitable. The delegates' handiwork seemed to become their master and there appeared to be little that anyone could do to alter its course.

The form which the convention took was especially obvious in the constitution which the delegates approved. Membership in the new organization was to be dependent on the payment of dues. For $20 an individual could be a life member, and for $100 a life director. A church could also appoint a delegate for the annual contribution of ten dollars.

Before closing the convention, there were a number of offices to be filled under the new constitution. Among the twenty men listed as vice-presidents was Tolbert Fanning, though he evidently was not at the convention. Campbell recorded his reaction when he received the news of the convention: "We are much pleased with the result, and regard it as a very happy pledge of good things to come."

In Tennessee, Churches of Christ continued their cooperation, using the church in Nashville as an agent for the other churches in the area. In 1850, they met in Murfreesboro in September and among other things discussed "views in regard to Bible, Missionary and Publication Societies and Cooperation Meetings." Fanning was still serving as corresponding secretary for the state publication society which by then owned the *Christian Magazine*.

The next year the Tennessee Churches of Christ met in Columbia in October. Church buildings belonging to the Methodists and Presbyterians were used for the meetings. Fanning was present as a messenger from the church at

Franklin College, and the minutes reveal that he played a prominent role in the proceedings. He made a motion, for instance, that a committee be appointed to consider the need for Bible revision and translation. Like many of the better educated preachers of his day who had worked closely with the original languages of the Bible, he felt the need for a more contemporary and accurate translation of the Scriptures to replace the King James Version.

Culminating the move toward organization in Tennessee was a meeting at Franklin College in April of 1852 to form the Tennessee Evangelizing Association. The constitution provided that membership could be obtained by the payment of one dollar annually, life membership with twenty dollars, or a life directorship with the payment of fifty dollars. The constitution further noted:

> The officers shall have authority to employ agents to collect and disburse funds, and do whatever may seem in their wisdom best calculated to promote the objects of the Society; and they shall hold their office for one year, and till others are elected in their place.[6]

J. J. Trott was the first president, Tolbert Fanning was corresponding secretary, and William Lipscomb was selected to be the treasurer. At the same time, a circular was sent out requesting churches to support the new organization. Since one purpose for the association was to encourage young men to preach, churches were asked to pay for the education of these students, supporting them through the association. The circular was sent out from Franklin College and was signed by Tolbert Fanning and two other teachers, F. M. Carmack and William Lipscomb. (Fifty years later, in 1909, David Lipscomb claimed that this society never collected any money and never convened a second time. However, there was some type of continuing cooperation, for as late as 1855 reports were published from that year's meeting of the "Christian Evangelizing Association of Tennessee.")

Later that year, in November, the state meeting was held in the buildings belonging to the Methodists and Baptists in Paris. Fanning continued to take an active part as a messenger from the Franklin College church. It should be remembered that this was the year that Campbell had launched his attack against Jesse B. Ferguson. It was at this state meeting that Ferguson tendered his resignation as the editor of the *Christian Magazine,* under the supervision of the Publication Society of the Tennessee churches.

There was an editorial silence during the years of 1853 and 1854. Ferguson edited the paper as a private enterprise during 1853, and it was not until 1855 that Fanning's *Gospel Advocate* appeared. That year the "Christian Evangelizing Association of Tennessee" held its annual meeting in October. The messengers of the congregations in the state met at the church in Philadelphia in Warren County, and the speakers were Fanning and W. D. Carnes, a prominent educator and preacher. But Fanning's attitude toward cooperation had undergone some radical changes during his silence. In an effort to understand his change, another strand must be picked up and woven into the fabric at this point.

When the American Christian Missionary Society was formed in Cincinnati in 1849, one of its earliest and most outspoken opponents was Jacob Creath, Jr. A nephew of Jacob Creath, Sr., who was also prominent in the Restoration Movement, Creath had been a Baptist preacher, but because of his acceptance of the Restoration position he was forced to leave that group. He was a companion of Alexander Campbell on several of his preaching tours, including one of his first visits to Nashville. He spent most of his later years in Missouri, where he died in 1866.

When Creath received an announcement of the plans to discuss the formation of a missionary society he wrote a series of articles opposing the plan. These were later carried in one of the brotherhood's periodicals, the *Proclamation and Reformer,* under the title, "Arguments Against Clerical Organization."[7]

In a typical article, written for the *Gospel Advocate* in 1866, Creath wrote,

> Did the missionaries of the New Testament ever hold a missionary meeting; ever form a society; ever preach

> a missionary sermon; ever make a collection for mis-
> sionary purposes; raise a subscription for that purpose?
> Let him that says they did, prove it from the New Tes-
> tament, or acknowledge himself deceived or a deceiver.[8]

Unlike Fanning, Creath wrote, "We will never attend one of these societies, nor countenance their men or measures." Creath also pointed to the fact that the cause had prospered in Kentucky and Missouri and had spread rapidly in other areas without these organizations. He never ceased to remind Campbell of his early articles in the *Christian Baptist* which opposed the missionary societies so violently.

Opposition to the new American Christian Missionary Society came from other quarters also. The Church of Christ of Connellsville, Pennsylvania, having received a copy of the constitution of the society, held a meeting to consider the propriety of associating with the new venture. The result was a list of ten resolutions renouncing the society. They expressed a desire to carry the gospel to foreign lands but stated that they could not do so through an organization which would "exclude from its membership many of our brethren and all of the apostles, if now on earth, because 'silver and gold they had not.' "[9]

While the members at Connellsville believed the society to be "necessarily heretical and schismatical," they also wanted everyone to understand that they felt a responsibility to cooperate with others. They resolved, "That for the missions, both foreign and domestic, we approve of a plan similar to that adopted by the brethren of Tennessee for evangelizing in that state (see *Christian Magazine,* Vol. 2d, page 223)."

Prophetically, the statement from Connellsville maintained that if vigorous efforts to promote the society persisted, division would inevitably result. Its effect would be the same, they maintained, as the creation of a creed. They were especially anxious for everyone to know that their resolutions were the result of long and prayerful consideration and were dictated only by a spirit of love and a determination to be guided by the Scriptures, "though they should fail to furnish a king like those of the nations surrounding us."

The Connellsville resolutions were immediately answered by several leaders. D. S. Burnet wrote that Paul established the office of "messengers of the churches" when he was carrying out the work of his "Jews' Relief Society." He added an accusation that those who opposed him were "do-nothingarians" and urged them to look to the work which other churches were doing through societies. Why couldn't the Church of Christ do just as much? Burnet later wrote, "I consider the inauguration of our Society system as one of the most important acts of my career."[10]

Another leader who hastened to the defense of the new society was Benjamin Franklin, influential Indiana preacher and editor of the widely circulated *American Christian Review*. For Franklin the societies were in the realm of "expediency," just as building houses of worship or selecting a place to baptize.

As Tolbert Fanning read these exchanges in the papers, he laid plans for the 1850 cooperation meeting to be held in the fall at Murfreesboro. As a member of the committee to make arrangements, he called for calm deliberation instead of sharp and bitter wrangling. He suggested that they spend their time that year discussing and studying "views in regard to Bible, Missionary and Publication Societies and Cooperation meetings."

As already suggested, the Ferguson defection caused a marked change in Tolbert Fanning. Alexander Campbell had called on the churches in Tennessee to act as a body in censoring Jesse Ferguson. They were organized, controlled the paper which Ferguson edited, and it was their place to discipline him. Referring to this demand, Ferguson wrote in the extra issue of the *Christian Magazine,* published in December, 1852,

> A brother proclaimer of this State, who may be called one of the Fathers of our Cooperation system— than whom there is no man who enjoys a more enviable reputation for sound scriptural knowledge and sincere

devotion to the religious interests of men—when it was thought that foreign influences would induce our State Meeting to take the matter in hand, avowed his determination to offer a resolution in opposition to all such meetings, believing that whenever they take under their charge the faith or opinions of their Brethren, they would become curses instead of blessings to the cause of Christianity.[11]

There is no way to know who this "prominent preacher" to whom Ferguson refers might have been. However, it is a matter of record that before this time Fanning, who was certainly one of the "Fathers" of Tennessee's cooperation system and whose reputation was higher in the state than any other man, took part in strongly organized cooperation, while soon afterward he began to express doubts. He never again took part in an organized cooperation by holding office, as he had done for several years. No doubt Fanning, among other things, could sense the dangerous attempts to control conscience and dictate to churches which could so easily grow out of such formal organizations. At any rate, the next time that he recorded anything about cooperation, it is not to urge his friends to continue in their work, as he had done so often before. Instead, he wrote,

It is well understood that for many years I have doubted the *practical results* of the cooperations in Tennessee, and indeed in other states, but I have yielded to my brethren of age and experience, and I should be willing to yield longer could I conclude it would be to the honor of God.[12]

In breaking his silence on the subject, Fanning said that those discussing cooperation appeared as "men at sea," without guide or compass. This, to him, was humiliating to a people who believed that the Bible was their all-sufficient guide! He was prepared to show that the Bible gives examples supporting church cooperation as well as demonstrations of the way in which it should be implemented. Accordingly, he suggested that they spend their time at the 1855 state meeting discussing their mistakes and searching for a more perfect way.

When Tolbert Fanning, with William Lipscomb as his co-editor, began publishing the *Gospel Advocate* in July, 1855, the paper was well received from the beginning. Fanning expressed a desire to merit the confidence which readers vested in him. Alexander Campbell commended the project, adding, "Under the editorship of Elders Fanning and Lipscomb, we anticipate for it a large circulation and liberal patronage."

The paper was printed by Cameron and Fall, job printers in Nashville, and Fanning made it his policy to send it only to those who paid cash for their subscriptions. Its name reflected his deep faith that in the world, all that men know of God is revealed in his word, and this "gospel" is "all or nothing at all."

At the end of 1855, the six month old periodical made no appeal for support. Rather than launch the inevitable subscription drive, the editors simply expressed gratitude for the unexpected popularity of their efforts.

Several objectives loomed large in Fanning's mind as he launched the paper. For one thing, he was searching for a more extended means of influencing those who had been affected by Ferguson. At the outset, he carried many articles on metaphysical speculations and emphasized that the Bible is God's only revelation to contemporary man.

Another objective was also important. As he continued to study the cooperation arrangements used by various churches, he felt compelled to further investigation. The *Gospel Advocate* was to provide an avenue of communication for his investigation.

The stated policy of the *Gospel Advocate,* as expressed also in the earlier *Christian Review,* was to print both sides of the controversies in which the paper became involved. (In 1857, when Fanning was carrying on an exchange with Robert Richardson at Bethany, he was deeply chagrined to find in his travels that readers who took only the *Millennial Harbinger* heard only one side of the discussion, while those who took the *Gospel Advocate,* heard both sides.)

In regard to Fanning's plans to discuss cooperation, J. W. McGarvey, an ardent supporter of the missionary society, wrote,

> There is one good thing in our circumstances, and that is, we are not so wedded to any particular system as to prevent our following the leadings of truth unhesitatingly and implicitly. Go ahead with the discussions, and be sure that there is no flaw in the argument. If there is we will make it snap.[13]

While Fanning was studying and writing about cooperation, he continued to announce numerous cooperation meetings in which his readers might have an interest. He also continued to attend and to take part in their deliberations as they studied and discussed their work. Several weeks after the paper started, for instance, David Lipscomb, secretary of the Mountain District Cooperation of Churches, announced their annual meeting where Fanning was scheduled to be a featured speaker. A few pages later William Lipscomb, secretary of the Christian Evangelizing Association of Tennessee, announced its annual meeting, with Fanning again listed as one of the main speakers.

As his friends continued to study with Fanning, there gradually came an alteration of action in Tennessee. Those who did not feel that societies were wrong still were convinced, no doubt to some degree by the humble and gentle manner with which Fanning handled their discussions in the meetings, that they should be prepared to work without the organizations in order to bring unity. By January, 1857, William Lipscomb could report, "There are some few brethren who do not yet see exactly how they can get along without a little human machinery, but we hope that these will soon see the way clearly."[14]

About this same time, Fanning began more and more to use the phrase, "consultation meeting," in the place of "cooperation meeting." It is true that before this time these phrases had been used, to some degree, interchangeably. But now there was a marked preference for the former phrase.

That Fanning saw a distinct difference between mere "consultation" meetings and the kind of meeting with which they had grown accustomed, was evident when, in 1856, he spoke of the coming meeting at Franklin: "Let this be the first meeting since 1842 for the purpose of the disciples consulting together THE DIVINE ORACLES, in reference to God's ways and means to save the lost." Fanning later explained that a "consultation" meeting was distinguished by its lack of formal resolutions and constitutions. From the beginning of the *Gospel Advocate,* he urged the churches to have two or three "consultation meetings" each year. It is in this unique setting, witnessing a shift in emphasis and arrangement, that Fanning made his oft quoted statement about his opposition to church cooperation. What he refers to seems to be the formally organized constitutions and authoritative resolutions.[15]

As a result of the Franklin meeting in 1856, Fanning reported a general feeling that the church, as he phrased it, was "fully adequate for all of our moral and spiritual wants." To Fanning this meant that missionary societies were superfluous. He was further encouraged because so many were anxious for more consultation meetings. He wrote, "The proper plan is for any congregation to call upon sister bodies through our paper, or otherwise, to meet in consultation. We have attended no meetings which are so profitable to the brethren." He then asked, "How many churches will call a meeting for July?"[16] He was convinced that if they could continue to study with an open mind, good would result and division might be avoided. However, he continued to attend the meetings of the various missionary societies, notably those in Kentucky, as well as the general convention at Cincinnati, and at the same time continued to plead for a further evaluation of their course of action. Most misunderstanding, he believed, resulted from a failure to consult and "socialize" together in Christ.

As the consultation meetings continued, Fanning participated in arrangements which he did not always feel were wise. But he thought that progress was being made, and by

1859 he was ready to say, "more good has resulted from consultation meetings in Tennessee for the last seventeen years, than from any other."[17] Sometimes Fanning appeared even elated by the mature fruit which resulted from patient labor. After a meeting that year with close friends at Murfreesboro, he described the occasion for his readers:[18]

> True, as on previous occasions, some three or four wished to transact the business by *voting* rules of action, and by adopting plans originating in human wisdom. . . . We were made happy however before the conclusion of our meeting by hearing the brethren who have long opposed what we regard the teaching of the spirit, say, that if we would not go with them into their *"resolves,"* "recommendations," "plans," etc. etc., they would act with us, who held that the church occupies every inch of ground which should be cultivated by Christians.
> . . . For the first time, so far as we are informed to the contrary, since the dawning of "this reformation," it pleased the churches represented, the elders, teachers, and brethren assembled to make the effort to cooperate by authority, in evangelizing Middle Tennessee.[18]

This accomplished Fanning's purpose in the consultation meetings. Now it would be possible for churches to carry out their work and yet also respond obediently to the biblical exhortation to "be of one mind." This was the result for which he had prayed so fervently and labored so tirelessly.

Early in his efforts Fanning became convinced that when Christians spend time together in prayer and study, with a sincere desire for unity, God will guide them to "speak the same thing." Since their consultation meetings were producing such a salutary situation in Tennessee, he decided to ask the whole brotherhood to consider a proposal for such a meeting on a nationwide scale. While statements calling for such a meeting began in the early days of the *Gospel Advocate,* his appeal at the close of the Civil War, when feelings of alienation were especially keen, was even more significant:

> What say you brethren in reference to a full and most thorough examination of all matters of difference,

somewhat after the manner adopted by the brethren in Nashville in 1842? We think we would be willing to travel a thousand miles, to England, or to any place on the earth to attend a general meeting of the brethren with such a purpose in view. What say you brethren who are officers of the missionary society? A large amount of talent of the brotherhood seems to question the authority of your proceedings, and many good men, who are not mere *youths,* really believe the tendencies of your labors are not favorable to spiritual progress.[19]

Fanning's plea for unity and his mild call for consultation and study stood in bold contrast to more vitriolic statements of others who were opposing the Missionary Society. He wrote to those who supported the missionary society in Kentucky: "If you had been disposed to let us live with you in peace, we felt no ambition to interfere with any of your schemes, and we had fondly believed that even slight mistakes amongst the brethren would soon correct themselves."[20] On both sides of the controversy feelings were beginning to become more and more heated. But in spite of the unchristian and radical manner of others, both among those supporting and those opposing the new societies, Fanning remained the Christian gentleman of the brotherhood. He concluded his appeal:

Our firm confidence in the authority of the Scriptures emboldens us to declare that it is our settled conviction, that if the brethren who now seem to differ across the whole heavens will come together a few days or weeks, or even months, if necessary, they will arrive at the same conclusion on every point. Remember, brethren, that "in the multitude of counsellors, there is safety."[21]

Amid darkening surroundings Fanning remained the idealist of the brotherhood, sincerely convinced that only time to know each other and talk together could heal what appeared to be differences separated by a whole world. "In the multitude of counselors, there is safety."

CHAPTER 12

BEFORE YOU DRIVE US FROM YOU

MISSIONARY SOCIETY DIVISION WIDENS

"Do brethren, read the New Testament more carefully, and study a little more of the history of the early Christians, before you drive us from you."
— *Tolbert Fanning*

TOLBERT FANNING was completely unprepared for the re-action evoked by his prospectus for the proposed *Gospel Advocate*. Thomas Munnel, an officer in the Kentucky Christian Missionary Society, wrote him to declare, "If the *Advocate* will come out and help us in our good work [the missionary societies] I could wish for it a large circula-tion in our state. Otherwise, my influence, much or little, will be against it." A similar letter arrived from G. W. Elly, also an officer in the missionary organization. While Fanning prayed for unity and feverishly purchased time for study, others obviously did not share his conciliatory mood. In-stead, he believed they had confronted him with a new creed in hand. He must be prepared to accept it or be thrust from their fellowship.

Fanning was stunned by the incident. He refused to answer immediately, not certain just what he should say. Finally he wrote, "Brethren, pardon us for very respectfully begging you to stop and think before you go too far. What have you done already?" In a final appeal for time to study and for an easing of pressure to permit contemplation, Fanning wrote, "We ask no fellowship but upon the au-thority of Christ. But if you are determined to impose upon us creeds, oaths, and tests to which no man, in full Chris-tian health can subscribe, after giving you a fair hearing, we may be compelled to bid you adieu." With almost final futility Fanning begged, "Do brethren, read the New Testament more carefully, and study a little more of the history of the early Christians, before you drive us from you."[1]

Tolbert Fanning always remained a staunch advocate of church cooperation. He stated, "In the apostolic age churches cooperated for various purposes, without thinking it at all necessary to form any new society to aid the cooperation." He maintained that "If any work should be suggested too great for the performance of one congregation, the Scriptures authorize the cooperation of any number of churches for accomplishing it." As to the scope of such cooperation, Fanning wrote, "We cannot for our life see anything to prevent the congregations from cooperating in sustaining evangelists, relieving the poor, building up and supporting schools, or even in translating, publishing, and distributing the Scriptures, as churches and not as societies foreign to the Bible."[2]

On September 15, 1857, after prayer and fasting, the church at Franklin College set apart its evangelist, J.J. Trott, to evangelize the Cherokee Indians. The Cherokees had recently been moved from their home in the South, along their "trail of tears" beyond the Mississippi. As the white man herded them to their new home, almost half died along the trail. Fanning asked, "How many congregations of Christ will cooperate in this noble enterprise?" The next month Trott himself appealed for cooperation through the *Gospel Advocate*. He urged, "If they are not disposed to cooperate through the agency of the American Christian Missionary Society of Cincinnati, why not cooperate as churches through the agency of some of the congregations according to primitive usage?"[3]

By 1859, the churches at La Vergne and Hartsville were cooperating with the church at Franklin to sustain Trott, who had baptized about one hundred persons. Whether or not the churches were dealing directly with Trott or sending their money through the church at Franklin College is not stated by Fanning. (Trott himself, in announcing plans for the mission to the Indians, had gone so far as to suggest that the church in Cincinnati serve as an agent for all other churches in doing mission work for the church at large and this was his antidote to the missionary society.)

Another example comes from Louisville, Kentucky. In 1856, the members there selected William Thompson as their agent to travel among the churches to collect funds for sending two or more evangelists to England, Scotland, and Ireland. They wrote,

> Taking the primitive churches as our model, we feel satisfied that each congregation is a missionary society in itself; and if unable by itself to raise means enough for any projected mission, to make an appeal to the brotherhood for aid. This we now do, by sending brother Thompson to you. The funds will be placed in the treasury of the church, and sacredly set apart and used for this mission by the congregation we represent.

As this notice appeared, Fanning was discussing the Missionary Society in an exchange of articles with Robert Milligan. Significantly, Fanning offered this plan of the Louisville church as an acceptable alternative to Milligan's support of the Society. Fanning added, "Thank the Lord that at least the members of one congregation regard the church as 'a *missionary society,*' and they appeal to the churches of the United States for cooperation in this good work."[5]

Thompson wrote Fanning to ask if there might be a church in Tennessee which could become a "center of co-operation for the churches in the State" in a role similar to that filled by the church in Louisville. Fanning simply replied, "The brethren in Louisville will have the hearty cooperation of many of the saints in the Southwest."[6]

Quite understandably the brotherhood took Fanning's remarks as an indication of his wholehearted support of the Louisville church's proposal to receive and disperse funds. But Fanning seems to have entertained another procedure. In answering an inquiry from G. W. Elly, he said the church in Louisville did well to propose "to encourage the sending of a few evangelists to England," but their sending Thompson through the country to collect funds for the Louisville church to appropriate made it the work of the Louisville church alone. This, he maintained, placed the Louisville church in the same position as the Missionary Society in Cincinnati. In effect they were saying, "We have a noble enterprise in view, and if you will send us your money, we will wisely appropriate it, and publish our proceedings in the papers and tell all the world what each member does."[7] Fanning believed that they should send the missionaries to England, *then* ask other congregations to cooperate with them. As the missionaries' wants were made known "to the respective congregations agreeing to carry out the good work," the needs would be met. "But each church must be left free to perform her own duty at her own time and in her own way."

Fanning is not here concerned (nor can it be proved that he *ever* was) with whether funds were to be sent directly from the various congregations to the evangelists or to be given for forwarding to the congregation which sent them out. This was not important to Fanning. If it had been, he surely would have mentioned it somewhere in his many articles on cooperation. His main point of concern, especially lucid in the light of his convictions on salaries for preachers, was that churches were not to be obligated ahead of time for a stated amount of money. Both the manner and the amount were to be determined by each congregation when the time for giving arrived. One thing was definite with Fanning. The evangelist should be appointed or "recommended" by some one particular congregation which would be responsible for his actions, and he was to reveal his needs to that church. She could ask other congregations to help, and then when they communicated to her their willingness to cooperate, it was her responsibility to inform them of the evangelist's needs. How they supplied these needs was their own decision. This, he believed, removed them completely from any semblance of outside control.

Thomas Munnell voiced the feelings of many when he

complained that Fanning had failed, even after fifteen years, to define exactly what type of church cooperation he favored! It almost appeared that he was not certain himself. If the Bible furnished a plan, they challenged Fanning, why did he not clearly show it to them with "book, chapter, and verse?" Fanning would answer that the home congregation should select a man and send him out. Then, "there is not a church in America, England, or even Australia, which would not rejoice to cooperate in such a soul-cheering service," if the sending church publicized the need.[8]

Elly sent Fanning a series of questions in an effort to clarify what he really proposed. Fanning answered them very directly:

> 1. May two or more congregations unite in their means and efforts to send the gospel to a destitute point, State or Nation? (Yes, T. F.) If so, state the authority of the Apostles for such a cooperation. (See 2 Cor. viii. 19, T. F.) And how the funds are with the evangelist to be controlled? (See Phil. iv. 16, T. F.)
> 2. If there is such permission, then say how all the churches in a county, district or in a State can cooperate in the work without infringing upon the individual congregational rights, and yet avoid what you call a "human organization," or one that is not specially marked out in the Oracles of God? (Any number of churches may cooperate, as churches, in any good work. T. F.)
> Shall we send the gospel to Jerusalem, China, or India? If so, how can it be done by church cooperation scripturally? (Send the gospel into all the world, and when a church is not able to send her missionary, let her ask the aid of others. T. F.)[9]

From Fanning's replies it appeared obvious that few would feel any more enlightened as to the mechanics of his ideas than before. But that Fanning believed that someway churches should cooperate remained just as obvious. He accepted the principle of selecting an evangelist to serve as a "messenger" sent out by one or more churches. In fact, the messenger could conceivably be involved in many types of work. Fanning stated, "We see nothing to prevent churches cooperating upon agreement in any good work. In the days of the Apostles a brother was chosen by the churches. Why may not churches, as churches, send missionaries to Jerusalem, or evangelize the State?"[10] He believed that "any number of churches" could even agree to translate the Scriptures and publish the results through "men chosen by the churches for the purpose, just as messengers were selected to bear the contributions 'into Judea.' "[11]

Out of these discussions there also emerged Fanning's major reasons for opposing the missionary society. He did not believe, for instance, that it was effective. To him the society was a clumsy piece of machinery which retarded efficient activity more than it contributed to effective cooperation. Thus, in his early exploratory objections, he expressed doubt about the "practical results" and the "competency" of the societies. By removing the work from the local church, the arrangement lost some of its challenge to the individual Christian. Since the individual was not close to the work, he could not feel the need for sacrifice and involvement. Fanning believed that "when people are called upon to act and to give their money, they must have some special object in view, so that they may be stimulated by a knowledge of the good they are doing." This was not possible under the society arrangement.[12]

Beyond the realm of judgment, however, and standing at the heart of his objections, was his conviction that the society was an unscriptural ecclesiasticism. He was convinced that through the machinery of the local congregation, and without the aid of "human organizations," the church could carry out the work God had given her to do. The missionary society was not a cooperative arrangement of separate churches but a separate body altogether. It had its own constitution and its own officers, and could, in fact, perpetuate itself completely independent of the churches. At one point Fanning wrote,

> From the many constitutions, articles, amendments, resolves, and magnificent plans that have been published

by the brethren—to say nothing of the more speculative
party bodies—one not acquainted with history might
conclude that the Heavenly Father had either left the
world in extreme darkness, or that if he had given
instructions for the government of his people, they were
not believers.[13]

Mirroring these doubts was his concern that the time and
attention lavished on the societies might tend to detract from
the church itself, actually providing "an outrage against the
church of Christ." He chided his brethren that they might
need,

> A few more *"central unions"* to regulate the faith and
> order of the churches; another society or two *"For the
> education of men for the ministry,"* with the creed
> somewhat elaborated, and a few other schools to "take
> care of the fatherless and widows in their affliction,"
> and especially one to teach the brethren how to *"keep
> themselves unspotted from the world."*[14]

"In the work accomplished by them" said Fanning, "the
credit is mainly given to them and not the church. Indeed,
according to President Elly's statement, these associations
plant churches, set them in order, and supervise them
generally."

Fanning believed it a misnomer to call the missionary
society "church cooperation" inasmuch as it was actually
made up of individuals (through the payment of a certain
amount of money) rather than churches.

If none of these objections was valid, the societies were
still unacceptable to Fanning because of the division which
they spawned. Those who argued for the missionary society
almost always called it an expedient, justified on the same
basis as a church building. Fanning replied that even in
expedients they were commanded to be of the same mind
and judgment. In building a meeting house "It is a matter
of expedience," he said, "whether we employ stone, brick
or wood, but Christians are to submit one to another, and
taking into consideration all possible conditions of the
question, they must yield to each other and be one."[17] By

choosing to continue with the societies instead of being of one mind, some elevated the societies to matters of faith, thus alienating those who could not conscientiously work through them.

Fanning gradually and thoughtfully reached a conviction which was to have far-reaching and long lasting consequences among those whose efforts were bent toward restoring the "ancient order of things." As Alexander Campbell, and others, urged strong cooperation arrangements between congregations grouped in districts, Fanning actually led the way in Tennessee. From 1842 until 1849, he not only acquiesced but *urged* the meetings which finally led to the selection of the Nashville Church of Christ as an agent for the other Churches of Christ in the state. In 1849, on the eve of the convention in Cincinnati, he personally introduced a resolution that even churches outside Tennessee be invited to send their funds to the committee in Nashville for distribution. But after this time Churches of Christ in Tennessee began to develop more formal arrangements involving constitutions and official "resolves." Plainly, this is what Fanning objected to.

His answer to this abuse was the "consultation" meeting where members met to study and discuss their mutual responsibilities and ways to cooperate as churches. The consultation meeting did not introduce official resolutions and government constitutions. Though his forebearance was extended toward such paraphernalia for awhile, he was never sure of its worth or its Scriptural basis. He continued to yield to others until after the Ferguson incident in Nashville. From that time, notably with the beginning of the *Gospel Advocate* in 1855, he freely expressed his convictions and urged that others follow him in studying and reappraising their actions. He continued to visit the society meetings and commended their good deeds while at the same time expressing his convictions that they had no basis in the Scriptures. He urged a national "consultation" meeting to discuss the possibility of bringing unity of action out of their differences. But he could never again participate, as he earlier had done, in arrangements which he now was convinced were wrong.

Tolbert Fanning spent himself totally in trying to cultivate unity in soil hardened by alienation. But his efforts toward peace were not always reciprocated. For instance, after the Civil War, at the same time that he was begging others to wait until they had studied a little longer before forcing their plans on fellow Christians, a missionary society was being formed by Northern leaders among freed Negro Christians. With great irony, either planned or accidental, they chose the city of Nashville to carry out their plans! Fanning attended the meetings and plead with his friends to study with him, but they insisted that they had come to "adopt some plan to get money" and they intended to do just that! There was no room for discussion. Led by a Negro preacher from Cincinnati whom Fanning himself had educated, they formed a missionary society. His counsel rejected, Fanning sadly left the building before the meetings were over. He was especially heartbroken because some of the men now led to "lift up their heel" against him were the very men whose freedom from slavery he had purchased with his own money and whom he had educated with his own funds and effort.

In 1859, determined to do all which was humanly possible to maintain an unobstructed rapport between himself and his society brethren, Fanning had attended the annual national meeting of the American Christian Missionary Society in Cincinnati. Ten years had elapsed since the first convention. Fanning was determined to express his concern but at the same time to continue to fellowship those with whom he differed.

As usual, the delegates gathered at "Christian Chapel" at the corner of 4th and Walnut Streets. It was October 19, and since Alexander Campbell was absent, Wm. P. Stratton presided at the meeting opened with devotional worship at 2 p.m. About three hundred were present. Fanning could not hide the thrill he experienced as he joined his voice in song with the elderly Samuel Rogers, the "veritable 'racoon' John Smith of Kentucky," Walter Scott, Moses E. Lard,

Ben Franklin, John Rogers, and others. Fanning was especially impressed with a host of younger preachers who were attending the meeting. "Never has it been my good fortune," he commented, "to associate with such a mighty host of strong and earnest men."[16]

At 7:30 that evening, they gathered for the major opening address which was delivered by D. S. Burnet. Fanning said that it was the "oration of the occasion. For artistic skill in composition and delivery and soundness of doctrine, it has rarely been our good fortune to listen to an address that would compare with it." Burnet stepped down from the pulpit, and at the close of the meeting Fanning was there to greet him. Overcome by the wonderful fellowship of the inspiring occasion, Fanning said, "You ought to die after that speech, Bro. Burnet, for you will never equal it again."[17]

Fanning drank deeply of the feast of fellowship with spiritual giants, admired from his youth for their long labor in the cause which was his life's first love. But other thoughts also clamored for his attention. He sincerely believed that their activities were moving them away from sound moorings. With the help of God, he was determined to talk with them about it.

On the third day, Fanning's opportunity came. Isaac Errett had been trying to keep Fanning silent, but he was finally recognized and admitted to the floor to give a report of the work in Tennessee. This Fanning did. But much of his time was spent emphasizing that in Tennessee they were accomplishing much without the use of missionary societies. He told of progress in overcoming the influence of Ferguson, and then proceeded to tell them about the work of J. J. Trott among the Indians. He admitted that there was much good in the missionary societies but said he was more impressed that the church, described as the "pillar and support of the truth," fully covers all ground which Christians should occupy in their labors of love.

While Tolbert Fanning continued to emphasize the church as the proper missionary society, he was also anxious that love and peace might continue to flourish. Before taking his seat he tenderly said, "But I am happy to say, that from what I have heard on this floor, we are one people."[18]

Fanning's remarks were made with the hope of provoking a discussion. Consultation in Tennessee had brought unity among those who were previously divided. Surely his friends here were capable of the same calm deliberation toward such peaceful fruit. At the close of Fanning's remarks, however, Isaac Errett was immediately on his feet with a resolution that Fanning's report be read into the minutes, printed with the annual proceedings, and that those present resolve "That there is no difference in fact, in doing our work through the church, as presented by Bro. Fanning, and through other agencies." Fanning was not at all impressed with Errett's stated devotion to peace and unity. Parliamentary procedure drove the wedge deeper, and Fanning winced at this "flattering trick of worldly wisdom" on the part of Errett, shrewdly designed to keep Fanning quiet.

This was the year of the execution of John Brown at Harper's Ferry, where a fanatical man became a myth and was enshrined as a hero. One nation, under God, was preparing its instruments of hate. As Fanning rode home to the peace of Elm Crag, he knew of the clouds which settled ominously over the nation. He sensed also the depressive atmosphere in the church as the winds of frenzied division were being driven to gale force and intensity. But with God's help, he would continue to plead for unity and peace and calm deliberation. Surely love could find a way. And love insisted, "We are one people!"

CHAPTER 13   **"BRETHREN,
WE ARE ONE"**
THE EVE OF THE CIVIL WAR

*"Brethren, we are one, and have but
one work to perform."*
— *Tolbert Fanning*

IN THE EARLY decades of the nineteenth century, the United
States was experiencing something of a cultural renaissance.
Colleges were coming into their own. The Industrial Revolution was well under way. Bancroft, Washington Irving,
Hawthorne, Melville, and Thoreau authored an indigenous
literature in an America which was impatient to prove its
sophistication. Transcendentalism, the German-made philosophical reaction to Calvinism, appealed to a self-conscious
country, telling its rugged individual that he was not totally
depraved, as the fathers of the Constitution had believed,
but that he was innately good and could hold his head high
as he walked the earth "as though he were a god."

In Massachusetts Horace Mann was campaigning to raise
the standards for teacher requirements and salary provisions in an effort to build respect for the profession. By
1860, two million copies of the famous *McGuffey Readers*
had been sold, and each year many were being transported
further west in wagons and saddlebags as the frontier tried
to attain some degree of respectable education. By 1860, the
population of the nation reached thirty-one million and then
moved on under the pressure of immigration from abroad.
Lincoln and Douglas were traveling through Illinois debating
the possibilities for a nation surviving half free and half
slave.

While men flocked to Pikes Peak in search of gold, and
others laid the transatlantic cable in search of interconti-
nental communication, still others were searching for re-

ligious meaning. Tolbert Fanning took a two-month tour and returned to report that he had never, in twenty-nine years of preaching, seen "half the anxiety generally to hear and examine the truth." He also reported that the Restoration plea was having tremendous effect even upon the denominations which it was designed to engulf. "The leaven is at work," he wrote, "which, we fear not, will leaven the whole lump of truly religious society."[1] He wrote later, "In spite of their hatred they begin to talk like us and they cannot help it."[2]

In Nashville, the meetinghouse which had burned in 1857 was being replaced, and by the end of 1859 the members were ready to move into their new structure. Fanning himself remained busy preaching in many places. On one tour he traveled south to be with the church in Selma, Alabama, which was just moving into a new building. Another tour, taken to provide for the family of a friend to whom he had made a promise on his deathbed, led him through several northern states. Having arrived home again, he mailed the first issue of the *Gospel Advocate,* with observations regarding the condition of the churches contacted on his trips. Illustrating the breadth of his interests he described the crops and geological phenomena as well. The *Gospel Advocate* joined what soon became a field of seventeen periodicals, all devoted to restoring primitive Christianity.

William Lipscomb, who was helping to edit the *Gospel Advocate,* in 1857 joined his brother, David, to pool their sources and purchase a five hundred acre farm from Fanning. Fanning had purchased the farm, which lay in the White's Bend in the Cumberland River, from his brother, A.J., and sold it to the Lipscomb brothers for $16,275, which included some machinery and stock.

When he started the *Gospel Advocate,* Fanning was forty-five years old and in the prime of life. He was especially optimistic about the future of Franklin College. The school enrolled as many as one hundred forty students and his schedule of work at Elm Crag moved along smoothly. According to one student, the singing in the chapel was the most stirring part of campus life, although it was not the only music to be heard. In 1851, J.J. Giers, who was teaching music there, wrote and published "The Franklin College Quick Step" for the band to play on its excursions and at special functions like the commencement exercises. The sheet music had a picture of the school on the attractive cover and was published in New York. Naturally, it was dedicated to President Fanning. Because of the academic reputation of the school its graduates found other educational institutions open to them without difficulty.

Drifting over these most encouraging years at Franklin College was a cloud whose darkness never quite lifted during the rest of Fanning's lifetime. In 1856, Robert Richardson, a professor in Bethany College, began a series of articles designed to show that the Restoration Movement needed to go on to higher enlightenment through direct intuitive knowledge from the Holy Spirit. At first, though registering his disagreement, Fanning said he would wait to see how Richardson was going to develop his ideas. He also wanted to hear what Alexander Campbell might have to say on the subject. As the articles were developed, he became convinced that Richardson was completely astray, and, to his dismay, the elderly Campbell remained silent.

Richardson taught that spiritual light can come from sources other than the Bible, since, he said, "The understanding can never rise to spiritual reality, till it goes beyond and above outward forms." Again, he wrote, "It is the spirit alone that can perceive the truth," and, "All attempts then to reduce spiritual truths to the forms of the understanding, must be futile and derogatory to the Divine word which addresses itself to our higher spiritual nature— to our self-consciousness, as the only auditor of its communications."[3] Richardson further implied that men like Fanning simply were not able to comprehend these higher communications of the Spirit. To Fanning's ear this sounded not only like the Transcendentalism, which had been bequeathed on the young nation during the early part of the century, but came too close on the heels of his experience with Jesse B. Ferguson's exploration into intuitive communication.

In Fanning, Richardson found one who had made a complete and thorough study of the German and French writers to whom the Transcendentalists were in debt. If he was not mistaken, Richardson had been influenced by some of the same type of philosophical reaction which had been so appealing to Jesse Ferguson. Since most men use past experience to interpret present events, Fanning might have assumed that a transcendental philosophy would lead, as it had with Ferguson, to a complete rejection of Christianity's uniqueness and possibly even to some macabre type of spirit-communion like that which finally made Ferguson the pitiful spectacle that he was in the end.

Before Fanning spoke out against Richardson, he made a trip to Bethany to visit with the aged Campbell. Campbell it will be remembered, had rebuked Ferguson mercilessly. Why was his pen now silent? Fanning had to find out. When he went to Bethany he did not let anyone know that he was coming. Instead, he went directly to Campbell's home unannounced and was shocked to discover that the aged giant was no longer the clear thinker which he remembered from his youth. Campbell's wife would not even let Fanning talk with him unless she too was present to prompt her husband. Fanning concluded that the younger men at Bethany were influencing Campbell in his senility and using his prestige for their own designs.

Having failed in his effort to have Richardson stopped, Fanning decided he must handle the question himself. He took the position that all "spiritual light" comes through the Bible. Even nature speaks of God only to the man who has seen him revealed through the message of the Scriptures. Richardson defended what he termed "Natural Theology" and spoke of God's spirit revealing spiritual truth directly to man as it dwells in him. He defended his position by saying that Campbell himself was teaching "Natural Theology" at Bethany. Fanning, who remembered the devastating debates and writings in which Campbell had earlier bludgeoned "natural theology," replied,

> Shall the Philistines take our greatest and best man, bind him with the fetters of brass, put out his eyes, and make him grind in the prison house of Natural Theology!!! . . . We have but little in the goods of this world, and less of its honors, and we say, in the sincerity of our soul, that we would greatly prefer becoming a beggar in the street, than to be satisfied that Alexander Campbell is teaching Natural Theology.[4]

With this note from Fanning, Campbell finally broke his silence to say that while a course which he taught at Bethany was called "Natural Religion," it was really only a class in biblical evidences and apologetics. As a "solid, substantive fact," he admitted, there was no such thing as "Natural Theology." After this acknowledgment, Campbell stopped Richardson from publishing his ideas on enlightenment in the *Millennial Harbinger* although he offered no apology to Fanning.

Richardson pointed out that Fanning was following the philosophy of John Locke, who believed that all knowledge comes through sensation and reflection. Thus, since Fanning believed that man is wholly dependent upon revelation for his ideas about God, he was classified by Richardson as a "sensualistic dogmatist," who was guilty of "Bibliolatry."

The question of how man receives his knowledge is, of course, an old one and the answers offered to it usually reflect an effort to be consistent with one's philosophical presuppositions. But in this case, Richardson carried his observations beyond an impersonal field of discussion and described Fanning's attitude and teaching as "an ignorant, pretentious adulation, a blind, unreasoning partiality, which, in reality, degrades the Bible."[5] According to him, Fanning had converted the Restoration plea into a "cold and heartless nominalism, prolific and unprofitable controversy but barren of religious fruits." Coming from one who had attained to spiritual enlightenment so much higher than most men, these bitter words sounded deeply ironic. Richardson continued to describe men like Fanning:

> Its advocates [revelation as the only source of spiritual enlightenment] have not a new thought, drawn from the Sacred Scriptures, with which to gladden the soul. If they are writers or preachers they continue to repeat themselves from year to year without the slightest improvement. They are ready to argue, debate, discuss, at all times, in the usual round of the stereotyped philosophy into which their minds have been cast, and will spend hours in the earnest defense of their favorite theories, but are indisposed to converse either with their own hearts or with one of the spiritually minded brethren, for five minutes, upon the character, the sayings, the doings, the perfections of Christ, or upon their own inward and spiritual state.[6]

As Fanning replied to the Richardson attack, he spent most of his time showing what Richardson's real teaching was. He also showed who his teachers were. Fanning, through many quotations from F. W. Newman, Henry James, and D. F. Strauss, tried to educate his brotherhood to the real danger of this philosophy which professed "direct spiritualism." The only time that Fanning approached a discussion of Richardson personally was in his statement that most men who hold these views "affect a haughtiness that is insufferable," while insisting that other men simply cannot understand the deeper things of the spirit.

Campbell was somehow led to attack Fanning also, and the picture which was drawn before the readers of his magazine, the *Millennial Harbinger,* portrayed Fanning as guided by evil motives of ambition and faction. He was "soured" against them and had a nature which drove him continually to find fault. He simply wanted to build Franklin College and the *Gospel Advocate* and was jealous of Bethany and the *Millennial Harbinger*!

Fanning's feelings of deep hurt under the realization that men with whom he had worked could attack him in this way was evident from several of his articles. He was especially disappointed by the fact that while he carried in the pages of the *Gospel Advocate* everything which Richardson and Campbell wrote, they did not carry his articles in the *Millennial Harbinger*. The readers of the *Harbinger,* for the most part accepted Richardson's judgment of Fanning's character and motives. Perhaps this was one reason that J. W. McGarvey, when he later met Fanning for the first time, was so surprised to find him such a courteous gentleman.

Many others, to be sure, feeling indignant at the treatment which Fanning had received, complained about it to Campbell. But Fanning, after visiting Bethany and seeing that the senile Campbell was now under the influence of others, wrote,

> Bro. Campbell is much devoted to those who have long cooperated with him, and he is reluctant to admit their abandonment of the Bible. . . . We still love him for what he has done, and though he should in the evening of life exhibit too warm an attachment for men unworthy of his confidence, we hope for the best. He must, however, rest assured that the brethren familiar with the controversy do not approve of his recent *attack* and *exit*.[7]

Fanning was at least thankful that others, like Benjamin Franklin and Jacob Creath, also recognized the situation and joined his efforts to stop Richardson's influence. He was also encouraged by Campbell's termination of Richardson's writing, even though Campbell never did apologize to Fanning.

By late in 1856, Fanning announced that he was making plans to change the administration of Franklin College. The next year the board of trustees was completely reorganized, including the addition of several of the alumni, who naturally had a deeper interest in the success of the school. At the same time, there was an announcement that the college (at least the business department) would become the property of all of the faculty. Since the efficiency with which they managed the school would determine their monetary returns at the end of the session, the teachers, Fanning believed, would have greater interest in its success. When the next session opened in September of 1857, Fanning was convinced that the college had never before enjoyed such great prospects for success. He was personally encouraged to know that much of the responsibility which in previous years had been his would now be shouldered by others. This year he was just another professor. By 1859, the school was actually sold to two of the professors, William Lipscomb and N. B. Smith, both graduates of the college.

Fanning revealed several reasons for his decision to divest himself of his heavy responsibilities at Franklin College. To begin with, he wrote, "As plainly intimated in years past, the fact that we have been pretty deeply involved in business of the world in order to accomplish what we have, many have regarded our purposes as merely selfish, and therefore, we have anxiously desired other brethren to take charge of the business department."[8] During the controversy with Robert Richardson, when even Alexander Campbell himself questioned Fanning's motives, saying, "It is a controversy between Bethany and Franklin College, the *Millennial Harbinger* and the *Gospel Advocate,*"[9] Fanning became so depressed that he confessed sorrow that he had ever *seen* a paper or *heard* of a college! Though convinced that the charges were unfounded, he decided he would rather have no further financial interest in schools or papers.

Fanning also wanted to change the emphasis of his work. His friends had always called for his help on far more occasions than he could possibly find time to answer. Some even criticized him because he did not spend more time preaching. Occasionally, when they criticized him for spending too much time with his business interests, he would answer that it was only through such strenuous efforts that he was able to keep Franklin College in operation. On the other hand, he expressed appreciation for their good motives and assured them that soon the situation would be remedied.

By 1860, members of the Church of Christ in Tennessee had formed a stock company to purchase Franklin College and to carry on the school as a business venture. Besides

Fanning, W. D. Carnes, David Lipscomb, and G. W. Cone figured prominently in the plans. Fifty thousand dollars in stock was to be issued, and the stockholders planned to select a better location and eventually to move the college.

Later that same year, however, the board of managers decided to purchase Franklin College and implement their plans there. David Lipscomb, who was secretary of the board, announced that while they were purchasing Franklin College, they would not buy Minerva College, built next to it, as they felt the price affixed to it was higher than necessary. At the same time the board also announced that the new president of the institution would be W. D. Carnes. Also, Mrs. Fanning's schoolrooms were to be used for a limited girls school. That summer N. S. Smith and William Lipscomb continued as the owners of the school, and Smith spent a considerable sum of money improving the main building.

When he came to Franklin College as the new president, W. D. Carnes was already an experienced school man. Almost thirty-five years before, at the age of eighteen, he started teaching, and at the age of thirty-seven he had gone back to college to secure his B. A. degree. For eight years he was the president of Burritt College, in Spencer, Tennessee, and from there he was called to the presidency of the State University at Knoxville. In 1859, he attended the consultation meeting held at the Franklin College church, and there he learned of the plans to build a large university in Middle Tennessee. The next year he accepted the opportunity to become its president, even though it involved great personal sacrifice on his part. The members of the church seemed to feel that they would eventually move the school from its location at Elm Crag and also that they would provide accommodations for a much larger campus.

During the summer of 1860 Carnes made an extensive tour, which was extremely successful in raising money and inciting interest in the new educational plans. When school opened that fall, almost every southern state was represented in the student body, and the year appeared to be the brightest yet for Franklin College. Carnes, whom the students affectionately called "Old Pap," established the first gymnasium on the campus and encouraged athletic sports among the students, which was something new at Franklin College. Only it was election year and the nation was deeply disturbed about its future.

Facing the year 1861, Fanning wrote,

> A storm has been raised by unwise and cruel leaders which they possess not the ability to control. The intelligent of the people are sound at heart, and they should not lose self-control through the influence of factions, in which exists not fear of God. Our glorious ship of State may not only be enabled to breast the raging surges, but be brought once more safely into the port of peace, and prosperity.[10]

That neighbors should be casting pronged words of hatred at one another was depressing enough. But that brethren in Christ were being sucked into the whirlwind of hatred was distressing beyond bearing. Most men felt helpless as they saw tornadic winds blow the nation toward a bloody precipice from which there was no return.

In 1859, John Brown marched on Harper's Ferry with plans to invade the South and free the slaves in a mass uprising. He entrenched himself in the fort only to be overpowered by Colonel Robert E. Lee and a company of marines. Found guilty of insurrection, murder, and treason, he was hanged on December 2. Before John Brown's body was cold in his grave, some leaders in the North, though not in sympathy with his bloody plans, nevertheless made a martyr of him. Their bells tolled the day of his execution and their flags flew at half-mast, lauding his "holy" cause.

It had been several years earlier, in 1852, that Harriet Beecher Stowe had written *Uncle Tom's Cabin*. The book appeared first in serial form in a Washington newspaper, and each installment was anxiously awaited by a people ripe to be roused. A quarter of a million copies of the book were sold in less than a year. Thirty "anti-Tom" books, published in the South, could not convince the North that *Uncle Tom's Cabin* had given a distorted view. At one time it took eight presses running night and day to satisfy the intense demand for the book. According to some, when Abraham Lincoln later met Mrs. Stowe, he referred to her as the lady who started the war. Even Fanning himself, usually completely aloof from political excitement, accused Mrs. Stowe's brother, Henry Ward Beecher, of using his pulpit to excite the people and to threaten the country with the sword. Fanning had been watching for a "quarter of a century, the black clouds of death rising as a result of such work." He wrote to brethren, both in the North and in the South: "Many engaged in the strife fear not God, and while they are blindly and recklessly plunging us into extremes, it is our duty to say to the troubled waters, peace, be still; and to men in their madness, listen to the reason and the voice of God."[11]

To be sure, slavery was a part of the land which Fanning knew as his own. In the 1850s he could visit New Orleans or Charleston and see a healthy young Negro sold for $1,500 or more. But like himself, over two-thirds of Southern white people had no involvement whatever with slavery. In fact in the year 1850 alone over two hundred forty thousand Negroes in the Southern states were set free. Many in the South would have reacted as young Tolbert Fanning had reacted during his early years of preaching, when he publicly rebuked a member of the church who sold his slave and thereby separated him from his family.

Fanning hated slavery not only because of what it did to the black race but for what it did to the white man as well. One of his relatives, who lost her husband and brought her family from Illinois to live at Elm Crag, wrote back to a friend in Illinois, "Slave holders here are emphatically the slaves. They are bowed down by a weight of cares and trials to which you are strangers." She continued, "Slavery in my humble judgment tends to degrade all classes of a community; but particularly the poor laboring class, who are not only placed on a level with the black but far beneath!"[12]

Fanning agreed with this evaluation. Shortly before he died, he wrote that his objection to slavery was evoked by the evils which it brought upon the white race "in physical and mental indolence, and the many moral evils springing therefrom." He was convinced that "every effort made to save the white race from toil, but the more effectually sinks our people into imbecility and moral degradation."[13]

In addition to these considerations, slavery was especially grievous to Fanning because of what it had done to divide men who should feel very close. Long before the Civil War slavery had been the source of division in the Methodist Church, the Baptist Church, and finally the Presbyterian Church. Fanning waged a relentless war, however, aimed both North and South, to stave off this same division in the Churches of Christ. He noted that Northern Christians could neither capably nor effectively lecture their Southern brethren because they were ignorant of the actual conditions. Yet, with the judgment that slavery produces great evil, Fanning said, "ninety-nine hundredths of the disciples of the south will have no controversy." But they could not prevent the course of affairs, and now, he said, they were trying to make the best of the situation. He warned Northern brethren, "The Christians in the north know not our condition, and therefore some reckless spirits may, in their zeal, which so far outstrips their knowledge, do us much injury by misdirected efforts." Furthermore, he said, "It is probable if we are let alone, a few years would show a wonderful revolution in sentiment and feeling in the South, but we do not lack foreign aid."[14] Many historians would today agree with Tolbert Fanning that slavery was dying from its own obesity at one point, until advanced methods of ginning made the demand for slaves again begin to grow.

But while he plead for understanding and patience on the part of Northern leaders, he also assured Southern brethren that he was personally acquainted with Northern leaders in the church who understood their problem, and they had no need to entertain misgivings about them. He relentlessly tried to nurture an atmosphere of trust and understanding between his friends in both sections.

Tolbert Fanning believed, as did many others of his day, that the Negro was a direct descendant of Ham and that the color of his skin was a part of his curse from God. This did not keep him from considering the African a creature of God, equal to himself and worthy of esteem and love in Christ. In fact, it was not until after the Civil War that the Negro members of the church, alienated from those they freely associated with before, began to meet for worship separately from their white brethren. Before the war it was accepted practice for both races to meet, work, and worship together in the same church building. The active church at Rock Springs reported in 1844 that it had ninety white members and thirty colored brethren (although their seating areas were separated with the Negroes in the galleries). This was also the pre-war situation for many years in Nashville. Fanning said,

> These people sat with their white brethren many years in heavenly places in Christ Jesus. It was a joyful season. Our colored brethren, some of whom at least we had educated in what seemed to us useful and good, without our agency were completely alienated from us and turned against us.[15]

Fanning made a trip through the North to observe the conditions of the Negro churches about which he had heard much. He returned convinced that "in the city of Nashville alone, there live and worship more educated, independent, refined, and earnest sons and daughters of Ham, as we have good evidence to believe, than in any other city on earth."[16] Fanning always expressed regret after the war that his Negro brethren would no longer meet to worship with him. (It will be remembered that one of the Negro members whom Fanning had personally educated, Rufus Conrad, began preaching and after the war was persuaded by members in Cincinnati to take the lead in forming a missionary society among his Negro brethren in Nashville.)

Fanning watched the political situation as it continued to deteriorate. In 1860, the Democrats were hopelessly divided, and so an air of victory hovered over the Republican Convention in Chicago during the latter part of May. Seward felt sure of the nomination and so was not prepared to contend with Lincoln's political prowess. Lincoln's backers, however, swamped the convention hall, and a judicious seating of delegates created a psychological benefit for Lincoln. Seward led on the first ballot, but on the second Lincoln was almost even with him, and by the third, amid a wild uproar, Lincoln was swept not only into the Republican candidacy, but for all practical purposes, into the White House as well.

Stephen Douglas knew that he was defeated before he began, but he courageously tried to save the Union anyway. He was well liked in the South, and toured there throughout the campaign, proclaiming that whoever the new president might be, he should treat all attempts to break up the Union "as Old Hickory treated the Nullifiers in 1832." The popular vote was close, but Lincoln won by a landslide of electoral votes.

The South was now, more than ever, convinced that it was time to secede. On December 20, 1860, at seven o'clock in the evening, the Institute Hall in Charleston, South Carolina, was brilliantly lighted by chandelier and candelabrum. D. F. Jameson watched as one hundred sixty-nine delegates to the special convention filed by and signed their names. Then he held the document aloft for the delegates and spectators to see. The people of South Carolina danced in the streets as though a great victory had been won. The document read,

> We the people of South Carolina . . . do declare and ordain . . . [the] Constitution is hereby repealed; and that the union now subsisting between South Carolina and other states under the name of the "United States of America" is hereby dissolved.[17]

That same day Tolbert Fanning was in Montgomery, the capital of Alabama, on a tour among the churches. It was a path he had trod many times during the past thirty years. But his heart was now heavy as he viewed what once had been a peaceful country with strong churches. He could not even preach in Montgomery because the city was "convulsed with revolutionary movements." Several days earlier he had been in Jackson, the capital of Mississippi. Two years earlier, the Senate chamber of the State capitol building in Jackson had been packed to overflowing with citizens who came to hear Fanning preach. Now it was different. He felt that by comparison he had never witnessed political excitement before! There was only one question in the air: "When, and how shall Mississippi secede from the Union?"

Fanning preached to very small audiences for two days and then moved on. In Atlanta, the day after South Carolina seceded, he met only one member of the church, and he already had his sword in his hand! How often Fanning had visited these same scenes and preached to sincere and honest people. Here he had planted churches, made them strong, and worshiped a God of peace. How different it was now. How thin was the veneer which covered human violence, even among Christians!

By the next February, South Carolina had been followed out of the Union by Mississippi, Alabama, Georgia, Florida, Louisiana, and Texas. On February 7, these states met in Montgomery to form the Confederate States of America. The *Gospel Advocate* continued to be printed all through that year, even after the first guns reported the inception of war. But by December, Fanning announced that influences beyond his control were forcing the termination of the paper. The last page contains a farewell which was saturated with Fanning's grief. He had survived great tragedy before. But now the whole future rested in a sea of uncertainty. As he entered an editorial silence of four long, weary years, his parting words were, "Brethren, we are one, and have but one work to perform."[18]

CHAPTER 14

AT DEAD OF NIGHT
THE CIVIL WAR

"We buried them darkly,
at dead of night,
The sod with our bayonets
turning."

— *Civil War Song*

WITH SLEEPLESS and lonely nights the new President began his stormy years in office with the burden of the country on his shoulders. Lincoln was inaugurated on March 4,
1861, and South Carolina had already beseiged the Federal
installation at Fort Sumter. Lincoln's efforts to send provisions were thwarted. At 4:30 on the morning of April 12,
a signal mortar was shot by southern troops. It described a
fiery semicircle in the night and exploded directly over the
fort. The country plunged into the dread abyss and brothers
promised to kill each other.

Fifteen years earlier, one of the propositions debated at
the literary society meetings on the campus of Franklin
College had been "Slavery should be abolished." With irony
one can still read the debating group's minutes where some
unsuspecting southern student had scribbled, "The affirmative won the debate."

When school opened in September of 1860, it was election
year and Nashville was a focal point of political strategy.
President Carnes tried to keep the young men at Franklin
College interested in their studies, but he soon saw that his
efforts were hopeless. At the rallies in Nashville the students
heard some of the most eminent political speakers of the
nation. There were Bell, Breckinridge, and Douglas, each
heading up his own splinter group of the Democratic Party.
The dogmatic William L. Yancey took his turn on the
speaker's stand along with John J. Crittenden. The students

also followed the course of events in the papers. They saw the "cotton states" secede one by one, and one by one they too left for home, trying to prepare for whatever might come.

Most were convinced that war was inevitable, and by June only a few students were left. With his own sons in the army, Carnes suspended activities at Elm Crag and moved to Pikeville. He left his library, his experimental apparatus, and his priceless collections of scientific specimens in the college buildings to gather dust. His library contained many rare books which were impossible to replace, but he had to leave them behind. Twenty graduates of Franklin College entered the Confederate army as commissioned officers and joined the stream of students migrating from the campus to the army camps.

One of the first men who said good-bye to Fanning was Pierce Butler Anderson, one of his faculty members at Franklin College. Anderson was a graduate of West Point who had served with distinction through the Mexican War and then became a legislator from McMinnville for the state of Tennessee. After he joined the faculty at Franklin College he became a great admirer of Fanning and through his influence became a Christian. When he left Nashville to become a captain of artillery under General Robert E. Lee, tears filled his eyes as he told Fanning that he did not expect to return from the war. He was one of the first of many companions whom Fanning lost in the struggle. When Fanning learned of Anderson's death he wrote, "A brave soldier of his country has fallen."

While Fanning stood by helplessly, the news became almost his daily enemy, bringing with it a mounting list of losses as one by one fine, promising young men gave their lives in what always seemed to him to be a senseless struggle. Some of the graduates of Franklin left large families to go to battles from which they did not return. There were also many like Turner Goodall, one of Fanning's most promising students who had planned to preach but would never have the opportunity.

Many members of the Church of Christ both before and during the war, were pacifists. They plead with their brethren on both sides of the conflict to refrain from introducing political excitement into the church. One of these in the North was Benjamin Franklin. As the editor of one of the church's most popular periodicals, the *American Christian Review,* Franklin's popularity was rivaled only by that of Alexander Campbell. He was also an active advocate of the Missionary Society. Franklin stubbornly refused when his northern brethren insisted that he discuss the slavery question on the pages of his paper. Members of the church accused him of disloyalty to the government, but still he refused, even though it cost him much of his popularity as an editor.

Tolbert Fanning assumed the same stance in the South. He and David Lipscomb both made extensive use of Franklin's articles of peace. By circulating them among the churches in the South they attempted to convince them that northern members were not becoming entangled in the hate of the world. Nothing, Lipscomb claimed, was so effective as this in keeping the attitude of brethren in Christ cordial toward one another.

Franklin and Fanning, though they differed in their view of the Missionary Society, found a sense of comradeship as both were maligned and threatened by more excitable members of churches in both sections of the nation. Both continued to maintain a position of pacifism. Then came October and the time for the annual meeting of the American Christian Missionary Society in Cincinnati. A series of war resolutions had been passed at most of the religious conferences, synods and associations of the other religious groups in the nation, and the clergy became an instrument to bolster the cause of their section. Special Sundays were set aside, both by Abraham Lincoln and Jefferson Davis, to be devoted to prayer for God's help on their sections' cause. At the close of the first morning session of the Missionary

Society in Cincinnati, Dr. J.P. Robinson of Ohio introduced a resolution:

> Resolved, that we deeply sympathize with the loyal and patriotic in our country in the present efforts to sustain the Government of the United States. And we feel it our duty as Christians to ask our brethren every-where to do all in their power to sustain the proper and constitutional authorities of the Union.[1]

The resolution was discussed briefly at the 2 P.M. meeting, and D.S. Burnet raised a question as to whether or not it was in order. Isaac Errett, who was chairman, decided that it *was* in order. On appeal from the floor by R.M. Bishop however, the chair was overruled and the resolution was considered out of order.

L.L. Pinkerton, aware of the finer points of parliamentary procedure, requested a ten minute recess and then called Burnet to the chair. As chairman, he could not now formally discuss the proposition. Great excitement prevailed, as a young soldier, a preacher who had become a lieutenant colonel in the Union army, rose to speak on behalf of the resolution. The members were then asked to vote for the resolution as individuals and not as the Missionary Society in official session. With only one negative vote, the resolution passed. The name of the young colonel who aided the measure through the parliamentary straits was James A. Garfield.

A Mr. Goodwin, in Iowa, called upon his Northern brethren to "put down the rebellion, peaceably if we can; forcibly if we must."[2] Isaac Errett referred to the war resolutions of the society as merely "abiding by the teaching of Paul in Romans 13:1-5." An elder of the church in Hopkinsville, Kentucky, was in the state legislature and urged his brethren to join the Union and use the bayonet, if necessary, to subdue the southern members of the church whom he rejected. He suggested that they hang all who did not sympathize with them.

Almost immediately, word of the Missionary Society's war resolution crossed the battle lines and raced to Fanning in Tennessee. He reacted by saying that the leaders at the Cincinnati meeting were "approving most heartily the whole-sale murder" of their own brethren who chose not to be governed as they themselves had chosen. (Southerners typically justified their secession on the same basis as the revolution against England by the thirteen American colonies.) Fanning concluded that without thorough repentance these preachers, who enforced political opinion with the sword, could only be considered "monsters in intention, if not in every deed."[3]

As if this were not enough, the action of the Missionary Society took away from Fanning and Lipscomb their ability to keep peace between churches in the two sections. They had been pointing to the peaceful attitude of northern members, but now this deterrent was wrenched from their hands. Lipscomb later wrote of the resolution:

> It we doubt not, sent men into the Federal army; we know it sent some brethren of good intentions, but strong impulses and feeling, into the Southern army. Some, too, who never returned. We felt, we still feel, that that Society committed a great wrong against the Church and cause of God.[4]

Conditions during the War violently touched the lives of everyone and created a culture resting almost wholly in the canon's mouth. In both the North and the South preachers often took an active part in the politics of dissension and even in the actual battles of the war. In the North, some gave their congregations weekly lectures on the holy cause of the Union. In the South, many had been preaching that slavery was justified in the Scriptures. The Confederate government was not slow in seizing this religious sentiment and utilizing it to bolster the morale of the people, praying for victory through divine providence. Periodically Jefferson Davis continued to declare various days to be set aside by the Southern people for prayer and fasting.

The chaplains were often active with weapons too. One

gave a soldier a gun with the advice, "If you get in a tight place and have to use it, ask God's blessing if you have time. But," he continued, "be sure and not let your enemy get the start of you. You can say "amen" after you shoot."[5]

While chivalrous southern writers may have overstated the patriotic spirit of the wives, mothers, and sisters of the South, the women were often as militantly secessionist as their fathers, brothers, and husbands. It is probably true that in the early months, especially, their fervor sent many an otherwise reluctant volunteer into the army camps. The southern women took over much of the hard work of the fields and the management of the plantations. One of their songs proclaimed:

> Just take your gun and go;
> For Ruth can drive the oxen, John,
> And I can use the hoe.

Fanning watched all of this. The continued course of so many of his friends made his grief especially heavy. At Lexington, for instance, John Shackleford belonged to the "Home Guards" and grabbed his gun every time that he heard that Morgan's Raiders were nearby. He learned that another member of the church, the preacher W. H. Hopson, was riding with the group, and he hoped to get a shot at him.[6]

B. F. Hall, the man who had been preaching the night that Fanning heard the gospel and decided to become a Christian, was with the Confederate Army at Fayetteville, Arkansas, just before the battle of Pea Ridge. He later liked to tell about a friend who had gone over the field after the battle had been waged there, and if he found a Union soldier begging for medical aid, would put a bullet through him. Having pictured the senseless scene, Hall would then laugh as though he thoroughly enjoyed the disgusting picture. He requested of his companions that if any "Yankees" appeared, he be given his opportunity to get his share. Hall openly advocated catching Yankee soldiers, cutting off their right hands, and sending them back across the lines with their severed hands tied to their saddlebags. Because of Fanning's criticism of this attitude, Hall died feeling that Fanning had become his enemy.[7]

Fanning's activities during the war illustrate that he was unwilling merely to sit by and bear the breaking of his heart without reaction. Early in the war he met with several others at Beech Grove in Williamson County. After they discussed how they might help members of the church to remain aloof from the conflict, Fanning penned the following letter:

To His Excellency The President of the Confederate States of America:

WHEREAS, A large number of the members of the Churches of Jesus Christ throughout this and the adjoining counties of the State of Tennessee, feel a deep sense of the responsibility they are under to recognize the Bible in its teachings as the only infallible guide of their life, and the supremely authoritative rule of action, and as being a superior authority to and more binding upon the subjects of the Kingdom of Jesus Christ than the rules and regulations of any human government or power, they would respectfully represent,

1st. That they are fully satisfied that God, through the Scriptures of Sacred Truth, demands of his servants that they should submit quietly, heartily and cheerfully to the government under which they may live, in all cases, except when compliance with the civil law would involve a violation of the law of God. They are deeply impressed with the truth that when there is a conflict between the requirements of worldly government and the law of God, the duty of the Christian is, upon the peril of his well-being, to obey God first, let the consequences be to him what they may.

2nd. They are firm in the conviction of the truth, that no man, who regards the authority of God, the spirits and letter of the Sacred Scriptures in their proper division and application, the life and teachings of the Son of God, or his Holy Apostles, as given for the guidance of his followers, can in any manner engage in aid, foment, or countenance the strifes, animosities and bloody conflicts in which civil governments are frequently engaged, and in which they often involve their subjects.

The measure and limit of their duty to, and connection with, the governments under which they live, as laid down in the Sacred Scriptures, is not an active participation in its affairs to destroy or upbuild, but simply a quiet and cheerful submission to its enactments, in the payment of tribute and any demands on our property or time, modified only by the first and highest obligation to obey God.

With these considerations of what our duty to God requires at our hands, the enforcement of the "Conscript Act" for the purpose of raising and maintaining an army, for the carrying on of this unhappy war, in which our country is involved, cannot fail to work indescribable distress to those members of our churches holding these convictions. Some of them will be driven as exiles from their homes, for no political preferences, but because they dare not disobey the commandments of God. Others may be thrown into seeming opposition to your government, suffering imprisonment and such punishment as may be inflicted on them. Others still, by the pressure of circumstances, may be driven into a deeply sadder fate, the violation of all their conscientious convictions of duty to their Maker and Master, whom they have, under the most solemn vows, pledged themselves to serve.

In view of these things, we are induced to make a statement of these facts to you, with the hope that some relief may be afforded to those of our members thus distressed.

We are the more encouraged, too, in this hope, from the fact that we perceive that Congress of the Confederate States of America, with a commendable regard for the conscientious convictions of its subjects, made provision upon certain denominations of professed Christians, from the performance of requirements repulsive to their religious faith. With the view, too, that this law might not act invidiously with reference to individuals not specially named in said act, the power was vested in the Honorable President, of making such further exemptions as, in his judgment, justice, equity or necessity might demand. We respectfully petition of you, that members of our churches who are now, and have been striving to maintain a position of Christian separation from the world, its strifes and conflicts, may be relieved on terms equitable and just, from requirements repulsive to their religious faith, and that they may be, at least, placed upon a footing similar to that in which denominations holding a like faith.[8]

The letter was signed by many elders and preachers of Middle Tennessee, and copies were sent both to the governor of the state and to President Lincoln, as well as to Jefferson Davis. Both governments were sufficiently influenced by the letter that it successfully permitted many members of the Church of Christ to remain aloof from the conflict.

Because of Fanning's position in regard to Christians participating in war, many of his own brethren accused him of disloyalty to the government. Fanning was encouraged that the Presidents of both North and South respected his position as far as possible for men in their positions. But he continually had difficulty from religious bigots. Even some of his own preaching brethren sneered at him for his "unsoundness." Others in the church told him that unless they repudiated him the church would not be respected by the rest of the world.

When the Union troops marched into Nashville and made that a base of operations for the greater part of the war, they demanded that its citizens swear allegiance to the northern cause. Fanning tried to explain to them that he would not swear with the oath although he had been loyal to four governments—the United States, Britain, the Southern Confederacy, and now the Northern Military power. But they still classed him as disloyal. As a result, although he was not placed in prison, all of his possessions were burned, and he was personally treated as an outlaw. Few men suffered more during the war. Because he was convicted of treason, he was not paid for honest work that he performed, and there were periods when he went for weeks at a time without bread in his house. Renegade bands of men roamed the countryside during the war, and many of

Fanning's neighbors were robbed. In several cases, whole families were murdered in cold blood. "We frequently saw openings to lose our life," he recalled, "and have our families outraged by miscreants, had we resorted to violent resistance. Many of our intimate acquaintances lost their lives by physical resistance."[9] The agony of these memories was compounded when, after the war, Isaac Errett accused him of thinking up his anti-war convictions because of his disappointment in the "lost cause."

In spite of his many hardships and difficulties, resulting mainly from his convictions regarding non-participation in war, Fanning found the strength during the struggle to serve others in distress. One young soldier was wounded and left among strangers in Tennessee, many miles from his loved ones. He had heard his father speak of Fanning, so he sent for him. Fanning talked to enough of his friends to obtain help to feed, clothe, and nurse the young man for many months. After almost a year in prison, the soldier was restored to his family but could never persuade Fanning to accept anything in payment for his help. Fanning replied that he was more interested in "laying up treasure in heaven."

Early in the war it became evident that the Federal troops were sweeping toward Nashville with great force. The southern general, A. S. Johnston, set up headquarters across the river from Nashville to await the fate of nearby Fort Donelson, since on its fate his tenure in Nashville would be determined. After a premature report that Donelson had stood, news came late at night on the 15th of February, 1862, that the fort was about to fall. The news was swiftly carried from street to street, and by daylight Nashville was filled with rumor and panic. Some carried the news that Federal gunboats would reach the city before morning and lay it in ruins. Others suggested that they immediately burn the city to leave only its ashes behind for the Federal army.

The next day, although Johnston assured the city fathers that he would make no military stand which would endanger the city, the state legislature decided to adjourn to Memphis immediately. The bridges across the river were destroyed and Johnston moved his men to Murfreesboro.

It was actually a week before the Northern troops appeared in Nashville. Buell, the Northern general, set up his headquarters across the river in Edgefield. He then called for the leaders of the city and gave them assurances of the safety of their town and its citizens. Throughout the rest of the war, Nashville remained an important base of operations and supplies for the northern armies.

Toward the end of the conflict, war-torn and weary, dressed in bloody rags and skin shoes, the southern troops made one last bid for Nashville. It was late in 1864, and they approached within sight of the lights of the city, seen through the smoke of innumerable campfires. Battle lines were drawn, stretching across the landscape near where David Lipscomb College now stands, and a bloody battle ensued. Again and again the Federal troops attacked the lines which the Confederate Army had set up. Finally, by sheer numbers, the northern troops broke up the southern lines and drove them back once and for all from the city of Nashville.

During the war, the main building of Franklin College was used for barracks by both the North and the South as they passed back and forth in the conflict. Into the four-year bloodbath the North sent many of her finest sons, and three hundred fifty-nine thousand of them never returned. Over two hundred fifty thousand never returned to their wives and mothers in the South. Their comrades cared for their bodies, far from home:

> "We buried them darkly, at dead of night,
> The sod with our bayonets turning."

As the war came to an end, Lincoln was planning a patient and peaceful period of reconstruction. At his second inauguration he concluded,

> With malice toward none, with charity for all, with firmness in the right as God gives us to see the right, let us strive on to finish the work we are in, to bind up the nation's wounds, to care for him who shall have

borne the battle and for his widow and his orphan, to do all which may achieve and cherish a just and lasting peace among ourselves and with all nations.[10]

Fanning's attitude toward politics and the state were largely settled before the war. One of the chief reasons for his plan to begin the *Christian Review* back in 1844 had been his desire to discuss the involvement of Christians in "political excitement." Even then he took the position that Christians could not become involved in politics without weakening themselves spiritually. He was certain that they could accomplish much more good in the world by laboring only in the eternal kingdom of God·rather than in the kingdoms of earth. The initial issues of the *Christian Review* reveal that wherever he went politics seemed to be foremost on the lips of the people. Families were divided, and Christians were quarreling among themselves about "Whiggery and Democracy," each believing that the other would ruin the country. Fanning wrote, "The Christians in Tennessee in the late presidential canvass gave enough to keep ten preachers in the field whereas, now, they have only two."[11] That same year, he addressed an open letter to his brethren:

> To describe the means employed by both the great parties . . . would endanger my safety . . . But alas! there are men who profess the Christian religion, employing their time, their talents and money in electioneering for political aspirants . . . I have never seen it otherwise than that Christians injure themselves by participating in political strifes. They become lukewarm, next dead to all holy emotions, and finally the mass give themselves wholly to some vicious practice . . . the present excitement is dangerous, and if men will give their hearts to such things, they should not, by their professions of Christianity, become stumbling blocks to others.[12]

Amid the excitement of campaign Fanning asked, "Has not prayer been troublesome, and Hurrah, Hurrah, been screamed to drive away thought?"[13]

One should remember that when Fanning's attitude toward politics was being formed, the nation was witnessing the birth of nationally organized political parties, party caucuses, stump speeches, and the herding and mass voting of drunks and helpless immigrants. It was his neighbor, Andrew Jackson, who first utilized the machinery of a national political party. Furthermore, seldom, if ever, has the nation witnessed such mudslinging in its presidential campaigns. Slogans were constructed and to emphasize their candidate, Jackson's supporters fashioned hickory brooms to remind people of the tough individualism of "Old Hickory." The hickory brooms were not only in evidence at rallies, but were set up at crossroads and even tied to church steeples. The opposition accused Jackson of living in adultery, and Jackson believed it was this charge and the strain which it engendered which killed his beloved wife, Rachel, before he moved into the White House. One should also remember that in Fanning's day, national figures engaged in duels to settle their political and personal differences. He could read in the paper of fist fights in the Congressional debates in Washington. He could remember how the frontier "common people" went to Washington to see Jackson inaugurated. An estimated ten thousand visitors thronged into Washington, then with a population of only eighteen thousand, and Jackson had to be whisked out a back window of the White House because of the party which had gotten out of hand. His supporters climbed over the damask furniture with their muddy boots, trod broken glasses underfoot, and imbibed ample amounts of alcoholic beverages in addition to what was spilled. In short, Fanning was witnessing what historians now see as a decided shift in national political activity. Fanning's nature made him more like the dignified and reasoned approach of the old Virginia aristocracy which had sent to the Presidency such stalwarts of the silk-stocking set as Washington, Madison, Jefferson, and Monroe. Even John Adams and his son, John Quincy Adams, although not from Virginia, were the opposite of the image which came to be prevalent among politicians after Jackson's day. Many have noticed that while Jackson was the first president to be born in a log cabin, many after him claimed to have been born there, even if they were not, because it became almost an unwritten requirement for the politician to claim lowly and uneducated beginnings.[14]

When the Civil War broke out, Fanning wrote again, "Who we ask in all charity, ever knew a brother that aspired to political preferment—to become even a member of the legislature that was not either greatly crippled in his usefulness, or completely killed to all that is ennobling in the church?" He continued, "We have had many excellent brethren who could not withstand the temptation to serve the world, but few if any of them have been able to serve their brethren efficiently afterwards.[15]

A rather amusing incident illustrates Fanning's ability not only to live above political strife but also to impress others with his disdain. A year or two before his death, one of his former students who was in the state legislature happened to see Fanning standing in the back of the hall while the legislature was in session. He hastened back to greet him and invited him to take a seat among the members. Fanning politely thanked him but declined his invitation with the remark, "I have four new shirts in this bundle under my arm, that cost me five dollars. I cannot risk a thing of such value among you fellows." Amusing as this may have been, it was not surprising. Fanning invariably surveyed politics with the highest contempt and remained convinced that mature Christians were too sensible and courteous to lower themselves to such petty activities.

When Isaac Errett charged that southern Christians, and particularly Fanning, opposed participation in civil government or war because they had sour grapes over their lost cause, Fanning understandably found the charge offensive and repulsive. It is difficult to understand how Errett could have hurled such distasteful accusations. Fanning, at great sacrifice, had held himself above strife during the war and, for many years previous to the war, had taken the position that civil government was not a proper channel for best Christian influence. Fanning had expressed this conviction as early as 1846. To him, the only influence and force which

Christians were to exert was "moral," and this could be done exclusively in the kingdom of Christ far better than through other agencies, such as human government. Said Fanning,

> Christianity, in Apostolic days, while it assailed no civil institution or political government, was equally scrupulous to approve of, in no special manner, or ask the aid of none. . . . It was the obvious intention of the Almighty to establish a religion entirely independent of human legislation, and separate from it. . . . The New Testament throughout teaches the one short and simple lesson that all that Christians had to do with worldly institutions, was to pay taxes, as the Savior and Peter did (Matthew 16:27), *"Obey magistrates,"* *"pray for kings,"* and men of "authority;" and that this was for the single purpose of avoiding offenses against governments, for which they might be punished, and that they might "lead a quiet and peaceable life" (I Timothy 2:29).

> . . . .

> Persons governed by the Law of God, need no other, at least as far as Christians are concerned; and were all men the servants of God, other governments than the divine would be useless. The Apostle informs us, "The law is not made for a righteous man, but for the lawless and disobedient, for the ungodly and for sinners, for unholy and profane, for murderers of fathers, and murderers of mothers, for manslayers,"[16]

When Fanning wrote these lines, David Lipscomb was a freshman student at Franklin College. Not only was he profoundly influenced by the message but he later developed its thoughts even further.

Tolbert Fanning believed that civil government was justified if it enforced its decisions physically. However, physical force was incompatible with the purely moral force to be used in the kingdom of God. Thus, if Christians had to resort to any type of physical force to attain good, they were acknowledging that the church had failed in its purpose. This type of reasoning was especially designed for those who, during the war, resorted to physical force to make their own brethren do what they felt was right. According to prophecy, Fanning pointed out, God's kingdom was to break in pieces, consume, and crush from the earth the governments of the world (Daniel 2).

Government was not devoid of good. It was simply outside the realm of the activity of the Christian. Fanning saw no vacuum left for activity toward good in any institution outside the church, whether this be a missionary society, a temperance society, a moral society, Masonry, or civil government. While he lived at a time in American history which was filled with efforts at social reform and new organizations designed to bring about improved conditions in almost every area of life, he still believed that Christians had a full-time citizenship in the kingdom of God and that their efforts in these organizations were somehow "outside" that kingdom and therefore a reflection on it. If all men were Christians, in fact, he believed there would be no need even for civil government.

Although one of his students, H. R. Moore, stated that Fanning never voted, Fanning once wrote, ". . . and although we see nothing improper in casting our vote, in elections, we are more than persuaded the early Christians needed neither to make war upon the powers that were, nor direct in the governments of earth."[17] Perhaps Fanning felt Christians could vote if they did not lower themselves to the "whirlpool" of "political strife." However, toward the end of his life he once said that he agreed with everything David Lipscomb had written in this area, and Lipscomb believed that it was wrong to vote.

Since war was an activity of civil governments, it naturally did not belong in the realm of Christian activity. But in addition to this, Fanning gave several other reasons for a Christian not engaging in war. To begin with there was the example of Christ. Christ was so gentle in his work that he would not bruise a reed. Recalling Jesus' command to Peter to put his sword into its place, Fanning found it difficult to believe that those using Christ for their example could kill. Then again, he pointed to the martyrs in the early church. The early Christians yielded to shameful and unjust death upon many occasions rather than take vengeance into their own hands. They were even willing to suffer for acts of righteousness—when their cause was just.

Fanning believed that the situation in the nineteenth century was even clearer. Christians were on both sides of the conflict in the United States. In 1846, when many of Fanning's neighbors were leaving for Texas to fight in the Mexican war, he wrote, "No doubt, should a war occur in reference to Texas or Oregon, all parties would lay the holy unction to heart, that they were performing the service to God." He warned, "Christians in England may soon be induced to make war upon Christians in America."

At the beginning of the Civil War, when members of the church in both the North and the South were excitedly preaching the holiness of their particular cause, Fanning wrote again,

> How dare brethren—the preachers—bring themselves to the fearful conclusion, to plunge their swords into the hearts of their brethren? We enter not into the question of right or wrong, in the present controversy. So far as our present object is concerned, we are not interested either way. Our purpose is to labor to satisfy Christians, that they are not to settle controversies by the sword.[18]

Fanning was also concerned about the Christian's example before the non-Christian. How could Christians go to war and kill and then appear with bloody hands before the world to preach a gospel of peace? He reminded his friends that Tom Paine used his great ability in the cause of infidelity because of the "bloody" activities of those who professed to be Christians.

Obviously, Fanning's views on civil government, politics, and war did not emerge from the Civil War. They were mature long before that shameful strife of brothers erupted. He never dogmatically insisted that all agree with his views. Such agreement would never have been a prerequisite to fellowship with him. But he did feel that few of his contemporaries had progressed to maturity in correctly comprehending the true nature of God's spiritual kingdom. Consequently he invested large blocks of his time and effort in trying to lead others to his view.

For Fanning, the kingdom of God demanded full time citizenship, and this ruled out active citizenship in any other kingdom. If one became active in kingdoms of this world, he not only damaged his strength as a Christian by diluting his interests but acknowledged that the kingdom of God was not sufficient to do all the moral good necessary. Fanning was not prepared to acknowledge such a deficiency in God's kingdom. On the other hand, if one supported an active Christian participation in civil government, he must be prepared to go all the way, even to participation in war. This, again, Fanning was not prepared to do. While his views were already mature and openly expressed before the war, the war provided more than ample illustration for his convictions. The bloodstains of sons and fathers, both North and South, killed by Christians who had laid down the sword of the Spirit to unsheath again the sword of Peter, gave telling testimony on behalf of the search for sanity woven into Fanning's teachings and actions.

At dead of night Fanning grieved over the insane slaughter which was destined to remain and help divide the church for a century to come. "How dare brethren—the preachers—bring themselves to the fearful conclusion, to plunge their swords into the hearts of their brethren!"

CHAPTER 15

NO INSURMOUNTABLE
BARRIER
ERA OF RECONSTRUCTION

"We at present can see no insurmount-
able barrier."
— *Tolbert Fanning*

AT THE CLOSE of the War, Isaac Errett moved to Cleveland, Ohio, to become the editor of the *Christian Standard,* a new weekly designed to rekindle the waning interest in the Missionary Society. The first issue of the paper, dated April 7, 1866, was doubly significant. Its front page announced that Alexander Campbell was dead. An era had ended.

But there was emerging during the postbellum years a new generation of younger men who approached maturity and took up the mantle which Campbell had laid down. There was the scholarly J. W. McGarvey, one of Campbell's students, who had listened to the artillery of the war near his home as he prepared the manuscript for a *Commentary on Acts* which would be read by thousands for several generations. Also in this second generation was Tolbert Fanning. When his copy of the *Christian Standard* reached Nashville, he was trying to put his affairs, so disrupted by the war, in order again. For one thing, he had more land than he could properly cultivate and more taxes than he could pay. Anxious to satisfy his creditors, he offered for sale several good building lots which combined an excellent view of Nashville with the educational advantages of Elm Crag.

But Fanning was anxious not merely for his own personal affairs. He was concerned about the prospects of the cause of Christ as well. In the fall of 1866 he made a preaching tour through Wilson and Sumner Counties and returned to report large audiences and intense interest. There had been twenty-five or thirty baptized at Franklin College during the previous winter, and P. S. Fall, who had remained faithfully at his post in Nashville all during the war, had actually seen a steady increase in numbers there. On every hand there were indications that men humbled by war, no longer too confident of the world's security, were developing a keener sensitivity to spiritual values.

Two things especially measure the direction and drift of events during this period of rebuilding. First there was the reappearance of the *Gospel Advocate,* edited this time by David Lipscomb and Tolbert Fanning. Fanning had hoped that the paper might break its four-year silence with a new voice, so he sent Lipscomb to the annual meeting of the Kentucky Christian Missionary Society to seek out J. W. McGarvey and ask him to serve as editor. McGarvey refused, but suggested another man. When this also failed to materialize, Fanning and Lipscomb, determined to see the paper published again, decided to use their own talents to give it rebirth, even though both men were extremely involved in other concerns. The paper was printed by J.T.S. Fall in Nashville. Fanning was aware that his editorial positions might not always reflect the thinking of all of his readers, and so he was careful to assure them that he intended to cultivate only the most cordial relationships in a "spirit of love and meekness." He insisted that since very early in life he had repudiated "human creeds," he could not conscientiously use the paper to encourage the missionary societies, even though such a policy could cost him a loss in circulation. He expressed once again, however, his determination to print both sides of any discussion which might prove controversial.

The other event which mirrors the temper of the times is the reappearance of the "consultation" meetings between the churches. Attending these gatherings after the war, one could sense the lingering desire for a larger fellowship than the local church could afford, yet at the same time a suspicion of ecclesiastical machinery which might turn on its creators and gorge itself on their cherished freedom of thought and action.

As early as February, 1866, Fanning suggested a consultation meeting for the approaching summer months and suggested Nashville as the logical location. He called for a mass meeting of all interested members of the Church of Christ in the South but recommended that no resolutions be made and no "political activity" be planned. He continued, "The purpose should be to renew old acquaintances and form new ones, and ascertain as far as possible, our ability for Christian co-operation."[1]

As the summer approached, hundreds of members began to make plans to attend the meeting. Interest came from outside the South as well. The Missionary Society in Cincinnati, formulating its plans to send J.S. Lamar to Georgia as an evangelist with a salary of $1,000 per year, expressed an interest in the consultation meeting. But Fanning hesitated to offer them a welcome. They had, he pointed out, used the "fist of wickedness" to slay sinners, and, when they could not muster enough bravery for that, they had passed resolutions in Christian missionary meetings! Fanning said that he was not sure that such men were ready yet for "genuine spiritual cooperation." From this it is obvious that wounds, left by the war, left by Fanning's great suffering during those horrible years, and left by Errett's charges against southern churches that they were poor losers, had not healed. Nor were they to heal for a century to follow.

As the meeting approached, the church in Murfreesboro rather than Nashville took the initiative, inviting area Christians to her community. Those who came from a distance were instructed to call at the Spence House where a member of the church, Mr. Cook, would be in charge of finding them homes for lodging during the meeting.

The first session got under way on June 6. The weary isolation of the long war had receded, leaving a deposit of deep craving for fellowship. They were so thrilled with the inspiration of the occasion, the largest meeting which anyone could remember, that they stayed together for seven days praying and discussing the tremendous challenges which the moment presented. Then they returned home, determined to use the momentum of the meeting to grapple with the grinding task which stretched before them.

Two avenues of attack were clearly defined at the meeting. One was ministering to those in physical need. The other was the educating of the younger men and women in the church. The latter group, which would become the new South desperately needed adequate tools and a proper spiritual perspective. David Lipscomb led the way in the first area, and Tolbert Fanning once again turned toward the education of youth.

The massive efforts necessary to try to reconstruct the bridges of commerce and economy, as well as the channels for distributing wealth to feed the people of the South, demanded the best of both public and private organizations. The Freedmen's Bureau provided the federal government with an opportunity to launch gigantic welfare programs designed to wage a relentless war on poverty. But the benevolent arrangements of the Church of Christ were massive too. To impress and inform members of the church with the great needs, David Lipscomb used the pages of the *Gospel Advocate* to publish a flood of letters from every section of the South, revealing conditions of want and starvation almost beyond belief. From every community they wrote,

> There never has been such poverty in this country. . . . members are actually suffering from the necessities of life . . . They are without meat, bread, or provisions of any kind, and not a single individual in the whole community is able to resist them.[2]

At the Murfreesboro consultation meeting, three Nashville men were asked to serve as a committee to forward all money and provisions which were sent there "for the relief of the destitute." The agent for forwarding would be V.W. Metcalfe, and all food and clothing was to be sent to Metcalfe Brothers and Company, marked, "For the destitute South." Selected to serve as advisors to Metcalfe were P. S. Fall and

David Lipscomb. At an October meeting in Franklin, three others were selected to travel to the North and discuss the plan with churches there. The elders and deacons of every congregation in the nation were urged to send their contributions of money and goods to the committee in Nashville for distribution to points where the help was most needed.

Lipscomb wrote, "Our object is to relieve first the destitute Saints; second, our suffering fellow mortal. Do good to all men, especially the household of Faith."[3] For many months the pages of the *Gospel Advocate* reflected the tremendous flood of response. Lipscomb published regular reports of the money and materials received and disbursed by the central committee. There is no indication that Fanning saw any inconsistency between the Nashville committee arrangement and the position he had taken in regard to the Missionary Society. But there was continuing indication, both from Fanning and Lipscomb, that the Society was, in their minds, inseparably related to the War and the havoc it had caused.

Thus the *Gospel Advocate* became not only an effective channel of communication after the War, but also entered its most demanding era of influence upon the Church of Christ. Two new special departments in the paper served to illustrate its expanding influence. One, the "Alien's Department," was designed for the non-Christian. The column, which confirmed in the vocabulary of the church the use of the term "alien" to refer to non-members, was edited by T.W. Brents (His articles were later issued in book form as the widely read, *Gospel Plan of Salvation*).

Another important department was the "Texas Department," edited by Carrol Kendrick, who was living in Bastrop, Texas, and was one of the most influential men among Churches of Christ in the Lone Star State. Kendrick had been editing his own paper, but when he decided to terminate publication, he made arrangements with Lipscomb and Fanning to incorporate his mailing list with that of the *Advocate*. It was not long until the names of Lipscomb and Fanning had become household names in most of the church families in Texas. Because of Kendrick's choice of the *Gospel Advo-*

cate for his Texas department, and also because of the vast immigration into Texas of Tennessee church members who so often brought copies of the *Advocate* with them, the paper and its conservative stance had tremendous influence in helping to shape the course which many in the Restoration Movement followed in Texas. Perhaps it is idle speculation, but one wonders what would have been the course of churches in Texas had Kendrick chosen a periodical other than the *Gospel Advocate* to take over his subscription list. It is sometimes upon such small hinges that history swings.

Since Tolbert Fanning had set his course toward continuing his educational activities, it is not surprising that the editorship of the *Gospel Advocate* fell more and more on the shoulders of David Lipscomb. By the spring of its first year, Fanning felt called upon to explain to his readers why he was not writing more. He was extremely busy with other important and pressing matters, he said, and then, too, he had tremendous confidence in the junior editor, David Lipscomb. By the time that they were ready to enter 1868, Lipscomb announced that he was taking over the editorship of the paper, and that he was making plans to enlarge its size.

After a four-year suspension, Fanning opened Franklin College again on October 2, 1865. Although the buildings had survived the war, Fanning's residence had burned to the ground in August, and then, about three weeks after school opened, a boy was burning out his chimney and let the fire get out of control. The main building of the college, valued at between $30,000 and $40,000, burned to the ground. Also destroyed was $20,000 worth of equipment and books, including W. D. Carnes' valuable library. Nothing was insured.

Tolbert Fanning had faced destruction before, and he had learned to rise above it. Perhaps the measure of the man, now nearing sixty years of age, is seen most clearly in his immediate response to this crisis as he promptly proceeded to purchase Minerva College from S. E. Jones. G. A. Kinnie and A. J. Fanning continued as teachers along with Tolbert

Fanning himself. Under the new arrangements, the Minerva property was used by Charlotte and two of her former pupils to operate a school for girls, while other buildings housed a small school for boys. One of the young men who graduated shortly after the new beginning was T. B. Larimore, who not only became such an outstanding preacher but also followed Fanning's example by beginning his own school, Mars Hill Bible School, which still continues one hundred years after Larimore was a student of Fanning.

Fanning's new school received its charter from the state legislature and was christened, Hope Institute. Although the enrollment of these schools was never high (three graduated in 1868), Fanning continued to believe that the classroom provided one of his most significant channels of service. With the dark of the war now yielding to the first rays of dawn, what better name could there be than Hope Institute?

But the name of Hope Institute provided only the small end of a wedge into much greater plans taking shape in Fanning's heart. The next month after the charter was granted, in December of 1866, Fanning called a meeting of the trustees of Franklin College. For three days they listened to Fanning's dreams as he carefully projected plans for the most ambitious educational undertaking he had yet attempted. An announcement of plans to establish a school equal to any other educational institution on American soil came at the climax of the three-day planning session. The school was to be located in Middle Tennessee, though probably not at Elm Crag, and would be designed to accommodate between five hundred and one thousand students who would enjoy its benefits without charge. "Our mind is at least fully made up," wrote Fanning, "and we at present can see no insurmountable barrier." The fact that he could face the sunset of his life, yet planning greater accomplishments than ever, is much more important than the size of any of the graduating classes at the school. By January of the next year, Fanning had obtained a charter and announced that the new school would be named, Peace College.[4]

These plans were much more ambitious than any others

which Fanning had attempted before. In at least one other way they were also radically different. He now began to emphasize the need for endowment. His plans demanded between two and three hundred thousand dollars, to be given by interested church members and friends. Then, counties in Middle Tennessee were to be given an opportunity to bid for the school by offering a gift of money to match the several hundred thousand dollars already to have been given by individuals and a minimum of five hundred acres on which to erect the school. Fanning's plans also called for the *complete endowment* of the professors' chairs!

By the fall of 1866, two counties had made offers of land. In addition, one offered $30,000 and the other $40,000 in cash. Fanning felt that when the time came either of them would be willing to offer at least $100,000 to bring five hundred youths to their area. He calculated that each of these students would spend $300 in a year's time thus infusing $150,000 into the economy of the county which had the school.

Fanning emphasized that the first step would be to endow the professors' chairs in order to assure the county that the project would be carried to completion. He estimated that this would take about $100,000. Gradually, gifts were pledged, and Fanning spent most of his time during 1866 traveling on behalf of the project.

But while Tolbert Fanning was making his grand plans for Peace College, David Lipscomb was facing worries of a more concrete nature. Before the war, a stock educational company had been formed to purchase Franklin College from Fanning. Then the war came, and much which had been pledged had not been paid. As a result, Lipscomb was deeply concerned that all the stockholders pay what they had promised before the war. He was especially concerned since he wanted to resign his post as secretary but was anxious to close the books first. Finally, Franklin College was offered for sale to satisfy the debts of the organization.

Just what happened to Fanning's ambitious plans is not too clear. There is evidence from statements made in the announcements that the trustees did not fully share Fanning's enthusiasm or optimism. No doubt many of them, like the South as a whole, found themselves without capital. Unlike the North, with its strong financial institutions, the South had placed the major portion of its capital funds in slaves and had depended upon loans from northern banks to finance its annual cotton crop. Divested of slavery, the South was also divested of capital for development. After the initial months of planning, Fanning's dream was not mentioned again. Soon, he was back at Elm Crag, the school and farm were his property again, and he was operating a small college for men beside his wife's Hope Institute for college women. Evidently, the war-ravaged South was straining merely to survive, and Fanning's ambitious dream was premature.

That Fanning was more determined than ever before to serve faithfully, regardless of risk and high hazards, makes the Peace College dream much more important than its realization. Here were men who, in spite of circumstances, were determined to remain valiantly at their post of duty, giving their Maker every opportunity to work mightily through them.

Two articles from the closing days of Fanning's life betray his attitude toward education after forty years' experience. One article, entitled, "The Education of Preachers," shows that while Fanning still did not like the idea of giving a young man a special ministerial course to make him a preacher, "We have not yet seen amongst the brethren such schools and preparations for giving instruction as seem requisite to make sound scholars and eminent Biblical critics."[5]

The second article was entitled, "Church Schools, or The Duty of Christians, in the Education of Youth." In the article, which appeared in the same month as his death, Fanning wrote,

> A volume of weighty reasons might be written in favor of the Christian training of children. If there is, in fact, a more important obligation resting upon the disciples of Jesus Christ than the proper instruction

and discipline of children, we cannot call it to mind. . . .
. . . .

> We can see no good reason why Christians should
> not have the exclusive control of all the higher schools
> of learning, to which their children are entrusted. We
> do not indeed, consider any man or woman at all
> *competent* to have the responsibility of educating youth,
> who fears not God, and who is not, in the fullest sense
> a Christian.[6]

In this article, Fanning noted that Campbell at Bethany, and
other church members at Kentucky University, had employed teachers who were not Christians, and he expressed
the conviction that it was a serious mistake. Yet Fanning's
faculty at Franklin College from 1845 to 1860 was not always made up altogether of Christians either. But in 1874,
his views were obviously different. When he started Franklin
College, he was more concerned about training farmers and
teachers and mechanics. He lacked experience. At the end
of his life, his own experience and his observation of others
had convinced him that Christians should entrust their children's education to the hands of Christians. Education
without direction was self-destructive. He closed his article,

> We need schools under Christian influence in every
> state, county, and section of our country, and we hope
> the time is not far distant when all who love our Lord
> Jesus Christ in sincerity will heartily co-operate in the
> momentous work of Christian education.[7]

Accompanying his plans for Christian education were
Fanning's dreams of a Christian publishing house in Nashville to encourage the publication of good books, tracts,
and journals. He also envisioned a huge library where
students could do comprehensive research and be challenged
to excellence in the field of biblical scholarship as much
as students at any other center of scholarship in the world.
The times demanded nothing less. Fanning sensed an even
greater opportunity for the church in the years toward the
close of the century, but he also sensed that the church
would be required to provide quality training if she was to

live up to the challenge. Even in death, his watchword remained the same: "Improvement!" He closed his article, "We need more profound scholars and sound thinkers."

CHAPTER 16

ON TO PERFECTION

TOLBERT FANNING AND THE
RESTORATION PRINCIPLE

"There is more to be done yet."
— *Alexander Campbell*

TOLBERT FANNING bridged the years between the first generation of leaders in the Restoration Movement and the younger group of preachers being schooled in Tennessee, Kentucky and Virginia. As a young man he was close to Alexander Campbell and knew the work and direction of Barton Stone as few others. Campbell, Stone, and Walter Scott all died while Fanning's life was at its midday. Then, in the decades that marked his closing years, he enjoyed ample opportunity to witness the attitude and direction of the younger generation of men.

While still a relatively young man of thirty-five, Fanning came to believe that the movement was already approaching a crucial intersection. In an article entitled, "The Crisis," he wrote,

> There is but one step between Christianity and sectarianism. One move from the Bible and its practices, and we are in the quagmires of party corruption. When reformers begin to boast of their respectability, they have started to the city of confusion,—when they court the smiles of corrupt denominations, they are at the very gates, and when they shake hands with sects, they are in the midst of "Babylon the great."[1]

Fanning was obviously troubled. He believed that determined decisions were mandatory as the movement encountered the inevitable intersection of every reform movement. Either they would find the resources to regain the momentum of reformation and continue toward the ideals of the New Testament, or they would call a truce and make concessions to some form of comfortable respectability. "Shall we, brethren, fall into the arms of Rome or her polluted daughters?" Fanning asked. "Or shall we glorify God in arousing our energies and determine never to rest till the churches of Jesus Christ be found walking in the pure light?"

As the Church of Christ paused at the crossroads, Fanning saw two hazards hovering near. One was the ever-present danger of an illegitimate purpose and direction. The movement could be derailed and reoriented. He entertained anxiety, on the other hand, over smug satisfaction with the past progress and present truth. Stagnation short of the ever elusive perfect goal always appeals to a pride which wants to believe that it has arrived. For him, the "restoration principle" produced perennial ferment, agitating each generation to view its positions critically in the light of the Bible and to place them in judgment before the spirit of Christ.

Toward the close of his life, in a series of articles entitled "Ancient and Modern Churches," he further developed his attitudes by contrasting the church of the first century with the church of his own day. He was clearly critical of his contemporaries when he wrote,

> We must either go forward and learn Christianity practically, as developed in the New Testament, or dwindle into a modern sect and make terms as best we can with the denominations of the age. Who that possesses a heart to love the ways of God, can be reconciled to an apostasy so degrading?[2]

Fanning spoke of Martin Luther, John Wesley, and others. But he added, though with obvious awe and admiration, that these had been too easily satisfied with their achievements and thus had "stumbled on the road to Jerusalem," in "clear sight of Zion's Hill."

> Both Luther and Wesley imagined that they had reached the *ne plus ultra* of spiritual discovery; and hence, each adopted the idea of making sure what he had discovered, by erecting his standard of truth and righteousness. Each became the author of a creed and a sect, and each possibly died satisfied that he had fulfilled his mission.[3]

Nowhere is this attitude more clearly expressed than in the changes reflected in Fanning's own concepts, and he never wavered in feeling that his changes were signs of strength and not weakness. To feel otherwise would be to claim personal ultimacy, which is the most deceptive type of idolatry. Fanning was impressed with Campbell's tremendous success in turning even those who did not fully agree with him back toward the Bible as a guide for religious beliefs and practices. Campbell had once told young Fanning, as they rode together on a preaching tour, "There is more to be done yet." The impression of that principle made a monumental mark. Fanning felt that his fearful responsibility was to perfect what had been initiated at such great cost during the first half of the century. "What does God require at our hands?" he asked.

Fanning's answer to this question was manifold. To begin with, there was an urgent need for greater maturity among churches. Most people one hundred years later would be surprised by the weakness of the churches which were contemporary with Fanning. An 1845 report from Kentucky, for instance, is typical. Of three hundred eighty congregations in that state, less than half of them were meeting every Sunday. Sixty-eight were meeting semimonthly, ninety-two met only once each month, and others still more irregularly.[4]

Tolbert Fanning believed that a genuine appreciation for the biblical message would create in a man a humility so great that he would continue to search for further understanding all of his life. He realized that the essence of human history is change and that a living God is in the rapids as well as in the quiet, rock-sheltered ponds along the river banks. He knew that institutions too brittle to meet new situations can do harm and, like all things, when they cease changing they cease to be living organisms.

Tolbert Fanning believed that the restoration principle leads a man to continue to appraise critically his position on every subject. When he starts to elevate his attained level of understanding as an example for others to follow, he has lost his right to be heard. Only as he calls men and women to be fellow searchers for mature understanding—as he elevates the perfect pattern which is God's alone in its fullness and as his daily renewal of the search is persistently nourished—only then can he continue the work which God has for him to do.

Closely related to the custom of sporadic assemblies was the need for better organization. "The great work for evangelists now," Fanning wrote, "is to set in order things lacking in the churches." He estimated that nine out of ten converts made during the summer "revivals" did not remain faithful through the first winter![5] Evangelists needed to have more concern for their converts and help the churches which they planted to become self-sufficient before going on to make more new members. Too often the new Christians were left to wither and die. Enmeshed with this was the pitifully patchy framework of local leadership. Fanning's wide experience compelled him to conclude that "not one bishop in twenty" was really qualified.[6] Much of his own effort was spent in visiting the churches which he established, to nourish and encourage them until they could carry on their work alone. Some of the strongest churches of the period were those which Fanning had planted.

Another area which, while receiving much attention throughout his life, was especially emphasized toward the close of his efforts, was the need for every member of the local church to be active as a "living stone" in both worship and work. Too many churches were guilty of what he called "proxy service" where a preacher or perhaps an elder so dominated the church that the members were kept "idle, inactive, and of course, ignorant and spiritless, till the whole moral heart ceases to beat."[7] At the end of his life he surveyed the scene again and wrote that "possibly the greatest religious error of the age" was to be found still in Churches of Christ. He said it was "evinced by the prevailing ignorance in the church members regarding the true spiritual division of spiritual labor." Continuing the judgment he wrote,

We consider it the privilege and duty of every Chris-

tian on earth to preach the good news of life and salvation from the hour of entering the kingdom to the
hour of death. It is true, we do not suppose it is the
privilege of every member, male and female, black and
white, old and young, to attempt religious orations, as
is the current practice. Indeed, we are assured that sermonizing as now performed was unknown in the Christian world in the primitive church.[8]

From his life as well as his writings it is evident that
Fanning regretted the current custom of long orations which
dominated the worship of the church. The only purpose
served was to "deaden true spiritual service" and worship.
By his emphasis upon every member participating, he did
not intend that all should speak. In fact, he discouraged
"sermonizing" on the part of *anyone*.

To Fanning, anyone committed to the restoration principle
should be willing to grow, however painful the process might
be. Campbell and the others had done a good work, but its
value would be lost if it were not used as a foundation for
further progress. They could not claim to be the Lord's
church unless they were willing to grow toward the true
spiritual body of Christ in which every member was an active citizen of the kingdom. "This, of all others," Fanning
urged, "we regard as the most important subject for the
consideration of the churches."

But others in his brotherhood were also speaking about
the movement going on to greater attainments, and some
seemed to Fanning to produce sounds of disharmony. While
there was a need to perfect the work begun, the progress
must be in the same vein, recognizing the Bible as their
guide. As has already been pointed out, Fanning saw the
Bible as man's only means of spiritual enlightenment. Any
concept which made shipwreck of this was to him a false
show of wisdom which foreshadowed no good end.

Another area of great concern to Fanning as he pursued
the New Testament ideal, was the growing practice of hiring
preachers in a professional way. The biographer of D.S.
Burnet boasts for Burnet the distinction of being the "father"

of the "pastor system" among the churches of the period, and to some degree, the distinction may be justified. Burnet himself wrote,

> The Bishop or resident preacher, who performs both the episcopal and the evangelical functions, must be looked to as the hope of the church in regard to its edification, both in knowledge and members. An effort —a series of efforts—should be made to furnish every city church, and as many of the rural ones as possible, the labors of a competent pastor.[9]

To admit that such an arrangement, without biblical precedent, was truly "the hope of the church," as Burnet claimed, would force Fanning also to admit that he had committed his whole life in the wrong direction. But Fanning did not believe he had gone so far afield. Of Burnet's teachings he wrote, "There is not a word in the Scriptures favoring such views." They were "plainly popish" in all their bearings. He continued, "We must add that the custom of the churches hiring lads, striplings, pert youths as pastors, elders or bishops of churches, is not only ludicrous in the extreme, but it is in fact subversive of the whole Christian order." As Fanning watched the group of men of whom Burnet was representative, he wrote,

> In the denominations, many had stood high in office, but in coming amongst the disciples, it was always difficult, and in some cases, impossible, to bring our new members to a level with those they were in the habit of calling "*laymen.*" Some, indeed, were so fond of the "official" "leeks," "onions," and "garlic," that they went back to their respective churches.[10]

Not only did this concept elevate a man to a position for which there was no Scriptural example, but it also damaged the spiritual fervor of the members, who, leaning on the "pastor," did not develop their own strength and talents. Fanning lamented the practice of the "elders" coming to the building and talking only of their merchandise, their banks, their crops, and their stock, while waiting for the appearance of "some youthful *Elder* or *Pastor* to take the chief seat in the synagogue and worship God for all the people." "This," he said, "is the state of the case with most of the denominations, Romish and Protestant, and it is getting to be the case with us."[11]

In the mind of Fanning, the concept of a "pastor system" had an obvious affinity with the disposition which some were showing to have "theological schools after the style of the denominations, to prepare youths for the preaching of the Gospel for making pastors for the churches." There was a time when there was "no official such as this amongst us as a fashionable pastor; and when we could not bear the idea of theological schools to manufacture preachers."

> But the times have changed and many have changed with the times. We witness these things in deep sorrow, but we have long been satisfied that many in this country, in addition to becoming influential with the world, have become worldly-wise and are strongly inclined to conform to denominational service.[12]

Another mood which disturbed Fanning was the growing tendency among leaders of the movement to accept a denominational concept of Christianity. It will be remembered that Fanning had been a Christian for some time before he ever heard of Alexander Campbell. Unlike the leaders of the first generation, he had never belonged to another religious group and had no denominational concepts to "unlearn." For several years he studied only his Bible. He made talks in the worship assemblies before he ever saw a commentary or a religious periodical. He was proud to be "freeborn." He could never tolerate the idea that the church was a denomination. He was a Christian—nothing more. Anything which tended to bring reproach upon the non-sectarian nature of the body of Christ was at once cast aside.

To understand why Fanning was so disturbed by some of the things he heard and read from others is not difficult. Moses E. Lard had written of "our denominational origin in this country." In an article for a book on American religious groups, Robert Richardson had said the church was established on Brush Run in Washington County, Pennsyl-

vania, on September 7, 1810, "under the superintendence of
Thomas Campbell of the Presbyterian Religion." Richardson
further spoke of baptism for the remission of sins as a
"prominent feature" of this new society which had begun
on American soil. Could this be the true attitude of one
who, at Bethany College, was training young preachers who
would soon be influencing and moulding the thinking of the
churches?

Fanning always suspected that even Luther, Calvin, and
Wesley had entertained the "proud thought of originating
respectable parties," and believed that their pride became
"the complete destruction of the cause of which they had, in
word, at least, been zealous advocates." Fanning believed
he saw the same "denominational" pride portrayed in the
concepts and the vocabulary of a group of men in the
church, who, like Burnet, continually referred to the church
as a "denomination." Others, like him, encouraged the
proud claim that theirs was the largest denomination originating on American soil. Fanning plead, "I speak this to
forearm my beloved brethren who are my seniors, of the
fatal rock on which so many have split. 'What I say unto
one, I say unto all, WATCH.' "[13] Tolbert Fanning never
failed to remind everyone that denominationalism had been
the very thing which Campbell had labored so long to overcome—he had never conceived of creating still another denomination. Fanning further emphasized that the real appeal
of their message to the world had partially been in their
emphasis upon the nondenominational nature of the one
body of Christ.

Probably no controversy in Fanning's closing years was
to have more far-reaching implications than the questions
clustered about the Missionary Society. His attitude toward
church cooperation has already been traced at length. That
he conceived of the society arrangement as an apostasy is
obvious. He bent some of his strongest efforts toward convincing others that they should and could carry out their
work through local churches without such auxiliaries. He
thought he sensed in the supporters of the societies a fail-

ure of commitment to a divine pattern. But the effect of this on his attitude of fellowship is also significant. One must remember that Fanning begged his brethren, for the sake of unity, to forsake their societies. He even attended the national convention of 1859 with the express purpose of discussing the problem with the leaders of the society. He commended the supporters of the societies for the good which they accomplished. In 1872, for instance, when he started his last paper, the *Religious Historian,* he pointed out,

> We would also be pleased to receive the results of all church co-operations, and all labor by the united efforts of the brethren. Although we have not seen proper to attempt any religious work through human organizations, such as Missionary and other like societies, we would be thankful for reports from such, as we will faithfully promise to do all full justice. The good, we would be pleased to place on record.[14]

He refused to shut the door of fellowship upon the society party. It was only when some, like Thomas Munnell and G. W. Elly, tried to make his approval a test of fellowship, demanding that he support their efforts, that Fanning rebelled and branded their demands as tantamount to a new creed.

When the Ohio Christian Missionary Society and the Ohio Baptist State Convention both passed resolutions expressing hopes for closer fraternity between their groups, Fanning printed their resolutions in the *Religious Historian,* with his comment:

> We most heartily approve of the efforts of the Brethren of the Ohio Missionary Society to bring the Disciples and the Baptists into more friendly relations; and we greatly rejoice in seeing the Spirit manifested by our Baptist brethren. It evinces most clearly an anxious desire to reconcile men who really love righteousness, in all sections of the earth.[15]

The suggestion has even been made that Fanning's interest in an ecumenical spirit of trust and openness was a century ahead of its time. As has been witnessed already, Fanning, like most others in the Disciples movement of his day, believed there were many Christians in the Baptist church who might be convinced to pursue a way toward nondenominational Christianity. What better way to reach them than to keep the lines of communication between them and the members of the Churches of Christ as free as possible from every obstruction of bigotry and prejudice?

His attitude toward his brethren in the Missionary Society was much the same. Back in the 1850s in Tennessee, when some supported the society and some did not, Fanning encouraged "consultation meetings." While some did not surrender their convictions that the society was valid, they agreed, for unity's sake, to work without them. Fanning continued to hope that this unity might also prevail through discussions at the national level. While this attitude of communication and fellowship with the Society party is apparent, it should not minimize the tremendous influence which Fanning exerted in keeping many from being engulfed in the end result. The commitment to the Societies, regardless of the effect, soon became apparent. Had it not been for the clear and decisive influence of Fanning, repeatedly voicing objection to the societies' direction, the Restoration Movement after the Civil War, notably in the South, would have been far different.

One of the Societies' staunchest supporters at their beginning was Benjamin Franklin, editor of the *American Christian Review*. He served as a corresponding secretary of the Society and used his paper to speak on behalf of its efforts. His paper might almost be considered the mouthpiece of the society during the first years. But it was also about the same time, as Lipscomb recalls, that Franklin paid a visit to Tolbert Fanning at Franklin College. Franklin was a popular preacher in the North and spoke the language of the "common" man. After Campbell died, he probably held greater influence in the churches as a whole than any other man. When he came to see Fanning, the two sat up most of the night and discussed the questions surrounding

the Missionary Society. We shall never know the full signifi-
cance of their conversation that night, but this much we do
know — when Franklin left Fanning, he offered him his right
hand as a pledge to join his resistance to the societies.

When Franklin began to speak out against the Missionary
Society, the effect was staggering. For a while the organization floundered for lack of financial support. Had it not
been for the artificial respiration administered by the new
Christian Standard (which struggled, even then, depending
upon heavy gifts from supporters of the society), the church
might remember the national Society as a part of the story
of the Civil War epoch which, by itself might not have inflicted as deep divisional wounds. But, as it happened, the
society remained as a reminder of the feelings nourished
during those senseless years of hysteria and hate, and hos-
tilities remained with some even after they had forgotten
their origin.

Fanning came to realize eventually that the society was
bringing division far more deeply than he at first suspected.
Although he went to his grave still seeking reconciliation
with his alienated brethren, he came to realize that the possibility was not too likely. His closing comments betray one
who is severely disillusioned (as idealists often are) and badly
broken because of the determined party spirit. He wrote of
the "rule or ruin" attitude which he encountered in some
and concluded, "The cooperation which seems current is
merely the union of parties to build up their particular sect,
or to carry into perfection their pet schemes, adopted in the
wisdom of men, to give place to their originators."[16] It is
difficult not to sympathize with Fanning's genuine concern
when one listens to the way in which he was handled by
those to whom he ascribed this party spirit. One of the supporters of the Missionary Society, C. L. Loos, wrote in the
Millennial Harbinger, and Fanning, quoting him, interspersed
his reactions:

> There will always be men opposed to every movement
> however justifiable and important. There are men in our

land even yet opposed to common schools, (Where in the name of heaven do they live? T.F.) and among these educated men (surely not, T.F.) as well as the lowest stratum of ignorance, other thousands opposed, on religious and secular grounds to colleges. So in the churches there is yet opposition to missionary associations and education of the ministry. (Did you say opposed to education and the ministry? T.F.) The few who have been of late days persistently and noisily denouncing missionary associations, have by their unsanctified bitterness and rudeness of their attacks, (Is this the spirit of missionary societies? Is this union? T.F.) given full evidence of the causes of their opposition—a lack of knowledge of an enlightened piety and a true spiritual culture. To attempt to teach such men is well nigh useless, as it is almost hopeless.[17]

With unmitigated bitterness Fanning was denounced by his brethren in the Society who classed him with an ignorant group of people who even opposed education! He was accused of lacking an enlightened piety and true spirituality. It was useless to try to teach anything to such a fellow! Subsequent histories of the controversy have too often parroted the judgment of Fanning's critics with little understanding of Fanning's position or personality.

In the maturity of life, Tolbert Fanning urged men and women to build on the work which Campbell and the others had done and to go "on to perfection" in emphasizing the spiritual nature of the church, with every Christian as a priest and a king. But at the same time, he labored ceaselessly against the encroachments of those who would change the course of the cause. He feared the dangers arising from two sources. One was ignorance of the Bible, and especially of the "spiritual organization, practices and enjoyments of God's empire." The other source of concern was the growth of "an ambition to have a name amongst men."

As "the crisis" came, with all of its uncertainty and misgiving, there was never the slightest doubt in Fanning's mind about where his allegiance was vested. In the midst of his controversy with Robert Richardson, he wrote of his own "perfect pattern":[18]

Once, in all human history, we meet a being who never did an injury, and never resented one done to him, never uttered an untruth, never practiced a deception, and never lost an opportunity of doing good; generous in the midst of the sensual, and wise far above the wisest of sages and prophets, loving and gentle, yet immovably resolute; his illimitable meekness and patience never once forsook him in a vexatious, ungrateful, and cruel world — *Christ in History*.

CHAPTER 17

A BETTER STATE
OF SOCIETY
THE CLOSING DAYS

> *"May sects cease, and all Christian
> forces be united against the common
> enemies of God and man, that a better
> state of society may exist in the
> world, than the annals of time have
> recorded."*
> — *Tolbert Fanning*

CHARLOTTE FANNING observed her husband: "He was· anxious to fulfill his mission—seemed to feel there was not much time left—that the night would soon come in which no man can work."[1] While those who knew Fanning found it difficult to associate his stamina with the thought of death, he noted, "We are too apt to flatter ourselves with security, when death walks in secret. We know not what a day may bring forth." Still, there was so much to be done.

In 1868, Fanning took what probably was his last tour down into Alabama and Mississippi to visit the scenes of both his childhood and the mature labors of his manhood. However, he did no preaching along the way for this time he was not riding in a carriage behind Jacob Faithful, but on the train. On July 3, he left Nashville on the Decatur train and the next morning was in Athens, Alabama. Since his last visit the god of war had visited the scene so that he hardly recognized the town. From every corner of Decatur he saw poverty staring at him and the death-like stare of drought-stricken crops was especially agonizing to one who loved the soil and its fruit.

Continuing along the valley of the beautiful Tennessee River, he passed the farm of J. T. Barclay, son-in-law of

Alexander Campbell and the first man sent out by the American Christian Missionary Society, who had returned from his work in Jerusalem. At Courtland the train stopped long enough for several people to enter Fanning's car. To his surprise, one of the new passengers was young T. B. Larimore, who had graduated from Fanning's school the year before and was preaching in the area. Larimore was on his way to Corinth to hold a meeting, and his reports of the work in northern Alabama were encouraging to Fanning. Larimore had also been teaching at Mountain Home. Fanning mused to himself that young Larimore seemed to be a "sensible, modest, and earnest advocate of the truth." At Corinth, he met William Anderson, an old friend from his days at Franklin, Tennessee, as well as the son of Allen Kendrick, another recent graduate of Franklin College, preaching at Corinth.

After a day on the train he reached Memphis and stayed over two Sundays, preaching in a series of meetings. He returned home disappointed with the results of his efforts in Memphis. He even entertained the suspicion that the failure was his own fault. Still, he continued to work diligently with the church at Franklin College. (In May, 1873, he reported between twenty and thirty baptisms within a few weeks' time.)

When Fanning began his third religious journal, the *Religious Historian,* in January, 1872, most of the material was written by Fanning himself, although there were also a number of articles by Charlotte. Fanning did not carry many news items and refused to give any notice whatever to local problems and controversies.

For some time he had wanted to write a history of the church. He now was planning to use the *Religious Historian* as a means for gradually unfolding the results of his study. As usual, he started at the beginning and progressed slowly, exhausting the territory he covered. He admitted that much of the preparatory labor was rather tedious. To enhance the Bible, he devoted most of the space in the first year's pages to concerted attempts to weaken confidence in speculative philosophy. His second volume was chiefly devoted to church organization and what he considered to be a number of false notions surrounding this subject. Then he began the third volume with an examination of the "only spiritual creed and system of religious government" recognized by God. He promised that if spared, the fourth year would find him commencing the historical work for which he was doing so much research and study. But even Fanning realized that man does not know what a day may bring forth.

Throughout the years following the Civil War Fanning continued Hope Institute, his school for girls. Operating under his charter for Franklin College, he also taught a limited number of young men. Each year he set his goal: "to make greater exertions in behalf of the next class" than he had made in any former year's work. "We are certainly very anxious in our few remaining days," he wrote in 1873, "to profit the youth of our times."

In January of 1872, Fanning went to Gallatin to attend a debate between his old student, David Lipscomb, and a Baptist named G. W. Griffin. He noted that Lipscomb was rather "slow and hesitating in speech," though he had a massive brain, went forward with the main object, and possessed no hedging ability or retaliatory power.

The next spring he attended a debate on spiritualism in Nashville just before the outbreak of a serious cholera epidemic. Between June 7 and June 21, three hundred ninety-seven people died in Nashville and business was brought almost to a standstill. About this same time Fanning received word from Texas that B. F. Hall was dead. He thought about how Hall had first come to his neighborhood to preach and how he, as a youth yet in his teens, had responded. He thought about what a difference that single act had made in his life. Later he had worked with Hall in and around Nashville. Silently now, his companions were tiring and laying down their tools.

Later that year, when J. M. Barnes came to Nashville, he naturally wanted to see Fanning, and, just as naturally, he knew where to find him—at the stock sale at the fairgrounds.

It was in 1872 or 1873 that E. F. (Pop) Geers, later a noted horse jockey in Tennessee, was at the beginning of his career. Fanning had a romantic pony-sized Morgan stallion, Davy Jennings, which he had bred for speed to drive on the road. Geers took "Little Dave" to the Wilson county fair in Lebanon and entered him for Fanning as a show horse. He won the stallion class and then, unknown to Fanning, Geers entered him in the trotting race. It was Geers's first race. Pulling an old skeleton wagon, Little Dave won the race for him. When Geers came home to Nashville, he gathered up his courage and told Fanning that Little Dave had won a race as well as a show class. Fanning is reported only to have smiled. Although he said nothing, some in the church who were critics of his enthusiasm for horses are reported to have said much!

In December, 1873, Fanning went to Franklin to attend a four-day debate between T. W. Brents and Jacob Ditzler, a Methodist. Beyond his interest in the debate he was especially cheered by the warm fellowship with old friends. He talked with J. T. Barclay, although he was disappointed that he was not doing more preaching. John S. Sweeney was there from Paris, Kentucky, in the very prime of his activities. Fanning's students, David Lipscomb and E. G. Sewell, now co-editing the *Gospel Advocate,* were there "ready and fully equipped to defend the faith once for all delivered to the saints." Fanning was especially glad to see and talk with a number of promising young men whose deep interest in the matters discussed at the debate was impressive to the aging debater.

At the debate those who knew Fanning well thought they could detect a loss of strength and a general stooping forward in his posture. He no longer moved with the elastic step for which he was noted. Then one day in the early spring of 1874, Fanning went to the lot to see his livestock. He asked Frank Manier, a farmhand, to lead out a fine bull for him to examine. Manier was afraid of the animal and so Fanning, showing signs of impatience with his farmhand, stepped into the yard to do the work himself. The bull made a lunge for Fanning and almost killed him on the spot. He was carried to the house and for a week or two remained in bed. But he was not accustomed to inactivity and hardly knew what it meant to be sick. By April 30, which fell on Thursday, he felt strong enough to be up again and so he went back to the lot. But when he returned to the house, he felt something tear inside his body as he started up the stairway. For several days he suffered great agony in his side. On Saturday the day was gloomy and rainy. Then, on Sunday morning he told the physician that this would be his last day. He summoned a group of his friends to his room and asked that they worship with him. Together they broke the loaf in memory of the death of Christ. But when Fanning asked them to sing, everyone was at first too filled with emotion. Fanning continued to beg, "Sing, sing." When they finally started the hymn, he was too weak to join them. Soon he went away into death.

His hands, so often busy, were folded by his friends to rest on the heart that "so long throbbed with earnest desire to do good to the church and the world." The next day, P. S. Fall spoke at his funeral.

> Two objects were near his heart—first to restore the service of God to the order God gave in the New Testament; second, to place a good industrial and literary education within reach of every youth. He labored to these ends during his life and desired his property devoted to them after his death.[2]

T. B. Larimore had judged Tolbert Fanning to be the most forceful preacher in the church in his day. His *Gospel Advocate*, having passed its one hundredth birthday, affirms the judgment of the subsequent church that his pen was not impotent. A host of Christian colleges and Christians in colleges can today trace an indelible ancestry to the classrooms of Fanning's Franklin College. There also remains a host of men who, like Fanning, are confident that Christ in history is man's best hope and surest example, even though the journey to their ideal remains, for the most part, still ahead of them.

Tolbert Fanning was not buried near the ashes of Franklin College, which had burned after the Civil War and were still visible at his death. Instead he was buried beneath the protecting trees of Hope Institute. There at Elm Crag, on Nubbin' Ridge, not far from the classroom where he had molded the lives of hundreds of young men who became leaders in the church; not far from the gentle pool just beyond the crag where his hands immersed young men and women as they committed their lives to Christ; not far from the chapel where for over thirty years he had preached and worshiped with the church, his body was laid to rest.

The earthly tabernacle of Tolbert Fanning, its oak-like six-foot six inch frame towering head and shoulders above his friends, was still. He no longer galloped, cyclone-style, down the lane on a fine steed to keep a preaching appointment or to lock the *Gospel Advocate* in the press. But many who persistently maintain the possibility of non-sectarian discipleship must be aware of his imposing shadow hovering over them. He still speaks through a body of people who believe, like him, that it is possible to be nothing more than Christians.

> All heaven was once pleased with this worship, and the same shining hosts must be again when it is enacted. I long to see the day come when it will be done. Then will Zion shine forth as the sun in his noon-tide majesty, and the world will be attracted by the light of God's revelation, pouring its golden rays through the church into the dark bosom of creation. May sects cease, and all Christian forces be united against the common enemies of God and man, that a better state of society may exist in the world, than the annals of time have recorded.[3]

IMPORTANT DATES
IN THE LIFE OF TOLBERT FANNING

Birth	1810
Nashville Baptist Church becomes Church of Christ	1827
Baptism	1827
Andrew Jackson inauguration	1829
Fanning leaves home to preach	1829
Mahoning Baptist Association dissolved	1830
Early preaching, Tennessee and Alabama	1831-32
Student at University of Nashville	1832-36
Marries Sarah Shreve	1835
Summer tours with Alexander Campbell	1835-36
Marries Charlotte Fall	1836
Girls School in Franklin, Tennessee	1837-39
Moves to Elm Crag, near Nashville	1840
Editor of the *Agriculturist*	1840-45
First Tennessee Cooperation Meeting	1842
Boys Agricultural School at Elm Crag	1843-44
Begins editing *Christian Review*	1844
Begins Franklin College at Elm Crag	1845
Begins editing the *Naturalist*	1846
Nashville Committee for Evangelism appointed	1847
End of U.S. War with Mexico	1848
Christian Magazine replaces *Christian Review*	1849
American Christian Missionary Society begins	1849
Jesse Ferguson-Alexander Campbell controversy	1852
New Nashville church building completed	1852
Begins *Gospel Advocate*	1855
Tennessee "Consultation" meetings begin	1856
Tolbert Fanning-Robert Richardson controversy	1857
Church building in Nashville burns	1857
Fanning visits tenth annual meeting of the American Christian Missionary Society	1859
Gospel Advocate and Franklin College interrupted by Civil War	1862-65

American Christian Missionary Society
    War Resolutions   1861-62
Tennessee Cooperation Meeting for
    Reconstruction plans   1866
Begins editing *Religious Historian*   1872
Death   1874

FOOTNOTES

Chapter 1—His Banner to the Breeze

[1]Tolbert Fanning, "Reply to Professor Robert Richardson," *Gospel Advocate*, 3:181-191, June, 1857.

[2]John I. Rogers, *Autobiography of Elder Samuel Rogers* (Cincinnati: Standard Publishing Co., 1880), p. 60. There are several errors surrounding the conversion of Fanning which have been passed down. H. Leo Boles, in *Biographical Sketches of Gospel Preachers*, states that Fanning heard James E. Matthews preach and was baptized immediately. It was neither Matthews nor was it immediately. At this time, in fact, Matthews was not preaching baptism for the remission of sins. H. R. Moore, in *Franklin College and Its Influences*, says that E. D. Moore baptized him in September of 1828. Both the preacher and the date are in error in this account, though it is possible that Fanning himself is to blame for this mistake. When Moore died, Fanning called him his "father in the gospel." This was evidently not intended to mean that Moore baptized him, but rather that he first taught him to study the Bible. In another article, "Notes on a Tour, South" (*Christian Review*, January, 1847), Fanning places the date as September of 1828. It appears that Fanning himself is mistaken in this date. Not only does Hall give the date as 1827, but Charlotte Fanning also gives this date. In addition, in several other places Fanning himself gives 1827 as the correct year: "Sketches in the Life of Alexander Campbell, No. 4," *Gospel Advocate*, 8:383, June 19, 1866; "Obituary of James E. Matthews," *Gospel Advocate*, 9:618, August 1, 1867; "Death of Dr. B. F. Hall," *Religious Historian*, 2:192, June, 1873. Not only does Fanning give 1827 in each of these three articles, but in the article on the death of Matthews he says it was in October of that year. Since Charlotte Fanning gave October 1, 1827 as the correct date, and Hall remembered that it was September of 1827 when he went to Alabama to preach, this seems to be the date which is correct. He heard Hall preach on the last day of September and was baptized the next day—October 1, 1827.

[3]Several clear discussions of this section of history are available, including: Winfred Ernest Garrison and Alfred T. DeGroot, *The Disciples of Christ, A History* (St. Louis: Bethany Press, 1948); James DeForest Murch, *Christians Only* (Cincinnati: Standard Publishing Co., 1962); and Earl I. West, *The Search for the Ancient Order* (Nashville: Gospel Advocate Company, 1946). An extremely helpful social history of the Restoration Movement is the more recent work of David E.

Harrell, *Quest for a Christian America* (Nashville: Disciples of Christ Historical Society, 1966). Harrell's book should be especially useful for those interested in locating a recent bibliographical survey for the movement. See also the special issue of the *Restoration Quarterly,* Volume 8, Number 4, 1965. Other issues of this journal will also be helpful.

[4]Obituaries, *Gospel Advocate,* 9:618, August 1, 1867.

[5]Rogers, *op. cit.,* pp. 58ff.

[6]Tolbert Fanning, "Obituary of E. D. Moore," *Gospel Advocate,* 6:31-32, January, 1860.

[7]Tolbert Fanning, "Reading the Scriptures," *Religious Historian,* 1:341, November, 1872; "Obituary of E. D. Moore," *Gospel Advocate,* 6:31-32, January, 1860.

[8]Thomas H. Olbricht, "The Invitation: A Historical Survey," *Restoration Quarterly,* 5:1, 1961, pp. 6-16.

[9]Tolbert Fanning, "Reading the Scriptures," *Religious Historian,* 1:141-146, May, 1872.

[10]Tolbert Fanning, "Reading the Scriptures,"*loc. cit.*

Chapter 2— The Hazard of the Die

[1]Material regarding Fanning's home life as a child has been gathered from many sources. Several helpful sources are: Charlotte Fanning, "Tolbert Fanning," unpublished manuscript in the possession of Miss Irma Batey of Nashville. This was to be Charlotte's biography of Fanning, but is only about twenty pages long. Since it was evidently written from memory, there are also several errors in it. See also: E. G. Sewell, "Brother T. Fanning," *Gospel Advocate,* 16:492-495, May 21, 1874; and James E. Scobey, *Franklin College and Its Influences* (Nashville: McQuiddy Publishing Co., 1906).

[2]Scobey, *op. cit.,* p. 120.

[3]*Ibid.,* p. 124.

[4]Charlotte Fanning, "Tolbert Fanning," An unpublished manuscript in the possession of Irma Lee Batey, Nashville, Tennessee.

[5]For an excellent and dependable discussion of the morals, social customs, and home life scenes of Fanning's day see Carl Russell Fish, *The Rise of the Common Man, 1830-1850* (New York: Macmillan, 1928).

[6]Tolbert Fanning, "The Christian Alphabet," *Gospel Advocate,* 9:67-69, January 24, 1867.

[7]Tolbert Fanning, "The Church in Nashville," *Gospel Advocate,* 3:70-74, March, 1857.

[8]F. Garvin Davenport, *The Cultural Life in Nashville on the Eve of the Civil War* (Chapel Hill: University of North Carolina Press, 1941), p. 92.

[9]Charlotte Fanning, Unpublished manuscript.

[10]Tolbert Fanning, "A Good Man Has Fallen," *Christian Review,* 1:288, December, 1844.

[11]Alexander Campbell, "Sketch of a Tour of 75 Days," *Millennial Harbinger,* 6:280, June, 1835.

[12]Tolbert Fanning, "Reply to Robert Richardson," *Gospel Advocate,* 3:181-191, June, 1857.

[13]Tolbert Fanning, *Discourse Delivered in Boston, July 17, 1836* (Boston: Benjamin H. Greene, 1836).

[14]Tolbert Fanning, "Sketches in the Life of Alexander Campbell, No. 1," *Gospel Advocate,* 8:305-309, May 15, 1866.

[15]Tolbert Fanning, "Reply to Professor Robert Richardson," *Gospel Advocate,* 3:181-191, June, 1857; "Sketches in the Life of Alexander Campbell, No. 1," *Gospel Advocate,* 8:305-309, May 15, 1866.

[16]Davenport, *op. cit.,* p. 15.

[17]Emma Page, *The Life and Work of Mrs. Charlotte Fanning* (Nashville: McQuiddy Printing Co., 1907), p. 34.

[18]Scobey, *op. cit.,* p. 346. See also: Emma Page, *The Life and Work of Mrs. Charlotte Fanning* (Nashville: McQuiddy Printing Co., 1907); Irma Lee Batey, "An Unbeatable Team," *20th Century Christian,* 4:24-26, September, 1942; Irma Lee Batey, "Charlotte Fall Fanning, Educator." An unpublished manuscript, Nashville, Tennessee; and Josephine Murphy, "The Professor and His Lady," *The Nashville Tennessean Magazine,* April 3, 1949.

[19]Tolbert Fanning, "Notes on a Tour, No. 3," *Christian Review,* 1:241-244, November, 1844.

[20]W. Woodford Clayton, *History of Davidson County* (Philadelphia: J. W. Lewis and Company, 1880), p. 453.

[21]Tolbert Fanning, *Discourse Delivered in Boston, July 17, 1836* (Boston: Benjamin H. Greene, 1836), p. 8.

Chapter 3 — The Truth is Prevailing

[1]Michael Kraus, *The United States to 1865* (Ann Arbor: The University of Michigan Press, 1959), p. 368.

[2]Mention has been made of Fanning's consideration of a position at the new Bacon College in Kentucky. There is some confusion about this relationship and part of it may be involved with the death of

Fanning's first wife, whose home was in Kentucky and whom he married the year the school opened. Dwight E. Stevenson has supplied a list of the faculty members taken from the first issue of the new magazine, *The Christian*, 1:23, January, 1837. The paper was published by Walter Scott and John T. Johnson in Georgetown and the school opened on November 14, 1836. The faculty, as listed, included:

> Walter Scott, President and Professor of Hebrew Literature.
> Dr. W. Knight, Professor of Moral and Mental Science, Belles Lettres, etc.
> T. F. Johnson, Professor of Math and Civil Engineering,
> S. G. Mullins, Professor of Ancient Languages,
> C. R. Prezriminsky, Professor of Modern Languages and Topography Drawing,
> T. Fanning, Professor of Natural Philosophy, Chemistry, Geology and Mineralogy,
> J. Crenshaw, Teacher in Preparatory Department,
> U. S. Phillips, Teacher in the Preparatory Department.

Since the session began on November 14, this did not appear until six weeks later, although it possibly could have been in the press long before that time. If Fanning was *not* on the faculty, it seems likely that this would have been reflected in the announcement. However, though this presents a difficulty, there seems to be even greater difficulties involved if one assumes that Fanning really was on the faculty for a while. To begin with, he was living in Franklin, Tennessee by January of 1837. Another difficulty has been pointed out by Dwight Stevenson, professor of homiletics at the College of the Bible in Lexington, Kentucky, who has made a study of the history of Bacon College. He points out that in April, 1837, *The Christian* notes that Elder Wm. Hunter had been elected to fill the vacancy occasioned by the death of Professor Knight. But this announcement, which covers the upcoming session to begin May 1, says nothing at all about filling a vacancy created by the removal of Tolbert Fanning. If Fanning had indeed served for a time, one would expect his replacement to be mentioned. (Personal letter to the author, July 9, 1960, from Dwight E. Stevenson, professor of homiletics at the College of the Bible, Lexington, Kentucky.)

[3]No author, "Nashville," *Agriculturist*, 2:218, October, 1841.

[4]Tolbert Fanning, "Elm Crag Agricultural School," *Agriculturist*, 4:132-133, September, 1843.

[5]Tolbert Fanning, no title, *Bible Advocate*, 1:112, February, 1842.

Chapter 4 — Paint Me As I Am

[1]James E. Scobey (editor), *Franklin College and Its Influences* (Nashville: McQuiddy Printing Co., 1906), pp. 11, 12.

[2]J. W. McGarvey, *McGarvey's Autobiography* (Lexington: *College of the Bible*, 1960), p. 63.

[3]Scobey, *op. cit.*, p. 268.

[4]Tolbert Fanning, "Education — No. 4," *Religious Historian*, 1:107-111, April, 1872.

[5]*Ibid.*

[6]*Ibid.*

[7]Scobey, *op. cit.*, p. 33.

[8]*Ibid.*, p. 136.

[9]Tolbert Fanning, "Reading the Scriptures," *Religious Historian*, 1:341, November, 1872.

[10]McGarvey, *loc. cit.*

[11]E. G. Sewell, "Brother T. Fanning," *Gospel Advocate*, 16:492-495, May 21, 1874.

[12]Scobey, *op. cit.*, p. 453.

[13]Editors, "Sad News," *Agriculturist*, 1:288, December, 1840.

[14]G. C. Brewer, "Tolbert Fanning and Foxhounds," *Gospel Advocate*, 79:386, April 29, 1937.

[15]Tolbert Fanning, "Great Men Are Generally Farmers," *Agriculturist*, 1:285, December, 1840.

[16]*Ibid.* See also a very enlightening article, David E. Harrell, Jr., "The Agrarian Myth and the Disciples of Christ in the Nineteenth Century," *Agricultural History*, 41:181-191, April, 1967.

[17]Letter from Tolbert Fanning to W. C. Huffman, in the possession of Earl I. West. See: Earl I. West, *Search for the Ancient Order, Volume I* (Nashville: Gospel Advocate Co., 1949), pp. 110, 111.

[18]Tolbert Fanning, "Opening to Make a Fortune," *Agriculturist*, 1:211, September, 1840.

[19]Tolbert Fanning, "Worldly Amusements," *Gospel Advocate*, 9:650-652, August 15, 1867.

[20]Letter in possession of Earl I. West, *loc. cit.*

[21]Tolbert Fanning, "The Immorality of Agricultural Fairs Considered," *Gospel Advocate*, 4:179-181, June, 1858.

Chapter 5 — Our Dangers are Greatly Augmenting

[1]Tolbert Fanning, "Political Strife Amongst Christians," *Christian Review*, 1:184-185, August, 1844.

[2]The original copy of this letter is in the Disciples of Christ Historical Society, Nashville, Tennessee.

[3]Jesse B. Ferguson, "Another State of Probation," *Christian Review,* 2:224, October, 1845.

[4]Tolbert Fanning, "Metaphysical Discussions, No. 2," *Gospel Advocate,* 2:326-329, November, 1856.

[5]Tolbert Fanning, "Metaphysical Discussions, No. 4," *Gospel Advocate,* 3:1-5, January, 1857.

[6]Tolbert Fanning, "Spiritual Light—No. 10," *Religious Historian,* 1:289-295, October, 1872.

[7]Tolbert Fanning, "A Knowledge of God Through Nature," *Gospel Advocate,* 9:29-31, January 10, 1867.

[8]*Ibid.*

[9]Tolbert Fanning, *True Method of Searching the Scriptures* (Nashville: McQuiddy Printing Co., 1911).

[10]Tolbert Fanning, *The Gospel of Christ* (Nashville: Cameron & Fall, 1857), p. 16.

[11]Tolbert Fanning, "Ancient and Modern Churches, No. 3," *Religious Historian,* 1:193-197, July, 1872.

[12]Tolbert Fanning, "Our True Position in Reference to the Different Religious Denominations," *Christian Review,* 1:2, January, 1844.

[13]Tolbert Fanning, "Ancient and Modern Churches, No. 3," *Religious Historian,* 1:193-197, July, 1872.

[14]Tolbert Fanning, *Discourse Delivered in Boston, July 17,* (Boston: Benjamin H. Greene, 1836), p. 19.

[15]No title, *Gospel Advocate,* 1:154, May, 1855.

[16]O. D. Williams, "Meeting at Alexandria," *Gospel Advocate,* 2:18-19, January, 1856.

[17]Tolbert Fanning, no title, *Christian Review,* 2:197, September, 1845.

[18]Tolbert Fanning, "Unprofitable Questions," *Gospel Advocate,* 9:483, June 20, 1867.

[19]Tolbert Fanning, no title, *Christian Review,* 2:208, September, 1845.

[20]Earl I. West, *The Life and Times of David Lipscomb* (Henderson, Tennessee: Religious Book Service, 1954), p. 124.

[21]Tolbert Fanning, "The Coming of the Lord," *Gospel Advocate,* 8:601-602, September, 1866.

[22]Tolbert Fanning, "Immortality—No Kingdom of God and Kindred Matters," *Gospel Advocate,* 9:431-432, May 23, 1867.

[23]Tolbert Fanning, "The Church of Christ, No. 9," *Gospel Advocate,* 2:193-199, July, 1856.

[24]Tolbert Fanning, "Geology and the Bible," *Christian Magazine,* 2:272, July, 1849.

[25]Tolbert Fanning, "Good Hits," *Gospel Advocate,* 2:239-240, August, 1856.

Chapter 6— Greater Than Storming a Castle

[1]The journal which Fanning kept at the college is now in the library of David Lipscomb College in Nashville, Tennessee.

[2]Tolbert Fanning, "Reply to Professor Robert Richardson," *Gospel Advocate,* 3:181-191, June, 1857.

[3]F. D. Srygley, *Letters and Sermons of T. B. Larimore* (Nashville: McQuiddy Printing Co., 1903), p. 365.

[4]*Ibid.,* p. 369.

[5]From the reports by both Fanning in the *Christian Review,* 3:186-188, August, 1846, and by I. N. Loomis in the *Naturalist,* 1:337-343, August, 1846, one can gain a fairly complete picture of the trip.

[6]Tolbert Fanning, *loc. cit.*

[7]James E. Scobey, *Franklin College and Its Influence* (Nashville: McQuiddy Publishing Co., 1906), pp. 217-218.

[8]*Ibid.,* p. 340.

[9]*Ibid.,* p. 273.

[10]Tolbert Fanning, "Institutions of Higher Learning," *Religious Historian,* 1:126-127, April, 1872.

[11]Tolbert Fanning, "Education," *Religious Historian,* 1:1-3, January, 1872.

[12]Tolbert Fanning, "Education," *Christian Review,* 1:34-35, February, 1844.

[13]F. Garvin Davenport, *The Cultural Life in Nashville on the Eve of the Civil War* (Chapel Hill: University of North Carolina Press, 1948), p. 44.

[14]Tolbert Fanning, "Education," *Christian Review,* 1:59-60, March, 1844.

[15]Tolbert Fanning, "Morality of Labor," *Christian Review,* 3:25-26, February, 1846.

[16]Tolbert Fanning, "Education," *Christian Review,* 1:228, October, 1844.

[17]Scobey, *op. cit.,* p. 290.

[18]Earl I. West, *The Life and Times of David Lipscomb* (Henderson, Tennessee: Religious Book Service, 1954), p. 46.

[19]Tolbert Fanning, "Endowed Institutions," *Naturalist,* 1:411-412, September, 1846.

[20]Winfred Ernest Garrison, and Alfred T. DeGroot, *The Disciples of Christ, A History* (St Louis: Christian Board of Publication, 1948), p. 251.

[21]Tolbert Fanning, "College Endowments," *Christian Review*, 2:280, December, 1845.

[22]Tolbert Fanning, "Education," *Gospel Advocate*, 2:142, May, 1856.

Chapter 7 — As A Giant Filled With His Theme

[1]Tolbert Fanning, "The Cause in Russellville, Ala.," *Gospel Advocate*, 7:149, May, 1861. H. R. Moore, *Franklin College and Its Influences*, edited by James E. Scobey, states (p. 131) that one hundred and twenty people were converted in this meeting in Russellville. L. C. Chisholm, in the same book, says there were two hundred and he was one of them, though he was a young boy at the time. Charlotte Fanning, in her unpublished biography of her husband, says one hundred and fifteen is the correct figure. Fanning himself, in reporting the meeting, gave two *different* figures. First, in 1845, he reported one hundred and five but three years later he put the figure up to one hundred and fifteen. Too often historians have taken the word of a participant without realizing that human memory is extremely unreliable in such matters.

Chisholm's number is obviously too high. Either he was overimpressed, as a boy, or else he confuses the number baptized on the whole trip with the number in his own town. While the number reported most often (twice) is one hundred and fifteen, this seems to have come to Charlotte from Fanning's report of it. When he himself gave this number sixteen years had elapsed since the event took place. The earliest report, two years after the event, gives one hundred and five.

[2]Scobey, *op. cit.*, p. 215.

[3]*Ibid*, p. 268.

[4]E. G. Sewell, "Brother T. Fanning," *Gospel Advocate*, 16:492-495, May 21, 1874.

[5]Scobey, *op. cit.*, p. 413.

[6]*Ibid.*, p. 225.

[7]Tolbert Fanning, "The Christian Alphabet," *Gospel Advocate*, 9:61-63, January 24, 1867.

[8]Tolbert Fanning, "Church of Christ, No. 10 — Evangelists," *Gospel Advocate*, 2:226-233, August, 1856.

[9]Tolbert Fanning, no title, *Gospel Advocate*, 3:266-267, August, 1857.

[10]Tolbert Fanning, "Co-operation — Comment," *Christian Review*, 4:214, June, 1847.

[11]Tolbert Fanning, "First Principles," *Christian Review*, 3:49-51, March, 1846.

[12]Tolbert Fanning, "First and Sacred Principles, and Two Orders of Preachers," *Gospel Advocate,* 7:161-167, June, 1861.

[13]J. W. McGarvey, *McGarvey's Autobiography* (Lexington: College of the Bible, 1960), p. 63.

[14]Tolbert Fanning, "The Christian Alphabet, Chapter 2," *Gospel Advocate,* 9:61-63, January, 1867.

[15]Tolbert Fanning, "Church of Christ, No. 9, *"Gospel Advocate,* 2:193-199, July, 1856.

[16]Tolbert Fanning, "To Young Preachers," *Christian Review,* 5:51-52, March, 1845.

[17]*Ibid.*

[18]Tolbert Fanning, "Letter, No. 1," *Gospel Advocate,* 9:267-269, April 4, 1867.

[19]Tolbert Fanning, "The Church of Christ, No. 10," *Gospel Advocate,* 2:226-233, August, 1856.

[20]*Millennial Harbinger,* Vol. 3, Series 5, July, 1860, p. 372.

[21]Tolbert Fanning, "Letter, No. 1," *Gospel Advocate,* 9:267-269, April 4, 1867.

[22]Tolbert Fanning, "Controversy and Interrogatories," *Christian Review,* 1:7-8, January, 1844.

[23]Charlotte Fanning, *Tolbert Fanning,* Unpublished manuscript in possession of Irma Lee Batey, Nashville, Tennessee.

[24]Tolbert Fanning, "Notes on a Tour, No. 3," *Christian Review,* 1:241-244, November, 1844.

[25]Scobey, *op. cit.,* p. 13.

[26]F. D. Srygley, *Letters and Sermons of T. B. Larimore* (Nashville: McQuiddy Printing Co., 1903), pp. 357-358.

Chapter 8—No Room for Repentance

[1]F. Garvin Davenport, *The Cultural Life in Nashville on the Eve of the Civil War* (Chapel Hill: University of North Carolina Press, 1941), p. 201.

[2]No author, "Opening of Our New House of Worship," *Christian Magazine,* 5:237-239, August, 1852. Davenport, *op. cit.,* p. 102.

[3]Tolbert Fanning, "The Church in Nashville," *Gospel Advocate,* 3:70-74, March, 1857.

[4]Davenport, *op. cit.,* p. 102.

[5]J. B. Ferguson, "Introduction," *Christian Magazine,* 1:1, January, 1848.

[6]J. B. Ferguson, "Editorial," *Christian Magazine,* 1:64, February, 1848.

[7]Several bound volumes of the *Christian Magazine,* with "regards" to the "editor" written on the fly-leaves, signed by J.T.S. Fall, are in the personal library of C.E.W. Dorris of Nashville.

[8]J.B. Ferguson, "Another State of Probation," *Christian Review,* 2:224, October, 1845.

[9]J.B. Ferguson, "Expositions of Scripture — 'The Spirits in Prison.'— I Peter III. 18-20 and IV. 1-3," *Christian Magazine,* 5:113-114, April, 1852.

[10]*Ibid.*

[33]*Ibid.*

[12]*Millennial Harbinger,* Series IV, Volume II, July, 1852, p. 414. Enos Dowling, who has made an exhaustive study of this controversy, was of great help in guiding me to needed materials. See: Enos Dowling, *An Analysis and Index of the Christian Magazine* (Lincoln, Illinois: Lincoln Bible Institute Press, 1958).

[13]J.B. Ferguson, "The Attack of the 'Millennial Harbinger' Upon the 'Christian Magazine' and Its Editor," *Christian Magazine,* 5:241-246, August, 1852.

[14]J.B. Ferguson, Extra of *Christian Magazine,* December, 1852, p. 21.

[15]A.S. Hayden, *Early History of the Disciples on the Western Reserve* (Cincinnati: Chase and Hall, 1875), p. 169.

[16]Ferguson, *loc. cit.*

[17]Davenport, *op. cit.,* p. 104.

[18]J.B. Ferguson, *History of the Relation of the Pastor to the "Christian Church" of Nashville* (Nashville: M'Kennie & Brown, 1855), p. 17.

[19]J.B. Ferguson, *Address and Correspondence, Delivered December 30, 1855, in the "Christian Church," Nashville, Tennessee* (Nashville: Smith and Morgan and Co., 1856), p. 5.

[20]J.B. Ferguson, *Spirit Communion* (Nashville: Union and American Steam Press, 1854), p. 12.

[21]*Ibid.,* pp. 234, 235, 238.

[22]David Lipscomb, "Death of Jesse B. Ferguson," *Gospel Advocate,* September 22, 1870.

[23]This information is from a personal interview with C.E.W. Dorris, of Nashville.

[24]Tolbert Fanning, "The Unpardonable Sin," *Gospel Advocate,* 8:263-265, April 24, 1866.

[25]Tolbert Fanning, "Religion, Old and New," *Gospel Advocate,* 2:48-52, February, 1856.

[26]Tolbert Fanning, "Reminiscences," *Gospel Advocate,* 1:27, August, 1855.

Chapter 9—Remember Nashville—And Lot's Wife

[1]Tolbert Fanning, "Church Organization, Light Wanted," *Gospel Advocate,* 8:593-596, September, 1866.

[2]*Ibid.*

[3]Tolbert Fanning, "Letters on Church Edification, No. 1," *Gospel Advocate,* 10:1040-1044, October 24, 1868.

[4]Tolbert Fanning, "Church Organization, Light Wanted," *loc. cit.*

[5]Tolbert Fanning, "Church Government," *Gospel Advocate,* 2:40-44, February, 1844; "Ordination and Installing Into Office," *Gospel Advocate,* 8:808-810, December18, 1866.

[6]Tolbert Fanning, "Church Organization—No. 3," *Christian Review,* 1:49-50, March, 1844.

[7]Tolbert Fanning, "Official Appointments and Service in the Church," *Gospel Advocate,* 8:788-792, December 11, 1866.

[8]Tolbert Fanning, "Notes on a Tour—No. 2," *Christian Review,* 1:193-197, September, 1844.

[9]*Ibid.*

[10]Tolbert Fanning, "Church Organization," *Christian Review,* 1:182-183, August, 1844.

[11]Tolbert Fanning, no title, *Gospel Advocate,* 5:255, August, 1859.

[12]Tolbert Fanning, "Church of Christ, No. 9," *Gospel Advocate,* 2:193-199, July, 1959.

[13]Tolbert Fanning, no title, *Gospel Advocate,* 1:94, September, 1855.

[14]Tolbert Fanning, "Church of Christ, No. 5," *Gospel Advocate,* 2:65-68, March, 1856.

[15]Tolbert Fanning, "Church of Christ, No. 1," *Gospel Advocate,* 1:134-137, December, 1855.

[16]Tolbert Fanning, "Church of Christ, No. 9," *Gospel Advocate,* 2:193-199, July, 1856.

[17]Tolbert Fanning, "Church of Christ, No. 4," *Gospel Advocate,* 2:45-48, February, 1856.

[18]Tolbert Fanning, "Zeal for God," *Christian Review,* 1:271-272, December, 1844.

[19]Tolbert Fanning, "College Endowments," *Christian Review,* 2:280,

[20]Tolbert Fanning, "Salary System—Reply," *Gospel Advocate,* 3:147-149, May, 1857.

[21]Tolbert Fanning, "Respectful Suggestions," *Gospel Advocate,* 3:147-149, May, 1857.

[22]*Ibid.*

[23]Tolbert Fanning, "Notes on a Tour, No. 4," *Christian Review,* 1:265-269, December, 1844.

[24]Tolbert Fanning, "Congregations Visited in December, 1859," *Gospel Advocate,* 6:22-23, January, 1860.

[25]James E. Scobey, *Franklin College and Its Influences* (Nashville: McQuiddy Publishing Company, 1906), pp. 24, 92, 111.

Chapter 10—Concert of Action

[1]Jacob Creath, "The Ancient Order of Things," *Gospel Advocate,* 8:201-202, March 27, 1866.

[2]Tolbert Fanning, "The Path of Safety," *Gospel Advocate,* 8:81-83, February 6, 1866.

[3]Tolbert Fanning, "State Meeting of the Churches of Christ in Missouri for 1846," *Christian Review,* 3:72, March, 1846.

[4]Tolbert Fanning, "Prospects of the Cause in America," *Christian Review,* 3:278-281, December, 1846.

[5]Tolbert Fanning, "Proposition for a Consultation and Co-operation (not for Preaching) Meeting to be held at Franklin College, Commencing the Friday before the First Lord's Day in May, 1847," *Christian Review,* 4:34, January, 1847.

[6]No author, "Circular," *Christian Review,* 4:287-288, August, 1847.

[7]J. B. Ferguson, "Our State Meeting," *Christian Magazine,* 2:424-428, November, 1849.

[8]G. W. McQuiddy (secretary), "Co-operation Meeting at Millersburg, Tennessee," *Christian Review,* 4:352-356, October, 1847.

[9]*Ibid.*

[10]Tolbert Fanning, "The Church of Christ, No. 1," *Gospel Advocate,* 1:134-137, November, 1855.

[11]Tolbert Fanning, "The Path of Safety," *Gospel Advocate,* 8:81-83, February 6, 1866.

[12]No author, "Meeting of the Disciples of Jesus Christ," *Christian Review,* 4:191-202, June, 1847.

[13]Alexander Campbell, "The Christian Religion," *Christian Baptist,* 1:6-7, August 3, 1823.

[14]Alexander Campbell, "The Cooperation of Churches—No. 1," *Millennial Harbinger,* 2:237, May, 1831.

[15]*Ibid.*

[16]*Ibid.*

[17]Alexander Campbell, "Convention," *Millennial Harbinger,* Third Series, 6:475-476, August, 1849.

Chapter 11 — In the Multitude of Counselors

[1]D. S. Burnet, "Reply to the Connellsville Letter," *Christian Magazine,* 3:173-176, June, 1850.

[2]Noel L. Keith, *The Story of D. S. Burnet: Undeserved Obscurity* (St. Louis: Bethany Press), 1954, p. 71 ff.

[3]Tolbert Fanning, "Christian Bible Society," *Christian Review,* 2:234, October, 1845.

[4]T. Fanning and others, "Meeting for General Consultation," *Christian Magazine,* 2:311, August, 1849.

[5]Keith, *op. cit.,* p. 91.

[6]No author, "The Tennessee Evangelizing Association," *Christian Magazine,* 5:187-188, June, 1852.

[7]Joseph Franklin and J. A. Headington, *The Life and Times of Benjamin Franklin* (St. Louis: John Burns, 1879), p. 334.

[8]Jacob Creath, "Missionary and Other Organizations Besides the Church, for Carrying Forward the Work of God," *Gospel Advocate,* 8:39-42, January 16, 1866.

[9]L. L. Norton and others, "Resolutions of the church at Connellsville, Pa., on Missionary and Other Societies," *Christian Magazine,* 3:141-143, May, 1850.

[10]D. S. Burnet, "Reply to the Connellsville Letter," *Christian Magazine,* 3:175, June, 1850; W. T. Moore, *The Living Pulpit of the Christian Church* (St. Louis: Christian Publishing Co., 1867), p. 45.

[11]J. B. Ferguson, "Proposed Action Respecting our Views," *Christian Magazine,* 5: Extra, December, 1852, p. 27.

[12]Tolbert Fanning, "Co-operation — Suggestions," *Gospel Advocate,* 1:109ff, October, 1855.

[13]J. W. McGarvey, "Correspondents," *Gospel Advocate,* 2:95, March, 1856.

[14]William Lipscomb, "Mountain District Co-operation," *Gospel Advocate,* 3:26-27, January, 1857.

[15]Editors, "Ministers and Elders Meeting?", *Gospel Advocate,* 2:96, March, 1856; Tolbert Fanning, "The Consultation Meeting at Franklin," *Gospel Advocate,* 5:267-269, August, 1859; Tolbert Fanning, "Co-operation Amongst the Preachers," *Gospel Advocate,* 1:188, December, 1855.

[16]Tolbert Fanning, "The Consultation Meeting in Franklin," *Gospel Advocate,* 2:154, May, 1856.

[17]Tolbert Fanning, "The Consultation Meeting at Franklin," *Gospel Advocate,* 5:267-269, August, 1859.

[18]Tolbert Fanning, "Co-operation Meeting at Murfreesboro, Tenn.," *Gospel Advocate*, 5:357-359, December, 1859.

[19]Tolbert Fanning, "The Path of Safety," *Gospel Advocate*, 8:81-83, February 6, 1866.

[20]Tolbert Fanning, "Missionary Societies," *Gospel Advocate*, 8:20-22, June 9, 1866.

[21]Tolbert Fanning, "The Path of Safety," *loc. cit.*

Chapter 12— Before You Drive Us From You

[1]Tolbert Fanning, "Missionary Societies," *Gospel Advocate*, 8:20-22, June 9, 1866.

[2]Tolbert Fanning, "The Lord's Treasury," *Gospel Advocate*, 3:65-70, March, 1857; "Answers to Brother J. T. Johnson's Enquiries," *Gospel Advocate*, 2:308-310, October, 1856.

[3]J. J. Trott, "The Indian Mission," *Gospel Advocate*, 3:330-331, October, 1857.

[4]Tolbert Fanning, "Reply to Robert Milligan," *Gospel Advocate*, 2:305, October, 1856.

[5]*Ibid.*

[6]Tolbert Fanning, "Mission to England," *Gospel Advocate*, 3:149-150, May, 1857.

[7]Tolbert Fanning, "Notes on Bro. G. W. Elley's [sic] Essay Regarding Co-operation," *Gospel Advocate*, 3:214-217, July, 1857.

[8]Tolbert Fanning, "Missions and Missionaries," *Gospel Advocate*, 3:229-232, May, 1857.

[9]G. W. Elly and Tolbert Fanning, no title, *Gospel Advocate*, 3:138-140, May, 1857.

[10]Tolbert Fanning, "State and District Association," *Gospel Advocate*, 4:168-170, January, 1858.

[11]Tolbert Fanning, "Notes on Bro. G. W. Elley's [sic] Essay Regarding Co-operation," *Gospel Advocate*, 3:214-217, July, 1857.

[12]Tolbert Fanning, "Report on Consultation Meeting in Franklin, 1856," *Gospel Advocate*, 2:175-184, June, 1856.

[13]Tolbert Fanning, "Christian Co-operation in Rutherford County, Tennessee for the Year, 1856," *Gospel Advocate*, 2:15-18, January, 1856.

[14]Tolbert Fanning, "Hints," *Gospel Advocate*, 2:316, October, 1856.

[15]*Ibid.*

[16]Tolbert Fanning, "Annual Meeting of the American Christian Missionary Society, for 1859," *Gospel Advocate*, 5:329-333, November, 1859.

[17]D. S. Burnet, "Is the Church of Christ a Denomination or a Sect?", *Gospel Advocate,* 6:272, September, 1860.

[18]American Christian Missionary Society, *Report of the Anniversary Meeting of the American Christian Missionary Society, 1859* (Cincinnati; G. B. Bentley, & Co., 1859). See also: Tolbert Fanning, "Annual Meeting of the American Christian Missionary Society, for 1859," *Gospel Advocate,* 5:329-333, November, 1859.

Chapter 13 — "Brethren, We Are One"

[1]Tolbert Fanning, "First Principles, No. IV," *Gospel Advocate,* 1:97-102, October, 1855.

[2]Tolbert Fanning, "The Secret of Success in the Church," *Gospel Advocate,* 6:234-236, August, 1859; "First Principles, No. IV," *Gospel Advocate,* 1:97-102, October 1855; "Prospects in Middle Tennessee," *Gospel Advocate,* 4:257-263, September, 1858.

[3]Tolbert Fanning, "Reply to Professor Robert Richardson, *Gospel Advocate,* 3:181-191, June, 1857.

[4]*Ibid.*

[5]Robert Richardson, "Professor R. Richardson's Second Notice of the Gospel Advocate," *Gospel Advocate,* 3:196-202, July, 1857.

[6]Robert Richardson, "Professor R. Richardson's Philosophy," *Gospel Advocate,* 3:241-251, August, 1857.

[7]Tolbert Fanning, "Personal," *Gospel Advocate,* 4:219, July, 1858.

[8]Tolbert Fanning, "Our School Relations," *Gospel Advocate,* 5:275-276, August, 1859.

[9]*Ibid.*

[10]Tolbert Fanning, "Duty of Christians in Reference to the Political Crisis of 1861," *Gospel Advocate,* 7:32-37, February, 1861.

[11]*Ibid.*

[12]This letter, from Margaret T. Fanning to a Mr. S. Henry, is in the Disciples of Christ Historical Society in Nashville, Tennessee.

[13]Tolbert Fanning, "Education, No. 4," *Religious Historian,* 1:107-111, April, 1872.

[14]Tolbert Fanning, "The Slavery Question," *Christian Review,* 1:184, August, 1845; "Christian Bible Society," *Christian Review,* 2:234, October, 1845.

[15]Tolbert Fanning, "The Colored People of the South," *Religious Historian,* 1:89-91, March, 1872. Cf. Beverly Wilson, "Order of the Church at Rock Spring, Rutherford Co.," *Christian Review,* 1:45, February, 1844.

[16]Fanning, *loc. cit.*

[17]Albert D. Kirwan (editor), *The Confederacy* (New York: Meridian Books, 1959), p. 21; Henry Steele Commager (editor), *Documents of American History, Volume I* (New York: Appleton-Century-Crofts, 1963), p. 372.

[18]Tolbert Fanning, "The Gospel Advocate," *Gospel Advocate*, 7:380, December, 1861.

Chapter 14—At Dead of Night

[1]*American Christian Missionary Society, Annual Proceedings, 1861,* as quoted by Noel L. Keith, *D.S. Burnet: Undeserved Obscurity* (St. Louis: Bethany Press, 1954), p. 162.

[2]Tolbert Fanning, "Defense of Government," *Gospel Advocate,* 9:213-217, March, 1867.

[3]Tolbert Fanning, "Ministers in the World's Conflicts," *Gospel Advocate,* 7:846-847, November, 1861.

[4]David Lipscomb, "I Did Wrong," *Gospel Advocate,* 8:170-171, March 13, 1866.

[5]Albert D. Kirwan (editor), *The Confederacy* (New York: Meridian Books, 1959), p. 85.

[6]Earl I. West, *The Life and Times of David Lipscomb* (Henderson, Tennessee: Religious Book Service, 1954), p. 84.

[7]William Baxter, *Pea Ridge and Prairie Grove* (Cincinnati: Poe & Hitchcock, 1864), pp. 113-123; Tolbert Fanning, "Death of Dr. B.F. Hall," *Religious Historian,* 2:192, June, 1873.

[8]Tolbert Fanning, "Church of Christ and World Powers," *Gospel Advocate,* 8:417-418, July 3, 1866.

[9]Tolbert Fanning, "Queries on War," *Gospel Advocate,* 9:23-24, January 10, 1867.

[10]Henry Steele Commager (editor), *Documents of American History, Volume I* (New York: Appleton-Century-Crofts, 1963), p. 442.

[11]Tolbert Fanning, "Political Strife Amongst Christians," *Christian Review,* 1:184-185, August, 1844.

[12]*Ibid.*

[13]*Ibid.*

[14]The comments about the Jacksonian "revolution" in politics are designed simply to help recapture Fanning's surroundings and not to enter the debate about who supported Jackson, how much of a "revolution" took place, or to discuss the true nature of the revolution. Interpretations of these questions since Frederick Jackson Turner and Charles Beard have added helpful insights and indicate that in addition to the frontiersman, there were city artisans and even New York City monied interests who helped engineer Jackson's popularity and political

power. Recently helpful has been the debate between Arthur Schlesinger, Jr. *(The Age of Jackson,* Boston: Little, Brown, 1945) and Bray Hammond (review of Schlesinger, in *Journal of Economic History,* 6:79-84; May 1946). A helpful historiographical sketch is Charles G. Sellers, "Andrew Jackson versus the Historians," *Mississippi Valley Historical Review,* 44:615-34; March, 1958. One of the better recent attemps at synthesis, avoiding the common temptation to confuse what democracy was with what Democrats thought and wrote that it was, is Glyndon G. Van Deusen, *The Jacksonian Era, 1828-1848* (New York: Harper, 1959). I have been concerned primarily with the manifestation of the political methods characteristic of Fanning's area and therefore most influential in forming his attitudes toward Christian participation in political activity.

¹⁵Tolbert Fanning, "Outward Pressure," *Gospel Advocate,* 7:174-176, June 1861.

¹⁶Tolbert Fanning, "The Kingdom of Heaven, a Spiritual Empire," *Christian Review,* 3:100-103, May, 1846.

¹⁷Tolbert Fanning, "The Danger of Political Excitement," *Gospel Advocate,* 2:217-218, July, 1856.

¹⁸Tolbert Fanning, "Duty of Christians in Reference to the Political Crisis of 1861," *Gospel Advocate,* 7:32-37, February, 1861.

Chapter 15 — No Insurmountable Barrier

¹Tolbert Fanning, "A General Consultation Meeting Suggested," *Gospel Advocate,* 8:140, February 27, 1866.

²David Lipscomb, "Destitution," *Gospel Advocate,* 9:175f, February 28, 1867.

³David Lipscomb, "Fellowship," *Gospel Advocate,* 8:720, November, 6, 1866.

⁴Tolbert Fanning, "Peace College," *Gospel Advocate,* 9:573-574, July 18, 1867.

⁵Tolbert Fanning, "The Education of Preachers," *Religious Historian,* 2:55-56, February, 1873.

⁶Tolbert Fanning, "Church Schools, or the Duty of Christians in the Education of Youth," *Religious Historian,* 3:147-153, May, 1874.

⁷*Ibid.*

Chapter 16 — On To Perfection

¹Tolbert Fanning, "The Crisis," *Christian Review,* 2:217-219, October, 1845.

[2]Tolbert Fanning, "Ancient and Modern Churches," *Religious Historian*, 1:193-197, July, 1856.

[3]*Ibid.*

[4]No author, "Christian Statistics of Kentucky," *Christian Review*, 2:238, October, 1845.

[5]Tolbert Fanning, "Meeting at Alexandria," *Gospel Advocate*, 2:18-19, January, 1856.

[6]Tolbert Fanning, "Setting Churches in Order," *Christian Review*, 3:193-195, September, 1846.

[7]Tolbert Fanning, "Church of Christ, No. 5," *Gospel Advocate*, 2:65-68, March, 1856.

[8]Tolbert Fanning, "Church of Christ, No. 6," *Religious Historian*, 2:289-316, October, 1873.

[9]Tolbert Fanning, "Church of Christ, No. 7," *Gospel Advocate*, 2:129-136, May, 1856.

[10]Tolbert Fanning, "The Path of Safety," *Gospel Advocate*, 8:81-83, February 6, 1866.

[11]Tolbert Fanning, "Franklin Consultation Meeting," *Gospel Advocate*, 2:175-184, June, 1856.

[12]Tolbert Fanning, "Difference in Manner of Worship in England and America," *Gospel Advocate*, 9:217-218, March 14, 1867.

[13]Tolbert Fanning, "The Origin of the Church of Christ is Not Modern," *Christian Review*, 2:4-7, January, 1845.

[14]Tolbert Fanning, "Religious Reports," *Religious Historian*, 1:96, March, 1872.

[16]Tolbert Fanning, No title, *Religious Historian*, 1:319, October, 1872.

[16]Tolbert Fanning, "Elementary Studies, No. 11, *Religious Historian*, 1:337-340, November, 1872.

[17]Tolbert Fanning, "Personal," *Religious Historian*, 3:32, January, 1874.

[18]Tolbert Fanning, No title, *Gospel Advocate*, 3:192, June, 1857.

Chapter 17— A Better State of Society

[1]Charlotte Fanning, *Tolbert Fanning,* an unpublished manuscript in the possession of Irma Lee Batey, Nashville, Tennessee.

[2]Epitaph on tombstone on the grave of Tolbert Fanning. When the property at Elm Crag was sold to make room for the new municipal airport outside Nashville, the remains of both Tolbert and Charlotte Fanning were moved to Mt. Olivet Cemetery, where the same inscriptions may be seen on the stone.

[3]Tolbert Fanning, *Discourse in Boston,* July 17, 1836 (Boston: Benjamin H. Greene, 1836), p. 28.

INDEX

INDEX